POLITICAL RISK

Also by Condoleezza Rice

Extraordinary, Ordinary People: A Memoir of Family

No Higher Honor: A Memoir of My Years in Washington

Democracy: Stories from the Long Road to Freedom

Also by Amy Zegart

Flawed by Design: The Evolution of the CIA, JCS, and NSC

Spying Blind: The CIA, the FBI, and the Origins of 9/11

Eyes on Spies: Congress and the United States Intelligence Community

POLITICAL RISK

How Businesses and Organizations Can Anticipate Global Insecurity

CONDOLEEZZA RICE
AMY ZEGART

NEW YORK BOSTON

Twelve
Hachette Book Group
1290 Avenue of the Americas, New York, NY 10104
twelvebooks.com
twitter.com/twelvebooks

Originally published in hardcover and ebook by Twelve in May 2018.

First Edition: May 2019

Twelve is an imprint of Grand Central Publishing.

Library of Congress Cataloging-in-Publication Data

Names: Rice, Condoleezza, 1954- author. | Zegart, Amy B., 1967- author
Title: Political risk : how businesses and organizations can anticipate global insecurity / Condoleezza Rice and Amy Zegart.
Description: First edition. | New York : Twelve, 2018. | Includes bibliographical references and index.
Identifiers: LCCN 2017054476 | ISBN 9781455542352 (hardcover) | ISBN 9781478914792 (audio download) | ISBN 9781549115547 (audio book) | ISBN 9781455542369 (ebook)
Subjects: LCSH: Risk management—Political aspects. | World politics.
Classification: LCC HD61 .R49 2018 | DDC 658.15/5—dc23
LC record available at https://lccn.loc.gov/2017054476

ISBNs: 978-1-4555-4234-5 (trade pbk.), 978-1-4555-4236-9 (ebook)

Printed in the United States of America

LSC-C

10 9 8 7 6 5 4 3 2 1

To our Stanford GSB 584 students,
for inspiring us to teach and asking us each year,
"Why isn't this course a book?"

Contents

POLITICAL RISK

I

The *Blackfish* Effect: Twenty-First-Century Political Risk

In April 2013, SeaWorld Entertainment, Inc., was riding high. The American theme park company had completed an initial public offering that exceeded expectations, raising more than $700 million in capital and valuing the company at $2.5 billion. "To many Americans, SeaWorld offers family fun amid penguins and killer whales," gushed the *New York Times*.[1] The story ran with a picture of two adorable penguins waddling around the New York Stock Exchange as part of a promotional tour.

Richard Drew, Associated Press

Eighteen months later, SeaWorld Entertainment's fairy tale had become a nightmare. The stock price had plunged 60 percent and CEO Jim Atchison announced that he was resigning. No adorable penguins this time: Instead, the pictures accompanying the headlines featured a giant orca. Suddenly, SeaWorld's famed killer whales were killing the company.

Orlando Sentinel, *Getty Images*

Atchison and SeaWorld were blindsided by political risk. Not just any kind of political risk, but twenty-first-century political risk, where the political actions of small groups, or even lone individuals, supercharged by connective technologies, can dramatically impact businesses of all kinds.

It all started with a Los Angeles documentary filmmaker named Gabriela Cowperthwaite, who liked taking her twins to see the orcas perform at the SeaWorld theme park in San Diego. In 2010, Cowperthwaite happened to read a tragic story about how an orca named Tilikum killed veteran trainer Dawn Brancheau in the middle of a show at SeaWorld's Orlando park.[2] Cowperthwaite spent the next two years making a low-budget investigative documentary called *Blackfish*, which depicted how SeaWorld's treatment of orcas harmed both the animals and their human trainers. The film cost a grand total of $76,000.[3] Released soon after SeaWorld's initial public offering in 2013, the movie captured the attention of celebrities and quickly went viral.[4] Actress Olivia Wilde was just one among many who took to Twitter.

Animal rights groups seized the initiative. Online petitions mounted. Public pressure grew. Musical groups including Willie Nelson, Barenaked Ladies, Heart, and Cheap Trick canceled shows at SeaWorld.[5] Corporations cut sponsorship ties, among them Hyundai, Panama Jack, STA Travel, Taco Bell, Virgin America airlines, and Southwest Airlines, which had enjoyed a twenty-six-year marketing relationship with the theme park and even painted SeaWorld animals on its airplanes.[6] Federal regulators and California lawmakers jumped into action, investigating safety practices and proposing bills to ban orca breeding in captivity. Attendance at SeaWorld parks declined and the company's stock price plummeted. While we often caution that correlation is not causation—two trends can occur simultaneously without one necessarily causing the other—the chart on page 4 indicates that the relationship between *Blackfish* and SeaWorld's trouble was causal.[7] Just before the film's release in July 2013, SeaWorld Entertainment stock was $38.92 a share. By the end of 2014, it had plunged to $15.77.[8] A $76,000 film triggered political action at the grassroots, state, and federal levels that ended up devastating the company. In 2017, SeaWorld's stock had still not recovered—all because one woman read a story about orcas. This cascading impact of the film has been dubbed "the *Blackfish* effect."[9]

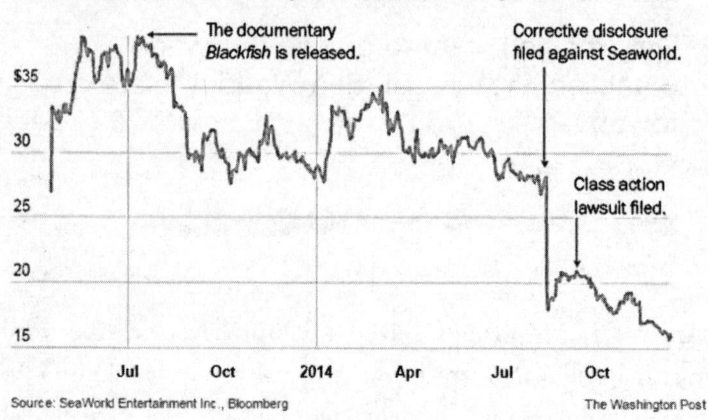

Washington Post

Political risk was once just about the actions of governments, such as dictators seizing assets or legislatures regulating industries. Today, governments are still the main arbiters of the business environment, but they are no longer the only important ones. Instead, anyone armed with a cell phone or a Twitter or Facebook account can create political risks, galvanizing action by other citizens, customers, organized groups, and political officials at the local, state, federal, and international levels. Events in far-flung places are affecting societies and businesses around the world at dizzying speeds. Anti-Chinese protests in Vietnam lead to clothing stock-outs in America. Civil war in Syria fuels a refugee crisis and terrorist attacks in Europe, leaving nations reeling and the tourism industry shaken. Video of a United Airlines passenger being forcibly dragged off a plane in Chicago goes viral in China. A North Korean dictator launches a cyber attack on a Hollywood movie studio. Russia wages an information warfare campaign against American democracy on Facebook, sparking congressional hearings and the company's most significant crisis since its founding.

This is not your parents' political risk landscape.

Simply put, twenty-first-century political risk is the probability that a political action could affect a company in significant ways.

> Twenty-first-century political risk is the probability that a political action could significantly affect a company's business.

This definition is more radical than it sounds. We chose the words "political action," not "government action," to highlight the growing role of risk generators outside of the usual places like capitals and army barracks and party headquarters. Increasingly, political actions that impact businesses are happening everywhere—inside homes, on the streets, and in the cloud; in chat rooms, dorm rooms, and boardrooms. Companies that want a competitive edge need to manage the risks generated by this widening array of global political actors, from documentary filmmakers to international institutions like the European Union. As we will see, the *Blackfish* effect is just one type of political risk. There are many others, from traditional risks like geopolitics to emerging risks that cross borders into boardrooms, like cyber threats and terrorism.

The idea of writing about political risk percolated between us (Amy and Condi) for a while. In 2012, we decided to create a new intensive MBA class examining what global political risks are, how they are changing, and how businesses can best navigate them. Condi, who has been on the Stanford faculty for over thirty years, had recently returned after serving as President George W. Bush's national security adviser and secretary of state. She had also served on the boards of Chevron, Transamerica, Hewlett-Packard, and Charles Schwab. Amy had recently returned to Stanford as well, joining the Hoover Institution as a senior fellow after spending several years at McKinsey & Company advising Fortune 500 companies and then serving on the faculty of the UCLA Luskin School of Public Affairs. For both of us, the chance to teach together and explore the intersection of global business and politics—twenty years after first sitting in the classroom together examining the changing security dynamics at the end of the Cold War—was exciting.

When we looked for readings to assign, however, we found slim pickings.[11] A search of Harvard Business School's publishing website returned nearly twenty times more materials on global business topics (such as building an effective team or developing an e-commerce strategy) than on the political dynamics that create global business opportunities and challenges in the first place.[12] So we began reading broadly and developing our own framework, cases, and simulations.

As political scientists, we naturally started with politics. Tectonic shifts in geopolitics over the past three decades have dramatically altered the international economic landscape. The opening of China and a market of 1.4 billion people has had the greatest impact. But so too has the collapse of the Soviet Union. Thirty years ago, a conversation on investment would not have included Poland or Estonia, let alone Russia. But today the promise of relatively sophisticated, industrialized economies with educated and consuming middle classes has brought these countries and others like them into view. Markets have been emerging at rates that nobody could have imagined, with the "BRICs"—Brazil, Russia, India, and China—growing at more than 8.1 percent a year even in 2010,[13] and China poised to become the largest economy in the world in 2019.[14]

Even in what was once called the "third world," opportunities abound. In Africa, Latin America, Southeast Asia, and even the Middle East, middle-class consumers and businesspeople alike are connected to the outside world, looking for products and investment opportunities, a state of affairs that would have been unthinkable three decades ago. In Silicon Valley, technology start-ups are moving into foreign markets at warp speed. As Marc Andreessen, cofounder and partner of one of the world's most successful venture capital funds, told us, "In the old days, it just would have taken companies a long time to get fully global, so the thinking and planning would have corresponded to the expansion. In the new world, the expansion happens first, whether you want it to or not. And so kind of by definition, the thinking and the planning are lagging...Internet companies might end up with 180 countries before they have 180 employees."

"Internet companies might end up with 180 countries before they have 180 employees."
—Marc Andreessen, cofounder and partner, Andreessen Horowitz

These major geopolitical shifts have brought politics and business closer together. When Condi was secretary of state, she spent a great deal of time on economic issues, not just matters of war and peace. She remembers discussing the protection of intellectual property rights with the Chinese, the opening of markets to American agriculture with the Russians and the South Koreans, and World Trade Organization rules and violations with just about everyone. In one particularly surreal encounter with Russian president Vladimir Putin, the subject was not ballistic missile defenses or NATO expansion. It was pigs. The Russians were putting up trade barriers to U.S. pork products because of professed concerns over trichinosis, a parasitic disease caused by undercooked meats. (Many U.S. producers believed that Russia's food safety restrictions were based not in science, but trade—intended to protect Russia's domestic pork industry.)[15]

"You wouldn't believe it," Condi reflected. "We spent an hour, an entire hour, on pork. I looked down at my talking points from the United States trade representative. They said, 'In thirty years, the United States has had only a handful of cases of documented trichinosis.' Putin kept going on about how Russians don't cook their pork as much as Americans do, which is why the trichinosis risk is higher. And we had this long discussion of cooking habits in Russia compared to Alabama, where I'm from." The meeting captured an emerging reality: International security challenges were no longer so distant from economics. With the Cold War's end, even between Russia and the United States, business and politics had become more tightly intertwined.

Of course, markets have never been just markets, sitting out there in the world, isolated completely from politics. Markets are created, molded, and constrained by rules, norms, and institutions in the political sphere. Trade regimes, sanctions, national laws—these things are highly contested and determine what playing fields exist, who can play on them, and how level they are. It matters whether you are operating in India, or China, or Brazil, or the United States. But globalization and the end of the Cold War have shrunk the distance between markets and politics just as they have diminished the distance between producers and consumers.[16]

In class, Condi taught our students about how political institutions at the local, national, and international levels—including the United Nations—channel conflict and cooperation and often inject high levels of uncertainty into business decisions. Amy, who has written three books about U.S. intelligence challenges, taught about how the security landscape was changing, from a half-century of superpower conflict to a more uncertain world of rising states, declining states, weak states, failed states, rogue states, and nonstate actors. She was also struck by how many leading businesses were developing their own intelligence threat assessment capabilities to deal with this new security landscape. Companies from consumer products manufacturers to law firms to high-tech firms were creating in essence mini-CIAs to assess global political trends and how they might pose physical, business, and reputational risks to a parent company.

We have been teaching the political risk class for several years now, but it has never been the same course twice. The more we've taught, the more we've refined our thinking. After Edward Snowden's revelations about National Security Agency surveillance activities, and a series of high-profile cyber attacks on Target, Home Depot, Sony, and other companies, we added a large cyber component to the course. In 2015, just after we finished role-playing a corporate board grilling our student "executives" about how they were going to handle a major cyber breach, Condi turned to Amy and said, "You know, we really ought to turn this course into a book."

Each year, we navigate the political risk landscape with thirty Stanford MBA students. Our hope is that this book will expand our classroom and help business leaders at all levels, in all industries, from founders and entrepreneurs to large multinational corporation executives and directors, to better manage political risks and opportunities. We share what we have learned from experience in government and the private sector; interviews with leading investors, CEOs, and risk managers on the front lines; academic research in psychology, organization theory, and political science about why people and organizations make the decisions (and mistakes) they do; and case studies and simulations that we have created and conducted in the course. Throughout, we ask you to walk in the shoes of hypothetical executives making hard choices about realistic risk scenarios. Should an American cruise line withdraw from the Mexican market as drug-related violence there rises? How can a fictitious Japanese telecommunications company mitigate the risks of partnering with the Burmese military in a country riven by ethnic conflict and facing a difficult transition to democracy? How should a tech company deal with early reports of a massive cyber breach? These are among the challenges this book considers.

We also share examples of real companies grappling with real political risks in real time across a range of industries. Some, like FedEx, Royal Caribbean International, the Lego Group, and Royal Dutch Shell, highlight best practices that can be borrowed. Others, like SeaWorld, Boeing, Sony Pictures, and United Airlines, offer cautionary tales and lessons to be learned. We also reach outside the business world to some unusual places, drawing insights from risk management successes and failures in nuclear force posture, aircraft carrier operations, the NASA space shuttle program, evidence-based medicine, and winning football coaches.

Our goal is not just to provide some interesting stories. It is to offer a useful framework that can be deployed in any company to improve political risk management. Our bottom line is your bottom line: Companies that best anticipate and manage political risks will have the strongest competitive edge. The four-part framework we provide is simple yet powerful:

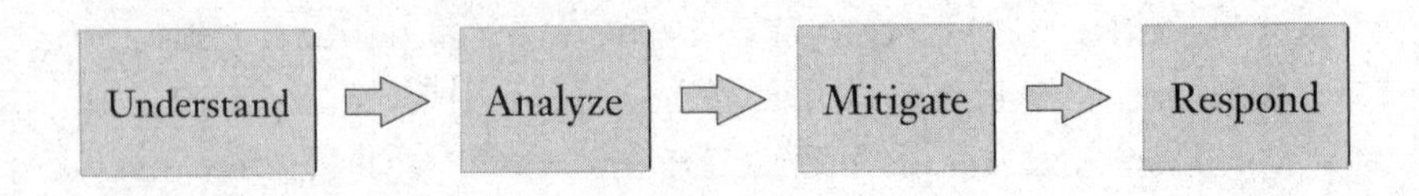

Before we take you step-by-step through the framework, we delve more deeply into understanding twenty-first-century political risks—what they are, where they came from, and why they are so challenging to manage. Chapter 2 examines the proliferation of risk generators and offers our list of ten political risks that every company should keep on hand. In chapter 3, we look at how political risk has evolved over time, examining megatrends in business, politics, and technology that have made political risks more diverse, pervasive, and consequential. Chapter 4 tackles a puzzle: Why do studies repeatedly show that most companies see the importance of managing political risk but have such a hard time doing it? We explore the key barriers to effective political risk management—what we call the "Five Hards."

Chapter 5 then introduces our framework with a closer look at two companies—Royal Caribbean International, which got political risk management right, and SeaWorld, which got it wrong. Chapters 6 through 9 cover each step in the framework, sharing insights from academic research and lessons from interviews with business leaders, class cases, and our personal experiences. Each of these chapters is organized around three guiding questions. The questions can be deployed in your own organization to improve political risk management, whether you are an entry-level employee, a mid-level executive, or a director on the board. We summarize them below.

Guiding Questions for Effective Risk Management

Understand	Analyze	Mitigate	Respond
1. What is my organization's political risk appetite?	1. How can we get good information about the political risks we face?	1. How can we reduce exposure to the risks we have identified?	1. Are we capitalizing on near misses?
2. Is there a shared understanding of our risk appetite? If not, how can we foster one?	2. How can we ensure rigorous analysis?	2. Do we have a good system in place for timely warning and action?	2. Are we reacting effectively to crises?
3. How can we reduce blind spots?	3. How can we integrate political risk analysis into business decisions?	3. How can we limit the damage when something bad happens?	3. Are we developing mechanisms for continuous learning?

In chapter 10, we offer some final thoughts about moving beyond intuition. Politics will always be an uncertain business, but managing political risk does not have to be pure guesswork.

While oriented to international business readers, this book is designed to be a useful primer for anyone wishing to better understand the changing political and business landscape. Topics we address include:

- Understanding and prioritizing political risks
- Taking advantage of global opportunities and efficiencies without unduly increasing vulnerability
- Harnessing tools like red teams and scenario planning to make better decisions
- Developing strategies for mitigating political risks and limiting the damage if something bad happens
- Creating a continuous learning cycle to anticipate, handle, and recover from political risk crises

As FedEx founder, chairman, and CEO Fred Smith told us, "People who don't pay attention to political risk who have any vulnerability to it ignore it at their peril."

As we will see, political risk management has been part of FedEx's DNA since the company delivered its first package in 1973. We hope that this book helps make political risk management part of your organization's DNA, too.

"People who don't pay attention to political risk who have any vulnerability to it ignore it at their peril."

—Fred Smith, founder, chairman, and CEO, FedEx

KEY TAKEAWAYS: TWENTY-FIRST-CENTURY POLITICAL RISK

- ☐ Twenty-first-century political risk is the probability that a political action could significantly affect a company's business.

- ☐ Governments are no longer the only important arbiters of business. Companies that want a competitive edge need to manage the political risks generated by a widening array of political actors. These actors include anyone with a cell phone and 280 characters at their fingertips.

- ☐ Our goal is to offer a useful framework that can be deployed in any company to improve political risk management.

2

Move Over, Hugo Chávez

In June 2009, Venezuelan health minister Jesús Mantilla announced that Coca-Cola's diet soft drink Coke Zero would be banned and production halted immediately "to preserve the health of Venezuelans."[1] Coke Zero, which was aimed at young men and marketed heavily with the James Bond movie *Quantum of Solace*, was a major move by Coca-Cola to capture the diet soft drink market. In Venezuela, that move did not last long: Coke Zero was on the shelves just weeks before it was yanked.

The decision to ban Coke Zero in Venezuela was not about health. It was about politics—namely, President Hugo Chávez's bid to pursue a radical socialist agenda. Chávez, who governed from 1999 until his death in 2013, embarked on an anticapitalist campaign that included attacking symbols of Western power and nationalizing large segments of Venezuela's economy. Coke Zero was just one of his many targets.

In the oil industry, Chávez imposed enormous windfall taxes as oil prices spiked, took a majority stake in four oil projects that caused ExxonMobil and ConocoPhillips to leave the country and file arbitration claims, and seized eleven oil rigs from Oklahoma-based Helmerich & Payne. In agriculture, Chávez nationalized a rice mill operated by U.S. food giant Cargill and took control of ranches and lands owned by Vestey Foods, a British meat company. Chávez also seized the local operations of Mexico's Cemex cement

Agência Brasil

company, Switzerland's Holcim, and France's Lafarge. He took over large swaths of the banking, manufacturing, and telecommunications sectors. The Venezuelan strongman even nationalized the gold industry.[2]

When most people think about political risk, they picture someone like Hugo Chávez, a dictator who suddenly captures foreign assets for his own domestic political agenda. But the truth is that Chávez is a throwback. Expropriating leaders still exist, but they are far less common than they used to be. Wharton Business School professor Witold Henisz and Maryland's Robert H. Smith School professor Bennet Zelner find that expropriation risk was prevalent in the 1950s, 1960s, and 1970s, but "has largely disappeared," thanks to more robust international law and more integration between developing and developed economies.[3]

When you think of twenty-first-century political risk, imagine instead a crowded landscape of different actors, not just dictators banning soft drinks and commandeering oil rigs. This landscape includes individuals wielding cell phones, local officials issuing city ordinances, terrorists detonating truck bombs, UN officials enforcing sanctions, and many more. It is complicated and messy, with overlapping and intersecting players generating risks within countries and across them, often simultaneously. We simplify the picture to five major "levels of action": individuals, local groups, national governments, transnational actors, and supranational/international institutions.

From Lone Rangers to International Posses: Five Levels of Action Generating Political Risks

- **Individuals** such as Twitter users, documentary filmmakers, activists, consumer advocates, celebrities, ordinary citizens, and bystanders
- **Local organizations** such as neighborhood associations, political groups, and local governments
- **National governmental actors and their institutions** such as presidents, executive agencies, legislatures, and the judiciary
- **Transnational groups** such as activists, terrorists, hackers, criminals, militias, and ethnic or religious communities
- **Supranational and international institutions** such as the European Union and the United Nations

Individuals

Activists and consumer advocates have been creating political risks for businesses for a long time. Ralph Nader took on the American automobile industry and succeeded in getting mandatory design standards, including the use of seat belts, implemented back in 1965.[4] Today, activists have new, more and more powerful technological tools that can dramatically increase the speed and scale of their efforts and the odds that they will succeed. Changing a company policy no longer requires face-to-face organizing, around-the-clock picketing, or testimony before Congress. Connective technologies enable people to organize and their messages to "go viral."

Individuals do not have to be part of activist groups to generate risks these days. They don't even need to consider themselves activists. They can be bystanders with 280 characters and a cellular network.

On Sunday, April 9, 2017, United Airlines oversold its afternoon flight from Chicago to Louisville, Kentucky. When no passengers volunteered to rebook so that four United staff members could make the flight, the airline decided to remove four passengers at random. One of them, Dr. David Dao, refused, explaining that he needed to see patients the next day. Police officers then forcibly removed him, pulling Dao out of his seat, causing him to hit his head, break his nose, gash his lip, and lose two teeth. Dao was dragged off the plane, dazed and bleeding, in front of shocked passengers. Some videotaped the incident on their cell phones and posted the footage on Twitter and Facebook. By Monday night, the videos had attracted more than nine million views, made international headlines, triggered a Transportation Department investigation, and prompted Congresswoman Eleanor Holmes Norton, a senior member of the House Transportation and Infrastructure Committee, to call for hearings.[5] The Internet exploded with memes like this one:

United CEO Oscar Munoz issued an apology that did not improve the situation. By Tuesday, United stock had lost $255 million in shareholder value[6] and some analysts began worrying about ramifications for the airline's Chinese market, after the incident attracted more than one hundred million views on Weibo, China's social media platform. Many commented that they believed Dr. Dao was discriminated against because he is Asian.[7]

What could have been resolved with a rebooking incentive ended up costing United Airlines far more, all because new technology platforms have amplified the voices of individuals, making it more likely that other customers, investors, and political actors will hear them and respond.

Local Organizations

As the old saying goes, all politics are local—and local politics can generate risks for businesses. In 2015, after intensive negotiations, the United Nations Security Council's five permanent members and Germany reached an agreement with Iran to lift UN sanctions in exchange for Iran's suspension of nuclear activities. On January 17, the day after sanctions were removed, Iranian president Hassan Rouhani tweeted euphorically, "The shackles of sanctions have been removed and it's time to thrive."[8] Foreign direct investment (FDI) did start to flow, with twenty-two new projects in the first quarter of 2016, boosting Iran's FDI ranking from twelfth in the region to third.[9]

Yet by April, Iranian leaders were complaining that they were not reaping the economic benefits of the deal, largely because many American unilateral sanctions remained. Which sanctions exactly? Not just federal government ones that had been on the books to condemn Iran's sponsorship of terrorism and development of advanced missile technology. It turned out that thirty-two American state governments had imposed sanctions of their own worth billions. California law, for example, prohibited state pension funds from investing in any company that conducted energy or defense business in Iran. California's public employee pension systems are among the largest in the United States, and if it were a country, its economy would be the sixth largest in the world.[10] Some estimated that the state's investment ban totaled close to $10 billion. Florida's state law similarly prohibited retirement fund investment in companies conducting oil business in Iran, resulting in $1 billion of divestment. Although the nuclear deal required that the U.S. government "actively encourage officials at the state or local level to take into account the changes in the U.S. policy...and to refrain from actions inconsistent with this change in policy," several governors made clear that they had no intention of lifting sanctions. Texas governor Greg Abbott was one of them. "I am committed to doing everything in my power to oppose this misguided deal with Iran," Abbott wrote to the Obama administration. "Accordingly, not only will we not withdraw our sanctions, but we will strengthen them to ensure Texas taxpayer dollars are not used to aid and abet Iran."[11] Analysts expected protracted litigation.

Labor union disputes are a more common example of how political risks generated locally can have reverberating effects globally. About half of all cargo entering or leaving the United States transits through ports on the West Coast, notably Long Beach and Los Angeles. In June 2014, the labor contract between the International Longshore and Warehouse Union, which represents about twenty thousand port workers, and the Pacific Maritime Association, which represents shippers and negotiates contracts with port employees, expired. For the next several months an impasse in negotiations led to work slowdowns, suspended night and weekend operations, and congestion in key western U.S. ports, leading many multinational companies to reroute shipments to Canada, Mexico, and the eastern United States. The situation became so serious that Labor Secretary Tom Perez joined the negotiations and threatened to force both parties to Washington if they could not reach a resolution. They eventually did, but not until February 2015, nine months later.

Big shippers like Walmart, Home Depot, and Target were able to capitalize on a diversified shipping strategy that enabled them to reroute cargo and avoid stock-outs. However, longer shipping routes increased shipping time and costs, doubling the typical two weeks it took to transport goods from Asia to Los Angeles. Smaller companies and agricultural businesses were particularly hard hit. Because farmers have to use ports close to where products are grown, many agricultural containers were stranded outside Los Angeles, where warm weather accelerated spoilage.[12] The Agriculture Transportation Coalition estimated that losses in agricultural sales reached $1.75 billion per month.[13]

Outside of local officials and labor negotiations, the most common examples of local-level political risk generators are "not in my backyard," or NIMBY, movements. In 2008, for example, Monterrico Metals, a London company acquired by China's Zijin Mining Group, was set to develop a copper-molybdenum project in northern Peru worth nearly $1.5 billion. Local opposition groups filed a referendum to block the project. As a result, the company found itself scrambling to bolster local support by adding local social programs. "We're trying to make friends," said company chairman Richard Ralph.[14]

Closer to home, a NIMBY movement led by rural landowners in Nebraska put a halt to TransCanada's Keystone XL pipeline, a twelve-hundred-mile-long project spanning an area from Canada to Texas. In 2012, ranchers whose land would have been impacted by the pipeline filed a lawsuit against the state challenging a new law that allowed the Nebraska governor to unilaterally approve the project. Local opposition sparked a national debate that led President Obama to nix it. In 2017, President Trump signed an executive order clearing a major hurdle for the pipeline to be completed.

As we will see, companies that manage risks well recognize the importance of building relationships with local stakeholders before opposition mounts. Being a good neighbor is good business. Alcoa, for example, initiated a major public outreach and communications campaign in Brazil two years before the company opened a bauxite mine there. In addition, it created a multi-stakeholder council to enable continuous communication with civil society organizations and local residents and established a $35 million development fund for initiatives proposed by the community. Alcoa executives had watched competitors face fierce local opposition in Brazil (including physical breaches that had temporarily shut down railroads and mines) and were determined to avoid the same fate. As one international mining investor put it, "You're in their backyard and they need to be on your side. Violent opposition on your doorstep is extremely disruptive."[15]

National Governmental Actors and Their Institutions

National governments pose evident risks through their power to tax, regulate, confiscate, expropriate, make or break commitments, and shape capital markets. Sometimes divisions within governments pose risks for businesses. Whether a regime is authoritarian, totalitarian, or democratic, all governments organize activities into offices with specialized portfolios and competencies to get the work done, each with its own incentives, interests, traditions, and ways of doing things that can conflict with others. Jurisdictional lines of authority between agencies at the federal level can at times be blurry or contested, generating uncertainty and facilitating corruption in specific industries and situations.

One of the more dramatic jurisdictional disputes arose due to the collapse of the Soviet Union. Practically overnight, assets and territory that had been under Moscow's control became the property of newly independent states.

Chevron was one company that felt this impact. The company acquired an oil and gas concession near the city of Atyrau in the Soviet republic of Kazakhstan in 1989. Before any production could take place, Kazakhstan became an independent state. Chevron faced thorny questions. Was the company's contract still valid in this newly formed nation? Would the Kazakhs have different regulations or requirements than the Soviets did? Clearly, negotiations would now go through Almaty, then the Kazakh capital, and its president, Nursultan Nazarbayev. Nazarbayev had been a member of the Soviet Politburo. Would Russia, the legal successor state to the Soviet Union, make claims to Chevron oil revenues as well?

More often, national governments as a whole pose risks. Most countries consider particular industries to be intimately tied to the national interest. These are called "strategic industries." Russia, for example, considers oil and gas to be a strategic industry, leveraging the full power of the state both to protect its state-owned gas giant, Gazprom, and to use the company for political advantage against European countries that rely on Russia for a substantial portion of their energy supplies. Long considered the Kremlin's hammer, Gazprom cut off energy supplies to Europe in 2006 and again in 2009 during times that coincided with rising political tension. Russia's "pipeline politics" were serious business.

Many European countries used to consider telecommunications strategic industries until technological advances led to the demise of landlines and the disintermediation of the business model. China's state capitalism model considers nearly every industry to be strategic, even the Internet. Lu Wei, who came from the propaganda department to serve as China's Internet czar until he was sacked in 2016, told foreign dignitaries in 2015 that "online space is made up of the Internets of various countries, and each country has its own independent and autonomous interest in Internet sovereignty, Internet security and Internet development."[16]

If China sits at one end of the strategic industry spectrum, the United States sits at the other. Where the state in China has a large hand in every important industry, the U.S. government has always been allergic to state ownership of industry. As Condi puts it, "We just didn't grow up as a country that way." Economic debates at the nation's founding were about charging government tariffs to private industry, not replacing private industry with state-owned "strategic" businesses. Vital industries to American growth, including most notably the railroads, remained in private hands. For the U.S. government, the "national interest" has always meant breaking up private monopolies, not asserting government ownership. Moments where the federal government has taken an ownership stake in private firms have been rare, temporary, and crisis-driven.

This American orientation nearly put Stanford University out of business in its earliest days. When Leland Stanford died in 1893, the U.S. government sued his estate to cover long-term government loans he had used to build the Central Pacific Railroad. While the case was being settled, Stanford's assets were frozen. As a result, his widow, Jane Stanford, scrambled to keep the family's fledgling university operating. She tried to sell her jewelry collection to purchase books for the campus library but found no buyers. She ended up funding the university for six years from her personal household allowance and put the faculty on her household payroll.[17]

The American experience is exceptional. Most countries consider some key industries to be within the national interest and will use the full power of the state to protect them. Companies seeking to move into a foreign market would be wise to understand whether their industry is one of them and plan accordingly.

Transnational Groups

Technology has enabled transnational groups of all types—nongovernmental organizations, activists, international labor unions, cyber vigilantes, criminal syndicates, terrorists, militias, and religious and ethnic organizations—to become more significant sources of risk for businesses. Cyber groups are newest on the scene. In February 2015, a cyber security firm discovered that an international group of cyber criminals, dubbed Carbanak, had stolen as much as $1 billion from a hundred banks in thirty countries over two years, the worst known cyber heist in history.[18] In addition to cyber criminal networks, the last decade has seen the dramatic rise of "hacktivist" organizations like Anonymous and LulzSec. Described by many as Internet vigilantes, these leaderless groups are loosely organized, global online communities that are driven by a shared sense of outrage against any action or entity that restricts the free flow of information on the Internet. They have vandalized, pranked, stolen data from, and waged distributed denial-of-service (DDoS) cyber attacks on a large and varied set of targets, including entertainment companies and industry associations, financial services companies, American military contractors, the Vatican, Arab dictatorships, pornography sites, the San Francisco Bay Area public transit authority, the CIA, and the FBI.

In cyberspace, membership in various communities and groups can be both fluid and anonymous. The relationship between individual hackers, groups, and governments is often unclear. And even when a particular breach can be traced to a computer, determining just whose fingers are on the keyboard and whether that person is part of an organization that is tolerated, encouraged, directed, or even employed directly by a nation-state is a significant intelligence challenge.

In June 2017, for example, a cyber attack called "NotPetya" disabled computer systems worldwide. The ransomware attacks disrupted everything from radiation monitoring at the Chernobyl nuclear site to shipping operations in India, and its victims ranged from Russian oil company Rosneft to American pharmaceutical giant Merck. The worm permanently encrypted the hard drives of tens of thousands of computers and demanded that owners pay a Bitcoin ransom to regain access. Except that the virus never allowed users to recover their data even if they paid the ransom. Instead, it permanently damaged the machines it infected. Exactly who was responsible for the NotPetya attack? Security researchers and law enforcement officials initially were not sure. The malicious code was for sale "in the wild," for anyone to buy and launch from the comfort of their personal computer. A group calling itself Janus Cybercrime Solutions authored the malware and got a cut of any ransom paid. Attackers also utilized a cyber tool called EternalBlue—a highly classified cyber vulnerability that the National Security Agency (NSA) was stockpiling until it was somehow stolen from Fort Meade and then leaked online by a shadowy group calling itself the Shadow Brokers. And just who are the Shadow Brokers? A corrupted insider at NSA? A nonstate actor group? A foreign government? Some combination of these actors or something in between? Were the Shadow Brokers responsible for stealing EternalBlue or just for releasing the secret code on the Internet for bad guys everywhere? These are just some of the vexing questions. Notably, even after investigators successfully traced the method of the global cyber attacks, clues about the intent of the attackers were harder to decipher. Since NotPetya initially targeted businesses and government offices in Ukraine before spreading globally, some quickly pointed to Russia. However, a major Russian bank and mining company were also struck and international companies were affected, costing billions in cleanup costs and lost revenue. It took eight months before the British and American governments publicly attributed this cyber attack to Russia as "part of the Kremlin's ongoing effort to destabilize Ukraine."[19]

As these examples suggest, politics, technology, and business can be a combustible mix. Technology is enabling groups to find, recruit, and galvanize like-minded members across geographic boundaries at little effort or cost. The ability of these groups to take politically motivated action—in virtual space, physical space, or both—poses new and rising challenges for governments and businesses alike.

Supranational and International Institutions

Supranational institutions, like the European Union, are made up of several countries who agree to participate in decision-making for the group as a whole. International institutions are bodies like the United Nations that function on behalf of essentially all nations in the world.

If individuals lie at one end of the "level of action" spectrum, supranational and international institutions lie at the other. Individuals start with the power of one. Supranational and international institutions start with the power of many. Individuals operate in informal ways, bringing others to the cause. Supranational and international institutions are formalized organizations that bind countries and hundreds of millions of people together. They have bureaucracies and offices, specific rules and procedures, and collective capabilities and punishments that can be directed at member states. With so many members, action is often difficult. But at times, these institutions can impose their will deep inside the economies and societies of member states, which is why they are so rare. Ever since the Treaty of Westphalia of 1648 established the principle of national sovereignty, countries have, for good reason, always been wary of relinquishing sovereignty to a collective.

The purpose of European integration was initially quite grand—nothing less than an effort to prevent war for all time on a continent that had experienced more than two hundred years of destructive conflicts. The EU and its forerunners were designed with the idea that if Germany and France were bound together, if their political and economic fates were tightly intertwined within broader European institutions, they would never go to war again.[20] From the point of view of its neighbors, Germany could be powerful but not dangerous. The idea was something akin to what political scientists call the democratic peace—the finding that democracies do not fight one another.[21] Not only did Germans accept this idea, they embraced it.

Condi saw this firsthand during negotiations for the unification of Germany. It was very clear that German chancellor Helmut Kohl was anxious to unify the country. The Soviet Union was in retreat and he knew that he would be the chancellor who delivered on the forty-year dream of Germans to live again as one people. It was equally clear that he was uncomfortable with any suggestion that Germany would again be powerful in its own right. Thus, whenever an American official said that we welcomed a unified Germany, Kohl would interrupt. "Within a unified Europe," he would say.

This explains in part the psychological attachment of Europeans, and particularly Germans, to the European Union. Yes, they have hoped that the common market will lead to greater economic growth. Yes, they have aspired to make the European Union a political force, equal to the United States and China in world affairs. But they credit the EU with something far more important: peace on the continent.

For those outside of it, whether countries or businesses, the European Union is more likely to be seen as a complicated entity that is difficult to navigate. Henry Kissinger is said to have asked, "When I have a problem, do I call Brussels or London, Paris, or Bonn [then the capital of West Germany]? As secretary of state, I found it better to call all of the above."

In many ways, Kissinger is still right. The EU actually has three key institutions: the European Parliament, the European Council, and the European Commission. The European Parliament consists of legislators who are elected on a Europe-wide basis. In truth, though, it has relatively little power to make consequential laws—that function is largely reserved for national legislatures. The European Council includes the heads of state and government, as well as other lower-ranking ministers. It is a powerful institution, but it meets only periodically, tends to reinforce sovereignty, and on the most important issues must achieve unanimity among states as varied as Germany and Spain, Slovakia and Sweden.

The European Commission (EC) is a permanent bureaucracy in Brussels with twenty-eight commissioners, nearly thirty-three thousand staff, and a budget of €155 million. The commission is arguably the most powerful and coherent of the EU's institutions. It is also the least democratic since its commissioners are appointed, not elected. Moreover, although the EC has a carefully delineated set of "competencies" or areas of jurisdiction, actual policy issues can overlap in confusing ways. For instance, energy policy is largely the purview of the individual states. Germany bans nuclear power, while France gets 80 percent of its generating power from this source. But environmental policy is largely within the jurisdiction of the commission. So, is the use of fracking technologies an environmental issue or a matter of energy policy?

The United Nations was founded in 1945 to promote international cooperation on issues such as peace and security, terrorism, humanitarian crises, and sustainable development. Today it includes 193 member states, nearly every country in the world. The five permanent members of the UN Security Council—the United States, the United Kingdom, Russia, China, and France—wield veto rights. The UN's large membership and its veto structure mean that Security Council resolutions are difficult to enact and enforce. But hard does not mean impossible. The UN has imposed multilateral sanctions twenty-six times on twenty-two countries since its founding.[22] UN sanctions can have an effect, and they at least inject greater market predictability by leveling the playing field. International binding sanctions are usually preferable—even with their drawbacks—to ad hoc arrangements by one nation or a few.

For example, following the Iranian revolution and the seizure of more than fifty American hostages in 1979, the United States imposed unilateral sanctions on Iran. The UN Security Council, however, did not impose sanctions until a 2006 resolution passed unanimously amid rising international concern about Iran's nuclear activities. One result of the lag between American and UN sanctions was that American companies were kept out of Iran while some of America's closest allies continued to do business there. When the Security Council's sanctions were finally instituted, Iran's two biggest trading partners were Japan and Germany.

Ironically, elaborate sanctions that are in place for a long time tend to get weaker. Those levied against Saddam Hussein after the 1991 Gulf War are a case in point. Everyone knew that the Iraqis were selling oil on the black market well in excess of what was allowed. But the UN and the international community turned a blind eye to the practice because it benefited so many countries. Moreover, sanctions on Saddam's ability to buy equipment with potential military applications eroded as the UN committee that was supposed to oversee these prohibitions became a place of constant bickering. By 2001, the sanctions regime against Iraq was in tatters.

Iraq is of course an extreme case, but sanctions regimes generally suffer from lax enforcement. This is due in part to the fact that countries are responsible for policing themselves. Not every state lives up to the letter (or even the spirit) of the law. And because the negotiations often result in least common denominator approaches with vague language, loopholes abound and states take advantage of them.

Types of Political Risk Today

What about the political actions that all of these risk generators take? What do businesses need to worry about most? Here, too, the list is long and growing. We summarize the ten major types of political risk in the table on pages 30–31 and discuss each one.

You will notice that two major risks are not on the list: climate change and economic risks. We excluded them for analytical reasons, not because we think they are unimportant.

Climate change is a global challenge that directly threatens agricultural production, vital ecosystems such as coral reefs, and the welfare of millions of people living in low-lying coastal areas. Rising temperatures are already spurring interstate rivalry over rights in the Arctic, where rapidly melting ice sheets have created a new ocean, and severe droughts and other major weather events are inflaming conflicts in weak states. But climate change is more of a risk multiplier than a separate risk category. It creates the environmental circumstances that trigger political actions, from social activism by environmental groups, to new environmental laws and regulations, to civil wars and interstate conflicts. Our top ten list covers these risks already.

The omission of economic risks to companies is also deliberate. Most businesses think about economic risks routinely, examining indicators like inflation, labor markets, growth rates, unemployment, and per capita income across markets. MBA programs teach about these risks, and Amazon.com is filled with business books about them. Our focus is different. We are interested in how *political* actions affect businesses, a topic that receives surprisingly little attention in MBA courses or business books but that causes a great deal of concern in boardrooms and C-suites. Corporate boards and executives often think about political risks but have few resources to develop a more systematic understanding or management of them.

Ten Types of Political Risk

Geopolitics	Interstate wars, great power shifts, multilateral economic sanctions and interventions
Internal conflict	Social unrest, ethnic violence, migration, nationalism, separatism, federalism, civil wars, coups, revolutions
Laws, regulations, policies	Changes in foreign ownership rules, taxation, environmental regulations, national laws

Breaches of contract	Government reneging on contracts, including expropriations and politically motivated credit defaults
Corruption	Discriminatory taxation, systemic bribery
Extraterritorial reach	Unilateral sanctions, criminal investigations and prosecutions
Natural resource manipulation	Politically motivated changes in supply of energy, rare earth minerals
Social activism	Events or opinions that "go viral," facilitating collective action
Terrorism	Politically motivated threats or use of violence against persons, property
Cyber threats	Theft or destruction of intellectual property, espionage, extortion, massive disruption of companies, industries, governments, societies

Geopolitical Events

First and most broadly, political risks arise from geopolitical events like major wars, great power shifts, and the imposition of multilateral sanctions or military interventions. These events can redistribute power among countries and generate reverberating effects across markets. Many market effects are direct and immediate—think back to what happened to Chevron with the collapse of the Soviet Union. But as we will keep underscoring, the indirect effects of geopolitical events are often hidden and yet just as important for businesses.

Dow Corning, an American silicone products manufacturer, provides a good example of the indirect effects from major geopolitical events and how to handle them. In the spring of 2003, it looked like the United States and Iraq were heading for war. Dow Corning executives were paying attention. They figured that war in Iraq would probably produce shipping capacity shortages across the Atlantic, since the United States would need to mobilize large numbers of troops and large amounts of equipment and materiel. This was exactly what happened. But before then, Dow decided to stockpile inventory and accelerate its own shipping schedule, actions that later enabled the company to mitigate the impact of wartime shipping capacity reductions on its operations.[23]

Internal Conflict

Conflicts within countries are often just as serious for businesses as conflicts between them. Internal conflicts include social unrest, ethnic violence, and federalist discord about the appropriate allocation of power between central and regional governments. In more extreme cases, federalist disputes evolve into separatist movements, such as Scotland's referendum to secede from the United Kingdom in the fall of 2014, or Catalonia's referendum to secede from Spain in 2017, or the Kurds' efforts to secure independence from the central Iraqi government, a struggle that has simmered and boiled over repeatedly since the end of British rule there in 1932.

Ultimately, internal conflict may lead to civil wars, coups, and revolutions, producing mass migrations into neighboring countries. The past several years have witnessed a dramatic rise in the number of displaced persons fleeing conflict zones resulting from enduring conflicts such as Chechnya, Darfur, Somalia, and Afghanistan, as well as newer conflicts such as the Syrian, Yemeni, and Burundi civil wars. In 2015, the United Nations high commissioner for refugees found that political conflict and persecution had displaced more than sixty-five million people, the highest number ever recorded in the agency's fifty-year history. That number amounted to one person in every 113 people on earth, or a population greater than that of Canada, Australia, and New Zealand combined.[24]

Mass migrations disproportionately affect neighboring states. In 2015, for example, six hundred thousand Ukrainians left Ukraine seeking political asylum or other forms of legal stay in neighboring countries.[25] In 2016, Syrian refugees were estimated to constitute

10 percent of Jordan's total population.[26] In 2017, more than five hundred thousand Rohingya fled violence and persecution in Burma by traveling to Bangladesh.[27]

It should come as no surprise that internal conflict can severely impact economic welfare. Coups are associated with a cumulative 7 percent reduction in national income.[28] Political scientist Jay Ulfelder finds that economic growth slows on average by 2.1 percentage points in the year of a coup.[29] Disruptions in business operations, displaced labor forces, sudden policy changes, corruption—these are just a few of the economic aftershocks that often add to human suffering in conflict-ridden areas. Even businesses with the best of intentions, robust corporate social responsibility programs, and strong relationships with diverse country stakeholders can find themselves facing significant challenges, including reputational risks.

Laws, Regulations, and Policies

Laws, regulations, policies, and the structure of business ownership vary considerably around the world. Global business investors and executives, of course, know this. For Marc Andreessen of the Silicon Valley venture capital firm Andreessen Horowitz, regulatory risk is top of mind. "Regulatory capture is probably the single biggest government risk that our start-ups think about," he told us.

Yet businesses can miss and get burned by legal, regulatory, or policy changes if they assume that political stability and policy stability are the same thing. They aren't. Even if a country's regime is stable, its ownership rules, taxation, environmental regulations, and other laws and policies may not be. Political risks for businesses exist even in seemingly

> "Regulatory capture is probably the single biggest government risk that our start-ups think about."
> —Marc Andreessen, cofounder and partner, Andreessen Horowitz

"safe" countries with relatively well-established legal regimes, well-functioning bureaucracies, well-respected currency controls, and low levels of corruption.

In our course, we first wrote a case in 2011 about a shale gas play in Poland by an Irish company called San Leon Energy. By all accounts, Poland looked like a good bet. Geologists estimated that the country had some of Europe's largest recoverable shale gas reserves. Poland also had a fervent desire for energy independence from Russia (which provided about two-thirds of its energy needs), a relatively professional bureaucracy with moderate levels of corruption, and more than twenty years of democratic rule. In fact, Poland had agitated against Soviet rule throughout the Cold War, and in 1989 became one of the first countries in the former Soviet bloc to democratize. In 2011, fracking was strongly supported by all of Poland's major political parties.

What San Leon did not expect was that strong domestic political support for fracking would lead the Polish government to overreach. Seeking greater revenues from shale gas exploration, the government in 2013 proposed dramatically increasing taxes to nearly 80 percent of profits and establishing a state-owned company that would take a compulsory minority stake in shale investments.[30] "What's been done here is what Poles call dividing up the bear hide before you've shot the bear," said Tom Maj, the head of Polish operations for Canada's Talisman Energy. "This has been hugely damaging to the shale gas project."[31] Essentially, the government was planning to increase the regulatory burden on an industry that had yet to develop.

Prime Minister Donald Tusk's government eventually reversed course, but not before Talisman and Marathon Oil pulled out in the spring of 2013.[32] Regulation, taxation, and state involvement in oil drilling added tremendous political uncertainty to the geological and economic uncertainty of shale gas exploration already at play.

In the summer of 2015, we were talking through the San Leon

case and its broader implications for this book when Condi commented, "Taxes aren't usually a sudden market-distorting risk. Governments are always adjusting some policies like taxes, and most companies watch that carefully. It's really about the suddenness and the gravity of change." The more we talked and thought about it, the more it struck us that businesses needed to think of policies, laws, and regulations along a continuum. At one end of that continuum are those that are almost always changing in some way, like taxes, and that typically result in incremental, manageable effects for global businesses. After the 2008 global financial crisis, for example, more than forty countries cut their corporate income tax rates, many of them temporarily, to stimulate business activity.[33] Another sixteen economies introduced new taxes such as environmental taxes, road taxes, and labor taxes.[34] In the middle of the continuum are policies like foreign ownership rules that change less frequently but when they do change are typically more consequential. At the extreme end of the continuum are major departures from the status quo like new "champion rules" that essentially close markets to foreign competitors. These types of policy changes occur more rarely, are harder to see coming, and are more difficult for a business to absorb. In these cases, policies create large market-distorting effects.

This is exactly what happened in 2002, when China proposed new policies stating that a Chinese government agency could buy only Chinese software. The government's goal was to stimulate the development of indigenous software companies. The effect, however, was to ban foreign software firms from selling to state-owned enterprises, which constituted 80 percent of the Chinese market.

Breaches of Contract, Expropriations, and Defaults

Sometimes governments need not go through the effort of changing national policy to create political risks for businesses. Instead, they can simply renegotiate, renege on, or violate existing contracts, or, in extreme cases like Hugo Chávez's, expropriate foreign assets entirely. As we noted at the start of this chapter, outright expropriations have become rare. But renegotiating or reneging on contracts, including politically motivated credit defaults, is more common. A 2004 World Bank study found that 15 to 30 percent of contracts in the 1990s involving $371 billion of private infrastructure investment were either renegotiated or disputed by governments.[35] And as Harvard economist Ken Rogoff notes, "Most countries have gone bankrupt at least a couple of times."[36] Countries defaulting on their national debt since 1995 include Russia, Pakistan, Indonesia, Argentina, Paraguay, Grenada, Cameroon, Ecuador, and Greece.[37] Argentina has defaulted twice in thirteen years. Ecuador and Venezuela have defaulted ten times in their history, and four other countries have failed to pay their debts nine times.[38]

In some cases, countries are simply unable to pay their debts. In others, countries are unwilling to repay foreign creditors for domestic political reasons. As our Stanford colleague Mike Tomz and his coauthor Mark L. J. Wright note, "When governments appropriate funds to service the foreign debt, they are making a political decision to prioritize foreign obligations over alternative goals that might be more popular with domestic constituents."[39] Sometimes, governments prefer to lose access to credit markets abroad rather than the support of constituents at home.

Russia, for example, defied economists' predictions in 1998 by essentially defaulting on its debt and allowing the ruble to float, which devalued the currency considerably and sent inflation surging to 80 percent. Many economic analysts were caught by surprise by this move because they examined only whether Russian leaders could pay off their debt, not whether they would. As it turned out, the Yeltsin government faced strong domestic pressures from striking workers, unions, and industry groups to devalue the ruble and stimulate exports.[40]

Ecuador in late 2008 failed to repay part of its national debt—for the second time in a decade—because the country's populist president, Rafael Correa, knew the move would be seen favorably by left-wing voters in the run-up to his bid for reelection in April 2009.[41] As Claudio Loser, the former director of the International Monetary Fund's Western Hemisphere department, noted, "The financial need wasn't so great that it was forced to declare a default."[42] In Ecuador, as in Russia, domestic political considerations trumped economic ones.

Domestic political factors also figured heavily into Greece's 2015 default woes. Although that nation had been confronting a looming economic crisis for years, the election in January 2015 of leftist prime minister Alexis Tsipras sent the country spiraling toward default. Tsipras's Syriza party ran on a single issue: rolling back Greece's austerity measures, which were a condition of the country's international bailout. And roll back he did, raising the minimum wage and cutting taxes, and in June 2015 making Greece the first developed country in history to default on its debt obligations to the International Monetary Fund.[43]

Russia, Ecuador, and Greece suggest why political risk analysis is so important, even with issues that are so intimately tied to a nation's economy. National decisions about economics are never just about economics.

Corruption

For the international community as a whole, corruption is a serious problem, hindering economic development, spurring transnational crime, and even fueling extremism and terrorism.[44] For individual businesses, it is a recurring and ubiquitous challenge. The United Nations estimates that corruption adds a 10 percent surcharge to the cost of doing business in many parts of the world, and the African Union found that in the 1990s a quarter of Africa's gross domestic product was lost to graft.[45]

The World Bank broadly defines *corruption* as "the abuse of public office for private gain."[46] As Sarah Chayes of the Carnegie Endowment for International Peace puts it, "That means when you have to be paid money on the side to do your job, or you can be paid not to do your job. It means the monetization systematically of public service."[47] Corruption includes, among other things, the payment of bribes or special favors by private interests to secure or breach government contracts; gain special access to schools, medical care, or other favorable business opportunities; reduce taxes; secure licenses or exclusive rights; or influence legal outcomes.[48]

Corruption cannot be avoided. In Transparency International's 2014 corruption perceptions index, no country earned a perfect score of 100 (on a scale where 0 is highly corrupt and 100 is very clean). Only two countries (Denmark and New Zealand) scored above 90. Two-thirds of all the countries in the world scored below 50. These included half of all G-20 countries and all of the large emerging-market BRIC countries (Brazil, Russia, India, and China), of which Russia scored so low, it was tied with Nigeria and Kyrgyzstan.[49]

Emerging markets are particularly prone to corruption for two reasons. First, their economic and political spheres are highly interdependent, which provides incentives for bribery. When public officials have discretionary power over the distribution of private-sector benefits or costs, the opportunities for corruption are high. Second, emerging markets typically have weak institutions. As a result, many laws are on the books, but the rule of law is not practiced systemically or predictably. A customs officer, for example, can appeal to the law to threaten punishment of a foreign company for not filling out a form correctly at the same time that he demands an under-the-table payment to overlook the transgression.

In addition to increasing the costs of doing business in foreign markets, corruption leaves companies at risk for criminal and civil prosecution as well as heavy penalties under the American Foreign

Corrupt Practices Act (FCPA) and the United Kingdom's Bribery Act 2010. For decades, the United States was the only nation in the world that banned bribery. In fact, bribes used to be tax deductible in Germany.[50] Those days are over. In 2005 the passage of the United Nations Convention Against Bribery signified changing international norms and a growing global anticorruption movement. The United Kingdom's antibribery law came into force in 2011. Enforcement of the U.S. law has increased substantially in recent years as well. Lockheed Martin's 1994 corruption fine of $25 million held the record for many years. In 2008, Siemens settled the largest FCPA case in history, paying voluntary fines, penalties, and profit disgorgements of $1.7 billion to U.S. and German authorities. In 2009, Halliburton settled a bribery case by paying a $559 million fine.[51] Corporate penalties in 2016 under the FCPA totaled $2.5 billion, the highest in history,[52] and included four landmark settlements that are among the ten highest in FCPA history. The largest, of $519 million, was paid by Teva Pharmaceuticals, an Israeli generic drug manufacturer charged with bribing government officials in Russia, Ukraine, and Mexico.[53]

Both U.S. and U.K. anticorruption laws are extremely broad,[54] banning gifts to any foreign government official even if the gift is given by a company contractor or third-party vendor and even if it is given in places where the practice is common. "Gifts" can be almost anything—a discount on a product, a donation to a charity, a used laptop, even payment for funeral expenses, which is a common form of tribute in many countries. The title "government official," moreover, may be held by just about anyone. In China, for example, doctors and university professors are considered state employees. The extraterritorial reach of both laws is wide, applying to the business dealings anywhere in the world of any company with a presence in either the United Kingdom or the United States.

"All along I thought our level of corruption fell well within community standards."

Bernard Schoenbaum/New Yorker.

Extraterritorial Reach

Corruption laws are one example of a more general political risk: the extraterritorial reach of powerful states into the affairs of others. American laws extend most broadly, as the 2015 arrests and indictments against fourteen international soccer officials showed. The arrests included a made-for-TV early morning international raid in which Swiss police descended on a luxury hotel in Zurich, nabbing seven high-ranking Fédération Internationale de Football Association (FIFA) officers. Hotel officials erected a shield wall of luxury bed linens in a futile attempt to protect the FIFA officials' identities as police carted them away—a moment captured on video and replayed around the world. The raid was a vivid display of the long arm of the law: Swiss police arresting soccer officials from Brazil, the Cayman Islands, Costa Rica, Nicaragua, Uruguay, Venezuela,

Pascal Mora/New York Times

and the United Kingdom so that they could be charged and tried in American courts for violating U.S. anticorruption laws.[55]

U.S. "311 sanctions" also have extraordinary reach. Developed as an antiterrorism tool shortly after 9/11, section 311 of the USA Patriot Act grants the Treasury Department's Financial Crimes Enforcement Network the authority to sanction countries and financial institutions anywhere in the world if they are linked to money laundering. No presidential action or new action by Congress is required. Perhaps most important, these sanctions bar any targeted institution from banking with any American financial institution, essentially cutting off the targeted country or bank from worldwide trade in U.S. dollars. What's more, any third party doing business with a targeted institution of a 311 sanction can also be barred from conducting business with any American financial institution. Targets of 311 sanctions include Iran, Burma, Ukraine, Nauru, and banks in Syria, Macau, and Latvia. The consequences of these sanctions can be severe. The Lebanese Canadian Bank, which was accused of transferring money for Hezbollah, was forced to close. Another targeted bank lost 80 percent of its business.[56]

The signaling effects of 311 sanctions can be powerful as well. In 2005 the United States put Macau-based Banco Delta Asia on the 311 sanctions list for its involvement in North Korea's illegal activities. Global banks took notice: North Korea was off-limits. However, when the United States later sought to lift the freeze on $25 million in North Korean assets at Banco Delta Asia as part of ongoing nuclear negotiations with the Hermit Kingdom, no bank in the world wanted to process the transaction.[57] Condi remembers how Chris Hill, U.S. envoy to North Korea, spent weeks trying to recruit a bank to execute the transaction, offering assurances that the United States would not punish any institution for its involvement in the deal. "Still, nobody wanted to touch it," Condi recalled. "Even the Central Bank of Russia wouldn't do it alone. So the Central Bank of Russia and the Federal Reserve Bank of New York worked together to process the transfer of North Korea's $25 million. Talk about an unusual partnership."

Manipulation of Natural Resources

In 1960, the Organization of the Petroleum Exporting Countries (OPEC) formed to take oil pricing out of the hands of the "seven sisters" multinational oil companies, which at the time controlled most of the world's petroleum extraction and shipping outside the communist bloc. OPEC's own website notes that in the 1970s, member countries "took control of their domestic petroleum industries and acquired a major say in the pricing of crude oil on world markets."[58] During the 1973 Arab-Israeli War, Arab members of OPEC launched an oil embargo against the United States, Portugal, South Africa, the Netherlands, and other countries that supported Israel. The effects were extreme and global: Oil prices quadrupled, triggering high inflation and economic slowdowns in the United States,

Europe, and Japan, giving rise to the term "stagflation." For energy companies, the crisis eventually triggered investment in new exploration outside of OPEC countries—in Alaska, the North Sea, the Gulf of Mexico, and Canadian oil sands—as well as investment in alternative power sources. Today, world oil production is 50 percent higher than it was in 1973.[59] For automakers, the oil shocks of the 1970s led to new American fuel efficiency standards that transformed the industry.[60]

While OPEC's influence has waned with the rise of shale gas exploration in non-OPEC countries, state manipulation of other natural resources poses increasing risks to a large number of industries. China currently produces more than 90 percent of the seventeen rare earth minerals, elements like europium and tungsten, which are vital components in most high-technology devices, including electric car batteries, mobile phones, computers, and military equipment such as missiles and night-vision goggles.[61] As former Chinese leader Deng Xiaoping once declared, "The Middle East has its oil, China has rare earths."[62] China has been accused of manipulating both the pricing and the production of minerals, charging foreign firms far more than Chinese state-owned enterprises for the same products and thus giving Chinese companies a competitive edge.[63] In 2002, the Molycorp mine in California was forced to close for nearly a decade when China flooded the market with cheaper minerals.[64] In 2014, the United States, Japan, and the European Union won a World Trade Organization case against China for Beijing's tight export controls on rare earth minerals.[65] China has also used its market dominance more directly as a foreign policy tool. During a territorial dispute in 2010, Beijing canceled all rare earth mineral shipments to Japan while Tokyo held a Chinese fishing ship captain in custody.[66] Today, many experts worry that China's concentrated control over rare earth minerals poses strategic vulnerabilities to specific industries as well as countries.

Social Activism

As SeaWorld's troubles made clear, social activism has become supercharged, generating sudden and sometimes large risks, particularly for consumer-facing businesses. The spread of social media, cell phones, and the Internet has empowered individuals and small groups in big ways. From the Arab uprisings to antifracking protests in Europe, technology has made it possible for civil societies to organize more suddenly, widely, and effectively. Technology-empowered social activism offers enormous potential benefits, enabling citizens to mobilize against repressive regimes, fostering greater democratic transparency and responsiveness, and bringing companies and stakeholders closer together. But it also poses new challenges. Governments and businesses alike must now contend with events that can go viral with little warning.

Greenpeace exemplifies the growing power of online social activism. In 2010, the environmental group used a creative social media campaign that took on food giant Nestlé and won. At issue was the sourcing of palm oil, a key ingredient of many of the company's products, whose production involved the destruction of the Indonesian rainforest habitat of orangutans. While Nestlé had committed to responsible sourcing, Greenpeace believed the company had not done enough to cut all ties to Sinar Mas, one of its suppliers. For two years, Greenpeace had been pressing Nestlé to take greater action. Then Greenpeace took its protest digital. "This is the place where major corporations are very vulnerable," said Daniel Kessler, press officer at Greenpeace.[67] On March 17, Greenpeace released a report about Nestlé's palm oil use featuring a cover picture of one of the company's signature products, KitKat chocolate bars, with the KitKat logo changed to the word "Killer."

The same day, Greenpeace protesters dressed as orangutans demonstrated outside the company's U.K. headquarters. And the organization posted a sixty-second video on YouTube mocking Nestlé's

Greenpeace

KitKat ad campaign and its tagline, "Have a break, have a KitKat." The video features an office worker opening the chocolate bar wrapper to eat a bloody orangutan finger, and ends with, "Have a break? Give the orangutan a break. Stop Nestlé buying palm oil from companies that destroy the rain forests."[68] Nestlé requested that the video be removed from YouTube, but Greenpeace then posted it on the video-sharing website Vimeo.com and spread the word on Twitter. The clip went viral, attracting hundreds of thousands of views. Meanwhile, protesters "brandjacked" Nestlé's Facebook fan page, many of them encouraging a boycott of Nestlé products. When Nestlé told Facebook users that it would delete any negative comments that included the doctored KitKat "Killer" logo, the number of protesting posts exploded. John Sauven, executive director of Greenpeace U.K. and the Greenpeace global forest team, reflected, "The moment that will forever stick in my mind was when Nestlé decided to ban our campaign on the fan site of their Facebook page. Fans of Nestlé products are only allowed to say nice things about chocolate bars. It backfired on them and helped us win our campaign."[69]

Social activism is not just for committed activists anymore. As we noted earlier, cell phones and social media are empowering ordinary citizens, too. "Companies are now being swept up into this

> "The moment that will forever stick in my mind was when Nestlé decided to ban our campaign on the fan site of their Facebook page. Fans of Nestlé products are only allowed to say nice things about chocolate bars. It backfired on them and helped us win our campaign."
>
> —John Sauven, executive director of Greenpeace U.K. and the Greenpeace global forest team

political consumer activism in a way that they have not been in the past," said Maurice Schweitzer, a professor at the University of Pennsylvania's Wharton School.[70] The Twitterstorm over United Airlines' passenger dragging incident was so fast and powerful that the airline quickly conducted a policy review. Just three weeks after fellow passengers posted their cell phone videos of Dr. Dao online, United announced that it would no longer force paying passengers off its airplanes unless safety or security was at risk and that it was increasing passenger compensation for overbooked flights to as much as $10,000.

It is worth noting that social activism is not always a threat. Sometimes it is a golden opportunity, galvanizing support for a company, a cause, or both. In 2014, Procter & Gamble launched an award-winning online campaign for its Always product line called "Like a Girl." Feminine hygiene products don't exactly spring to mind as winning social media topics. Nobody likes to talk about them. But the company created an Always-branded three-minute video on YouTube that transformed the insult "like a girl" into a message of female empowerment. The video depicts a casting call for boys and girls who are asked to do athletic activities such as running and throwing "like a girl." Ten-year-old girls give it their all, brimming with self-confidence, while teenage boys and girls follow the stereotype, interpreting "like a girl" to mean "weakly," or "not as good as a boy." They run flapping their arms and legs, throw poorly, giggle, and flip their hair. The video caught fire, reaching ninety million viewers in more than 150 countries. P&G

launched a #LikeAGirl Twitter campaign and aired a Super Bowl ad. Always's product brand equity rose by double digits, its Twitter following tripled, and surveys found purchase intent grew more than 50 percent among the target demographic. In surveys, two out of three men who watched the video said they would now think twice before using "like a girl" as an insult. Procter & Gamble harnessed the power of social media activism to change minds, not just sell products.[71]

Terrorism

Terrorism comes in many forms—hijackings, kidnappings, bombings, beheadings, and shootings, to name a few. Terrorist attacks are also conducted by a variety of actors, from transnational organizations like al-Qaeda, which operates in over sixty countries, to nationalist movements like the Tamil Tigers, to "lone wolves." But all terrorists use violence or the threat of violence for political purposes. All terrorists deliberately target innocents. And all terrorists seek to instill fear, terrorizing societies and their leaders. There is a strong psychological component to terrorism, which is why terrorists often strike victims and targets that have symbolic significance—like the Houses of Parliament in London, the 1972 Munich Olympics, the Taj Mahal Palace hotel in Mumbai, and the *Charlie Hebdo* magazine offices in Paris. Terrorists also frequently select "soft" targets. The more that governments harden the defenses of government buildings and installations, the more terrorists turn their sights on relatively vulnerable locations like hotels, restaurants, markets, and even marathon races.[72]

Terrorism has become a growing economic and security concern for governments, particularly in Europe. In 2015–16 the Eurozone saw a record number of successful and foiled terrorist plots, including attacks in Turkey, Belgium, and Germany, and a wave of mass-casualty attacks in France that slowed French growth to a halt in the second quarter of 2016 and played a major role in cutting

Eurozone economic growth in half.[73] In their July meeting, finance ministers from the world's twenty largest economies emphasized that geopolitical conflicts and terrorism had become growing threats to the global economy. The French finance minister, Michel Sapin, singled out terrorism as an economic risk, telling reporters, "Today the frequency of attacks creates a new situation of uncertainty, which is at least as damaging as regional destabilizations or a regional conflict."[74]

Terrorist attacks often trigger cascade effects for specific companies that can be widespread, long-term, and surprising. Consider the tragic attacks of September 11, 2001. For Wall Street trading firm Cantor Fitzgerald, which lost 658 of its 960 New York employees that day—almost two-thirds of its workforce—the damage could not have been more direct or searing.[75] (As we discuss in chapter 8, Cantor survived, and its incredible turnaround after tragedy reveals important lessons about communicating in crises, aligning incentives, and creating organizational resilience.) For Ford and Chrysler, the effects of 9/11 were immediate but indirect: These two American auto manufacturers suddenly found themselves confronting the first total grounding of American air traffic in history, disrupting shipping in their supply chains. For Boeing, the full effects of 9/11 took six years to surface. It wasn't until 2007, when orders for a new airplane took off, that the company discovered its principal supplier of specialized nuts and bolts had laid off nearly half its workforce after 9/11 and could not keep up. Four American companies in three different industries were all affected by the 9/11 terrorist attacks in very different ways and along very different time frames.

Cyber Threats

John Chambers, executive chairman and former CEO of Cisco, famously said, "There are two types of companies: those who have been hacked, and those who don't yet know they have been hacked."[76]

> "There are two types of companies: those who have been hacked, and those who don't yet know they have been hacked."
> —John Chambers, executive chairman and former CEO, Cisco

He's right. Experts estimate that at least 97 percent of Fortune 500 corporations have been hacked already.[77] In 2016, a Google director revealed that Google notifies customers of four thousand state-sponsored cyber attacks on its systems each month. That's about one attack every eleven minutes just from state actors, and just from attacks Google is telling its customers about.[78] Brad Smith, president and chief legal officer of Microsoft, noted in February 2017 that 74 percent of global businesses expected to be hacked in the coming year.[79] Most cyber victims will not know for months that they have been breached: The typical time between a cyber penetration and its detection is 205 days.[80] Costs are hard to measure, but by all accounts are large and growing. The Center for Strategic and International Studies, a well-regarded think tank, in 2014 estimated that the annual global cost of cyber crime was as high as $575 billion[81]—the equivalent of the entire GDP of Sweden.[82] A Juniper Networks study found that cyber crime is now worth more than the global illicit drug trade.[83] For individual companies, the cost of a single incident can be large, including everything from customer notification, forensic investigations, legal fees, and fines to lost business and long-term reputational damage. The Target breach of 2013 has cost the retailer $292 million so far, with only $90 million covered by insurance.[84] The 2017 breach of credit reporting company Equifax compromised the personal information of 143 million customers and could become the most expensive in history, with estimated costs in the billions.[85]

And that's just crime. Countries, criminals, hacktivists, and others wage cyber attacks in many ways for many reasons. Official government systems are major targets. The United States fends off millions of attempted cyber intrusions into military and other government networks each month.[86] In 2015, hackers most likely acting at the behest of the Chinese government stole the highly classified security clearance information of twenty-two million Americans from the Office of Personnel Management. Many believe it was a massive intelligence operation to find foreign contacts and compromising information about government officials that could be used to coerce them later. In 2016, the mysterious Shadow Brokers started releasing a treasure trove of secret computer vulnerabilities that had been stolen from the NSA.[87] That same year, the Russian government waged an unprecedented influence operation to disrupt the American presidential election and undermine American democracy. Russia's efforts included hacking into campaign-related websites and servers, releasing data from those breaches online, penetrating multiple state and local electoral boards, disseminating propaganda overtly through Russian state-backed media outlets RT and Sputnik, and inflaming social cleavages by covertly spreading deceptive information with botnets, fake accounts, and unwitting users on American social media platforms.[88] According to Facebook's general counsel Colin Stretch, Kremlin-instigated content may have reached 126 million Americans—more than a third of the U.S. population. "We're obviously deeply disturbed," said Joel Kaplan, Facebook vice president for United States public policy. "The ads and accounts we found appeared to amplify divisive political issues across the political spectrum."[89] Experts expect that attacks on elections and government systems worldwide are likely to grow.[90]

For companies, attackers and motives vary widely. Some steal, some spy, some disrupt, others destroy. Some attack a company to protest a particular product or action, some to steal intellectual property, some to turn a quick profit by stealing customer credit card information, some to help a foreign government, some to gain information that will advantage another business in an upcoming negotiation, and some simply because they can. The threat landscape is evolving rapidly and dramatically, raising business and reputational risks for companies. As U.S. director of national intelligence James Clapper noted in February 2015, despite improvements in cyber defenses, the frequency, severity, sophistication, destructiveness, and scale of cyber breaches all are increasing.[91] The cyber dark arts are growing darker.

Although headlines focus on major breaches in large corporations like Target, J.P. Morgan Chase, Anthem Insurance, Home Depot, Sony Pictures, and Equifax, nobody is immune. As Enrique Alanis, chief risk officer at the Mexican building materials giant Cemex, put it, "You don't have to be a sexy company anymore to be hacked. Cyberthreats are real for everybody and for every company. It could impact any brand."[92] Any company that relies on information and communications technology—and nearly all companies do—is inherently vulnerable. Exposure is global: Any device that is "smart," any phone or computer or printer or machine that is connected to the Internet (and even some that aren't),[93] can be used as an attack vector into your company's networks. From anywhere. Hackers pulled off the Target attack of 2013, stealing credit card and personal information from forty million customers during the peak holiday shopping season, by getting into the computer system of a Target third-party vendor—a small family-owned refrigeration, heating, and air-conditioning company called Fazio Mechanical Services in Sharpsburg, Pennsylvania.[94]

Many cyber threats are intimately connected to political actors and actions. By far the most sophisticated cyber attack capabilities reside in the hands of governments—namely, Russia, China, Iran, North Korea, and the United States. As a matter of policy, the United States does not conduct espionage to aid specific companies. But other countries do. And lest anyone think that cyber

Reddit

attacks on companies are only about profit, talk to Amy Pascal. She was the studio chief of Sony Pictures Entertainment during one of the worst cyber attacks in American history. The 2014 hack, which was eventually attributed to the government of North Korea, stole terabytes of Sony trade secrets, including upcoming movie scripts and celebrity contract information; revealed embarrassing internal emails; forced the company off the grid for days; publicly released personal information of thousands of Sony Pictures employees; destroyed data on thousands of hard drives and servers; and threatened violence in movie theaters if the studio released *The Interview*, a comedy depicting the assassination of North Korean leader Kim Jong-un.

By the end, the Sony hack was not just about Sony. It became a national security incident involving the highest levels of the U.S. government. It erupted into an international crisis. And it provided a sneak preview of cyber threats facing all companies today. As *Fortune* magazine reported, "What happened at Sony…struck terror in boardrooms throughout corporate America, and for all the unique elements in Sony's situation, the lessons apply to every company."[95]

Risks from Within

A final word about the risk landscape. Our list above focuses on external challenges—on political risks "out there." But it's important to underscore that sometimes the biggest political risks come from within. Organizations can hurt themselves by paying too little attention to their own corporate cultures and practices. In 2017, Uber and Fox News faced firestorms of criticism and business crises over their treatment of female employees. At Fox News, sexual harassment scandals led to the firing of cofounder and chairman Roger Ailes as well as twenty-year veteran host Bill O'Reilly. Over a fifteen-year period, O'Reilly (and Fox executives) had settled six complaints of harassment against him. When a *New York Times* investigation made some of these settlements public, more women came forward with allegations, and an advertiser boycott soon followed.[96] In Uber's case, twenty people were fired, and Uber founder and CEO Travis Kalanick was forced out, after a blog posting by a former employee triggered a string of reports describing sexual harassment, discrimination, and "Silicon Valley start-up culture gone awry."[97] For both companies, these "sudden" crises were self-inflicted and years in the making.

KEY TAKEAWAYS: MOVE OVER, HUGO CHÁVEZ

☐ Political risk used to be driven mostly by the actions of governments. Not anymore.

☐ Today's risk generators operate at five intersecting levels of action: individuals, local organizations and governments, national governments, transnational organizations, and supranational and international institutions.

☐ The risks they create are more varied now, too. Old political risks remain, but new risks have arisen alongside them.

☐ Today's top ten types of political risk are: geopolitics, internal conflict, policy change, breaches of contract, corruption, extraterritorial reach, natural resource manipulation, social activism, terrorism, and cyber threats.

3

How We Got Here: Megatrends in Business, Technology, and Politics Since the Cold War

On February 5, 2014, Manila mayor Joseph Estrada signed a new law to provide relief to local commuters. Manila, the sprawling Filipino metropolis of several million residents, was growing so fast that it was being overrun by traffic. Gridlock was everywhere. Commute times of five hours or more

Greg Elms/Getty Images

were common. To ease congestion, the city government passed an ordinance that banned cargo trucks on main roads from 5 a.m. to 9 p.m.—sixteen hours a day. "The days when buses and trucks were king of the road are over," Estrada proudly declared.[1]

But the truck ban quickly led to trouble. Manila was also home to the country's most important port, responsible for handling half of all overseas freight transiting the Philippines. Before Estrada's truck ban, up to six thousand containers could be moved in and out of the port each day by truck. Now the number was closer to thirty-five hundred. Shipping containers were quickly piling up. Loading equipment was getting stressed. Streets inside the port complex were clogged with containers, further impeding the flow of equipment and the efficiency of operations.[2] At one terminal, cargo processing time ballooned from six days to ten.[3]

Eventually, the national government had to step in. Philippine president Benigno Aquino III publicly blamed city officials for the port congestion, noting that the truck ban was "a city ordinance that perhaps, nobody envisioned how bad this would amount to."[4] In September, after seven long months, Mayor Estrada finally signed an executive order lifting the ban.

Among those affected was Toyota, the world's largest automaker, which had made the Philippines a hub for Toyota suppliers who shipped auto parts to Thailand for final production. In 2014, thanks to the truck ban and a political crisis in Thailand, Toyota experienced a 10 percent decline in shipments from the Philippines, and its exports fell noticeably short of the company's $897 million forecast.[5]

It was a very different world than in 1933, when Sakichi Toyoda started the Toyota Motor Corporation. In 1950, Toyota sold just 492 cars outside of Japan.[6] The year's top-selling car in the American market was the American-made Chevrolet Bel Air. In Moscow it was the Russian-made GAZ Pobeda, and in Paris it was the French Renault 4CV.[7] By 2009, in contrast, Toyota was selling 80 percent of its vehicles outside of Japan.[8] By 2015, the automobile industry was so globalized that the top-selling car in the United States was a Japanese model (the Toyota Camry) and, for the first time since the 1970s, the top-selling car in Russia for a given month was not the Russian Lada, but the South Korean Kia Rio.[9] The globalization of production and markets for automobiles meant that a Japanese automaker selling cars in other Asian countries had to worry about the political actions of a mayor in the Philippines.

Toyota's cargo container woes in Manila illustrate just how much business has changed, even for traditional industries like automotive companies. As venture capitalist Marc Andreessen told us, "There is no substitute for having some sense of a global perspective" today.

"There is no substitute for having some sense of a global perspective."
—Marc Andreessen, cofounder and partner, Andreessen Horowitz

In this chapter, we take a step back and look at history, examining three trends that have profoundly shaped this landscape over the past thirty years: supply chain innovations, the communications revolution, and dramatic changes in politics since the end of the Cold War. The convergence of these megatrends has created a best-of-times/worst-of-times moment for businesses: unprecedented economic opportunities coupled with unprecedented political risks.

Business Trends: Globalization and Supply Chain Innovation

The past thirty years have witnessed a revolution in supply chain management. Today's supply chains are longer, leaner, and more global than at any time in history. Even very small businesses can have long global supply chains, enabling them to seize opportunities and profits by taking advantage of lower wages offshore, low shipping costs, and better inventory management to customize products for different segments. Fairphone is one of them. A twenty-seven-employee cellular phone company based in the Netherlands, Fairphone aims to minimize the social impact of manufacturing smartphones by carefully understanding its supply chain. A Fairphone smartphone requires thirty-nine minerals. Some, like tungsten and tantalum, come from notoriously conflict-ridden countries like Rwanda and the Democratic Republic of Congo. Other components travel from North America, Europe, and the Middle East before arriving at a handful of factories in China for production. In total, Fairphone parts travel nearly once around the world before the phone ever gets turned on by its owner for the first time.

We interviewed Fairphone's director of impact and development, Bibi Bleekemolen, about how Fairphone designed its supply chain. She told us, "We are different in that we view political risk as maximizing opportunity rather than minimizing the risks. We don't shy away from risky places, but instead find what's wrong in the world and go after it to try to fix it." Fairphone carefully selects its Chinese production partners based on their willingness to uphold various social and environmental practices and works closely with local partners in Africa to ensure that Fairphone is using conflict-free minerals and metals in its phones. Fairphone has nearly as many nodes in its supply chain as it does employees in the company.[10]

Supply chains are leaner now, too. Sparked by Toyota's innovations in the 1980s, companies have developed just-in-time inventory management systems that have substantially improved profits by reducing inventory storage costs and ensuring that this year's model, or this season's hottest item, makes it out of a warehouse and into the hands of consumers while they still want it. Efficiency and customization are at all-time highs. With AmazonFresh, you can order Granny Smith apples grown in New Zealand and have them sitting on your doorstep by morning. Interested in purchasing a mobile phone handset? There are nine hundred more varieties to choose from now than in 2000.[11]

But there is a dark side to the supply chain revolution: Longer, leaner, more global supply chains have increased supply chain vulnerability to disruptions in faraway places. As companies extend supply chains to more locations in search of margin, customization, and speed, chances are that a political action someplace, sometime will occur, impacting the distribution of goods and services to customers. Often, these disruptions are immediate. In 2014, for example, China moved an oil rig just 130 miles off the coast of Vietnam and 70 miles inside Vietnam's exclusive economic zone, near the disputed Paracel Islands. Anti-Chinese protests erupted in Vietnam, leading to the ransacking and preemptive closing of several factories that sourced everything from Nike shoes to iPads.[12] Li & Fung Ltd., the world's largest supplier of clothing and toys to retailers like Walmart and Target, was forced to close its factories in Vietnam for a week during the riots, halting delivery of goods to American retailers. What began as a conflict over disputed territorial waters between China and Vietnam quickly ended up affecting store shelves in American cities.[13]

Sometimes, supply chain disruptions take longer to work their way through a business. Remember Boeing's troubles in chapter 2? In 2007, the company's new 787 Dreamliner became a business nightmare, with unprecedented three-year delays in production. The root cause: Declining air travel after the 9/11 terrorist attacks led to reductions in airplane manufacturing, which in turn triggered layoffs and consolidation in the fastener industry making the super-strength nuts and bolts that hold airplanes together. When Dreamliner production finally started to take off years later, Boeing's main fastener supplier, Alcoa, could not keep up, because it had cut its division by 41 percent. Fasteners accounted for only about 3 percent of the cost of an aircraft, but ended up throwing a wrench in Boeing's $136 billion Dreamliner program.[14] Even worse, Boeing's workaround—buying temporary fasteners from Home Depot and Ace Hardware to try to keep production going and then removing them later—ended up damaging the planes.[15] CEO Jim McNerney admitted to investors that executives did not see this slow-motion supply chain disruption coming. "The fastener industry got consolidated, post 9/11," said McNerney. "The consolidators misjudged the demand swingback—a lot of us misjudged the demand swingback—post 9/11."[16] The fastest-selling airplane in company history became the most delayed airplane in company history because of a supply chain disruption that started six years earlier.

Perhaps the most important thing to remember about supply chain vulnerability to political actions is *cumulative risk*: The risk of disruption in any one node of a supply chain may be low, but the cumulative risk of disruption across the entire supply chain is much higher. With global businesses, some political action somewhere is nearly always putting a kink into the smooth flow of business, whether it's an election, a coup, a local protest, a territorial dispute, a scandal, a diplomatic crisis, a regulatory change, a cyber breach, a referendum, a disease outbreak, a government intervention into the economy, or a terrorist attack. Consider the following list of events that occurred in 2018, many of them viewed as highly unlikely beforehand.

- China and the U.S. launch a trade war, with the U.S. imposing tariffs on $250 billion worth of Chinese goods and threatening tariffs on $263 billion more.
- The U.S. slaps aluminum and steel tariffs on allies and adversaries alike and President Trump calls himself "Tariff Man" on Twitter. Canada, China, the European Union, and others impose retaliatory tariffs on U.S. goods.
- Just hours before an American deadline, Canada, Mexico, and the U.S. sign a replacement to the North American Free Trade Agreement.
- Japan and the European Union sign an Economic Partnership Agreement, creating the largest free trade bloc in the world, affecting 30 percent of global trade.

- British prime minister Theresa May suffers a stinging defeat of her Brexit deal with the European Union, throwing the Brexit process into tumult.
- Right-wing candidate Jair Bolsonaro wins Brazil's presidential election while former president Luiz Inácio Lula da Silva goes from candidate to convict, imprisoned on corruption charges.
- Leftist Andrés Manuel López Obrador wins Mexico's presidential election in a landslide and promises radical change.
- German chancellor Angela Merkel announces that she will not run for re-election in 2021, ending what will be 16 years at the helm of Europe's most powerful economy and sparking concerns about Europe's future leadership.
- Thousands of "yellow vest" protesters flood the streets of French cities to oppose new economic policies, sparking a crisis for President Emannuel Macron.
- Record-setting turnover in the Trump administration continues, with the resignations or dismissals of the secretary of defense, secretary of state, United Nations ambassador, national security adviser, attorney general, White House counsel, and chief of staff.
- Democrats pick up forty seats and regain control of the U.S. House of Representatives, the biggest gain for the party since the Watergate class of 1974.
- The European Union's General Data Protection Regulation goes into effect, imposing wide-ranging data protection and privacy standards on companies.
- Major cyber attacks hit Marriott, T-Mobile, Quora, Google, and Orbitz, compromising the personal information of hundreds of millions of people.
- Executives for Google, Facebook, and Twitter are called before Congress and questioned about security and privacy concerns following Russia's foreign influence operations during the 2016 U.S. presidential election.

- Saudi journalist and *Washington Post* columnist Jamal Khashoggi is assassinated at the Saudi Arabian consulate in Istanbul by agents of the Saudi government.
- Chinese and American Navy warships come within 45 yards of each other in the South China Sea, marking the closest call yet.
- After a historic Singapore summit between North Korean leader Kim Jong-un and President Trump, denuclearization talks stall and commercial satellite imagery reveals Pyongyang has continued its secret ballistic missile program in 16 hidden bases.
- Russian president Vladimir Putin announces the successful test of a hypersonic nuclear weapon that can reach any point on the planet and evade missile defenses.
- The U.S. formally withdraws from the Iran nuclear deal.
- Humanitarian crises continue in Yemen, Venezuela, Syria, South Sudan, Myanmar, the Central African Republic, and Congo.
- Ethiopia and Eritrea sign a peace deal, reopen embassies, and begin demilitarizing their borders after eighteen years of talks and a war that killed nearly 80,000.
- Climate change warnings grow more alarming in new UN and U.S. government reports as hurricanes, heat waves, massive wildfires, and other extreme weather events increase.
- FreedomHouse reports that 71 countries suffer net reductions in political rights and civil liberties, marking the twelfth consecutive year of a decline in global freedom.

As FedEx founder, chairman, and CEO Fred Smith told us, "You should take very seriously political risks to your business that seem far-fetched." In 2016, FedEx's own risk analysts estimated that there was a 25 percent chance of Brexit and a 25 percent chance that Donald J. Trump would win the 2016 American presidential election. But as we'll see in chapter 8, FedEx's business requires planning for the unexpected so often that the company always has contingency plans on hand in the event the unlikely becomes reality.

Natural disasters are even more frequent disrupters and more commonly the focus of supply chain management. Taken altogether, supply chain interruptions from rare events turn out to be not so rare after all. As the saying goes, lightning does not strike in the same place twice. But it does strike someplace nearly all the time.

"Just in time" inventory management magnifies these disruption risks. Supply chains have grown so lean that each key link often keeps just days or even hours of inventory on hand, which means there is no cushion if something bad happens to a supplier.[17] Political scientists Martin Landau and Donald Chisholm presciently warned that "just in time" has displaced "just in case."[18] The search for short-term profits has generated longer-term risks.[19]

In the last chapter, we noted how Ford and Chrysler had to contend with the grounding of all U.S. flights after the 9/11 terrorist attacks. For both auto manufacturers, the sudden elimination of air shipping threw a wrench into production lines. Chrysler acted fast, asking logistics suppliers to switch from air to ground transport. Ford waited, and by the time it tried to switch to ground shipping, none was available. Ford had to shutter five U.S. plants for several weeks and reduce its production by 13 percent that quarter.[20] While Chrysler managed the sudden disruption better by responding immediately, both Chrysler and Ford were extremely vulnerable to disruption in the first place because their supply chains were so lean. They had almost no slack in their inventory to keep the production lines moving more than a few days before new shipments could arrive.[21]

Supply chain visibility is also a challenge. With so many suppliers outsourcing to so many sub-suppliers in so many places, business executives often have only vague ideas of exactly how far their supply chains extend or just who is doing what where and when. Here, too, Boeing's 787 Dreamliner provides a cautionary tale. Fasteners were a major problem for Boeing, but they were not the only problem. The company also famously suffered from an exceptionally complicated and opaque supply chain with poor measures to ensure accountability and coordination. To meet the unprecedented demand for the 787, Boeing decided to try a new supply chain system designed to cut delivery time from six years to four and production costs from $10 billion to $6 billion.[22] Using a tiered structure, it contracted with approximately fifty first-tier partners, who assembled major parts of the aircraft from sub-systems they received from second-tier partners, who received the individual components from third-tier suppliers. In total, Boeing used more than a hundred partners across twelve countries on five continents in manufacturing and delivering the 787.[23] Parts shortages or shipping delays at any of the second- or third-tier suppliers meant significant production setbacks. To help manage the supply chain, Boeing utilized a Web-based program to track each component in the chain. It sounded good. The problem was that second- and third-tier suppliers often failed to enter accurate and timely information into the system, which meant that the first-tier partners were often unaware of delays or shortages. As of February 2016, Boeing had fulfilled only 380 of the 1,143 orders placed since 2004.[24]

Boeing has plenty of company when it comes to supply chain visibility challenges. In a 2008 IBM survey, supply chain executives from twenty-five countries and twenty-nine different industries—including retail, industrial products, pharmaceuticals, food and beverage, telecommunications, and electronics—complained that poor supply chain visibility was their number one concern. Seventy percent of respondents said that visibility issues impacted their operations "to a significant or very significant extent."[25]

In addition, the widening geography of supply chains is making them more vulnerable to production interruptions. The quest for lower production costs has led many companies to use suppliers in places like Bangladesh, Indonesia, and Brazil, parts of the world that are more prone to political instability, natural disasters, and other nasty surprises. "We buy stuff from all over the world," said John Hach, risk manager at Lincoln Electric Co., a Cleveland-based manufacturer of welding products. "I'd estimate we have suppliers from about 50 different countries other than the United States, many of them third-world nations, which is where a lot of mining takes place."[26]

All of these factors explain why supply chain disruptions caused by political risks are becoming increasingly prevalent. A 2013 World Economic Forum report noted that more than 80 percent of executives and corporate directors were concerned about supply chain resilience to geopolitical instability, extreme weather events, unstable prices, and other disruptions.[27] With good reason. Increasingly, businesses are reporting lost income from supply chain disruptions, and surveys repeatedly find that companies do not think enough about supply chain risk management, especially disruptions arising from civil unrest, policy changes, regime instability, interstate conflict, terrorism, and other political risks. A 2013 survey conducted by APQC, a leading business practices nonprofit, interviewed 196 companies in 22 different industries and found an overwhelming majority of companies—83 percent—were caught off guard by a supply chain disruption in the previous twenty-four months. In the majority of these cases, disruptions were serious enough to attract the intervention or sustained attention of C-suite executives. Perhaps most interesting, 86 percent of companies surveyed said they were concerned specifically about political events that had a high impact their supply chains. Why? Because in the search for margin, they had moved to lower-cost suppliers in parts of the world known for more political instability and extreme weather events. Only about a quarter of businesses surveyed thought that they were well prepared to anticipate and mitigate these disruptions.[28]

Small Groups, Big Effects: The Rise of Connective Technologies

The second megatrend shaping the political risk landscape is technological: The spread of social media, cell phones, and the Internet has empowered small groups in big ways. Already, 48 percent of the world is online. There are more cell phones on the earth than humans.[29] By 2020, more people in the world are expected to have mobile phones than running water or electricity.[30] Connectivity is here to stay, and it is generating profound transformations in politics, business, and society.[31]

In 2006, *Time* magazine's Person of the Year was You. This was a radical departure from the magazine's tradition, in which it chose world leaders and other well-known public figures who had impacted the world—in good ways or bad—during the previous year. In years past, for example, *Time* had selected Martin Luther King Jr., Adolf Hitler, and Nikita Khrushchev. But by declaring everyone the 2006 Person of the Year, *Time* was onto something. Its editors realized how much innovations in technology were empowering individuals. Managing editor Richard Stengel said that the editors wanted to highlight that "individuals are changing the nature of the information age, that the creators and consumers of user-generated content are transforming art and politics and commerce, that they are engaged citizens of a new digital democracy."[32]

Economists and political scientists have conducted a great deal of research about the costs of collective action—the effort it takes for people to join forces in pursuit of a common cause. What they find is that normally, such costs are high, even for a cause that every member of a potential group believes in deeply. Organizing is hard. It drains time away from family and work. It requires effort up front for benefits that come later, if ever. It often costs money. It can be difficult, and even dangerous, to try to discover who might be on your side, to meet with them, and to take action, particularly if potential members are geographically dispersed or not already known to one another. What's more, the bigger the group, the more concerned each member becomes that others won't do their share.[33] Because everyone worries that everyone else will shirk, shirking becomes rampant, and not much gets done. On a societal scale, people often feel that their individual contribution cannot make much of a difference (this is one of the reasons why only about half of eligible American voters actually vote on Election Day).[34] The costs of collective action help explain why mass movements historically have been so rare, even when large sectors of a population might share the same views and goals.

Connective technologies, however, have sent the costs of collective action plummeting, making it much easier, safer, faster, and cheaper for like-minded people to find one another, share information, organize, and take individual actions in loosely coordinated ways toward a common goal, even across vast geographical distances. Transnational movements of all stripes, from human rights activists to Taylor Swift fans to jihadi terrorists, are able to recruit, organize, and act more easily and effectively, in large part because communications technologies have driven down the costs of collective action. It is one thing to travel each week to a meeting across town; quite another to click "send," "like," or "upload" on your smartphone.

The Arab Spring of 2011 revealed just how transformative communications technology can be in powering collective action. The protest movements that swept the Middle East and North Africa and led to the downfall of the Tunisian and Egyptian regimes all started with a rural Tunisian fruit seller named Mohammed Bouazizi. On December 17, 2011, Bouazizi was stopped by a police officer. After she demanded that he give her several free bags of fruit and confiscated his scale, an altercation ensued. The officer hit Bouazizi with her baton and slapped him across the face, a public humiliation. Fed up with having to face constant police corruption and deeply shamed by this particular encounter, Bouazizi went to city hall and demanded to see an official. Nobody would meet with him. The next day, he walked to the municipal building, poured paint thinner over his body, and set himself on fire. Small protests quickly erupted nearby. Bouazizi's cousin went to one of them. He took out his cell phone, recorded a video of it, and posted it online. A thirty-three-year-old blogger in Tunis named Slim Amamou saw the video and posted it on his Facebook account. From there, the Facebook postings spread like wildfire. That evening, the cable television channel Al Jazeera, with a large Arab audience, started broadcasting the video repeatedly. Protests in Tunisia grew. Within weeks, Tunisian president Zine El Abidine Ben Ali had fled the country, and Bouazizi's self-immolation had ignited rebellions in Yemen, Syria, Egypt, Libya, and Bahrain.[35] As Marc Fisher of the *Washington Post* wrote, "This wave of change happened because aging dictators grew cocky and distant from the people they once courted, because the new social media that the secret police didn't quite understand reached a critical mass of people, and because, in a rural town where respect is more valued than money, Mohammed Bouazizi was humiliated in front of his friends."[36]

Connective technologies have made it more likely that one person's act can have outsized and even unintended effects, and not just when it comes to protesting long-running corruption in Middle Eastern countries. On April 24, 2013, the eight-story Rana Plaza factory in Bangladesh collapsed, killing more than eleven hundred garment workers inside. The tragedy was not a black swan—a bolt from the blue that could never have been expected. At the time, Bangladesh was the second-largest garment exporter in the world, with a $20 billion industry, five thousand factories, and 4.5 million garment workers. Safety problems in the country's factories were both widespread and widely known. In 2011, just two years before the Rana Plaza disaster, hundreds of garment workers were killed in a rash of fires and other incidents caused by building safety lapses. International unions proposed an Accord on Fire and Building Safety to global retailers, suppliers, unions, government officials, and NGOs at a meeting in Dhaka. No retailers signed it.

But in 2013, after the Rana Plaza collapse, the unions' stalemated safety plan suddenly gained traction. Why? Because this time, news of the collapse, and the resulting public outcry, went viral over the Internet. Within twenty-four hours of the tragedy, the Worker Rights Consortium started a "name and shame" campaign, listing retailers who had produced garments in the collapsed factory.[37] At the same time, a disturbing photo from the tragedy taken by a local *Time* photographer also went viral. The photo, under the headline "A Final Embrace: The Most Haunting Photograph from Bangladesh," depicted an unidentified deceased couple holding each other, half of their bodies buried in the rubble and a trickle of blood running down one of the man's eyes like a teardrop.[38] International labor unions, leading NGOs, and a United Nations expert group collaborated virtually, using connective technologies to reach their supporters, launch online petitions, and coordinate. Within a month, companies, including Swedish retail giant H&M (the largest buyer of Bangladeshi garments), began signing a legally binding, five-year accord on fire and building safety that required retailers to undertake independent safety inspections, publish public reports on their findings, offer safety training for workers and management, pay for mandatory repairs, and terminate business with any factory that refused to make necessary safety upgrades.[39] By summer, the United States had announced the suspension of Bangladesh's trade benefits under the Generalized System of Preferences until the country improved its monitoring and inspection of factories and increased fines and other sanctions for noncompliance. By fall, one hundred retailers in Europe and the United States had signed the accord, and other retailers, including Walmart and The Gap, had reached a separate nonbinding safety accord.

Greenpeace/YouTube

The Lego Group's experience with Greenpeace shows that the effects of connective technologies can reach across industries—sometimes in surprising ways. At first glance, the Danish company known for its Lego brick toys does not seem like a prime target for an environmental group known for scaling oil rigs at sea. But the Lego Group was a longtime partner of Shell, and that gave Greenpeace an idea. In July 2014, as part of its campaign against Arctic drilling, Greenpeace produced a digital video depicting a pristine Alaskan Lego brick wilderness, replete with Santa Claus, polar bears, ice-skaters, and children, being covered in toxic oil sludge. Greenpeace's strategy was clear. The organization declared on its website:

> Every company has a responsibility to choose its partners and suppliers ethically. LEGO says it wants to leave a better world for children and has a progressive environmental policy. But it's partnered with Shell, one of the biggest polluters on the planet, now threatening the Arctic. That's a terrible decision and it's bad news for kids. We're calling on LEGO to stand up for the Arctic—and for children—by ditching Shell for good.[40]

The video caught on, attracting six million views. Greenpeace's social media activism worked.[41] The Lego Group eventually ended its fifty-year partnership with Shell. And then it did much more. As we will see, the Lego Group is one of the world's companies who are best at managing political risk, constantly looking for "risks around the corner." The Greenpeace video suggested that environmental activism and consumer preferences for sustainable products, even in the children's toy market, were likely to rise. The Lego Group had already started a sustainability effort that included a strategic partnership with the World Wildlife Fund, but Greenpeace's video kicked these efforts into overdrive. A year after the video, the Lego Group announced a major new initiative that included ambitious environmental goals for its materials, packaging, and operations and the creation of a new Sustainable Materials Center with $150 million in funding and a hundred employees to implement sustainable alternatives to its materials by 2030.[42]

Whether it's the Arab Spring, a Bangladeshi factory collapse, or a toy company's remote association with Arctic drilling, connective technologies are lowering the costs of collective action, making it possible for seemingly distant events or actions by small groups of people to have substantial effects. Today, it is far more likely that the word will get out. "News travels very fast," noted Enrique Alanis of Cemex, the Mexican building materials company. "Bad news in Nicaragua is going to be known in the U.S. and in Mexico, as well as in Europe. And because we are a global player, we have to manage our brand."[43]

These changes in connective technologies offer new hopes for citizens seeking freedom in repressive societies and new challenges and opportunities for businesses everywhere.

Key Trends in Politics Since the Cold War's End

This is the most complex security environment in modern history. During the Cold War, superpower rivalry between the United

States and the Soviet Union set relatively clear dividing lines between adversaries and allies. Trade politics and security politics were more sharply delineated, too, with the world largely split between Western capitalist markets and the command economies of the Soviet bloc. China's rise, Russia's aggression, strains within the Eurozone, nuclear proliferation, the disintegration of the state in parts of the Middle East and North Africa, and the rise of non-state terrorist groups and cyber criminal networks, to name just a few trends, make the current global context far more complicated.

Security is not just about security anymore. International economic challenges have become tightly connected to security politics. States, led by China, are playing a more direct role in the world economy, investing in the infrastructure of other countries, making strategic investments using sovereign wealth funds and state-owned enterprises, and purchasing other governments' debt.[44] Sanctions have become a more frequent tool of statecraft across the globe. Prior to 1990, the UN Security Council imposed sanctions against only two countries: Southern Rhodesia (now called Zimbabwe) in 1966; and South Africa in 1977. Since then, the UN has established over twenty sanctions regimes, with the United States also implementing its own sanctions in some cases. In 2015, the United States and the European Union imposed sanctions on Russia for invading Ukraine at the same time that Russian, European, and U.S. negotiators lifted sanctions on Iran in exchange for a nuclear deal. And it gets even more complicated than that. In 2016, the United States lifted nuclear sanctions against Iran but at the same time imposed new sanctions on the regime for conducting ballistic missile tests in violation of a UN resolution. And while global international economic policy issues used to be the province of just seven advanced economies, the rising importance of emerging markets has expanded the club: The G-7 has become the G-20.

Specifically, four distinct external or "exogenous" shocks have affected the political world—and by extension the business world—in serious ways.

The most significant shock to the international system was the terrorist attacks of September 11, 2001. It was a day that no American will soon forget.

For Condi, who was serving as President Bush's national security adviser at the time, the biggest effect of 9/11 was the realization that the United States was threatened by weak and ungoverned spaces, not just powerful states. This was a radically new world. Once the Treaty of Westphalia marked the beginning of the modern state system of international relations, great powers had always been most threatened by, and most focused on, other great powers. Not anymore. While you could count on states to control their territory, places like Afghanistan operated as breeding grounds and safe havens for groups that wanted to do serious harm to the United States. September 11 also marked the first time since the War of 1812, when British troops burned the White House, that the United States had been the victim of such a large attack on its own soil, changing Americans' perceptions of what constituted security.

Seven years later, the global financial crisis caused a second shock. The financial crisis increased political risks to businesses in a different way, leading to greater government intervention in the form of austerity measures and new regulations of firms and industries. It also created a heightened sense of awareness among populations of the impact of the global economy on their personal well-being. When you lose your house because of the global financial system, international economics becomes personal.

The other two major shocks involved changes to the international order. The Arab Spring and the subsequent unrest that unfolded across the Middle East made it more difficult for both governments and businesses to figure out how to handle operations in that part of the world and put enormous pressure on the state system's ability to endure in the region. Artificially constructed at the end of the Ottoman Empire by the French, British, and Italians, the national borders of present-day Saudi Arabia, Yemen, Turkey, Iraq, Syria, and the Gulf

States were drawn on the back of an envelope and cut across regional concentrations of Shia, Sunni, and Kurds. The Syrian civil war added an additional level of complexity as nearly seven million displaced people need shelter. The strain on Turkey, Lebanon, and Jordan was direct and immediate. But the impact on Europe and the politics of the refugee crisis may end up being more long-lasting, fueling a strong sense that the European Union no longer protects its borders and its citizens from the dangers of the Middle East.

The last shock was what Condi likes to call "Great Powers Behaving Badly." With the rise of China and the reemergence of Russia as major world powers, both governments have become increasingly assertive, reigniting long-running territorial conflicts—Ukraine in Russia's case, the East and South China seas in China's.

Russia and China have presented different challenges. The former is essentially an extractive industries giant with only a marginal impact on the international economy beyond the production of oil, gas, and minerals. Tensions over Russia's annexation of Crimea have led to sanctions, making the business environment there less certain and significantly more challenging.

China, on the other hand, as we discussed, has been a critical hub for manufacturing as well as an essential market for growth. Several years ago, in conversations with CEOs in almost every industry, China was the hot topic—the place to be and the future for growth and investment.

Today, there is greater caution about the People's Republic of China. In part, this is due to a growth of economic nationalism and continuing problems in the protection of foreign intellectual property. But it is also due to rising unease with China's more assertive foreign policy in the Asia-Pacific region. The United States and China seem to be on a collision course over Beijing's claims in the South China Sea and other territories in the region and America's determination to defend freedom of navigation and protect its allies. Many ask whether these old-fashioned geopolitical differences will ultimately lead to a less stable environment for commerce and business in China.

These four shocks have been evident in the international system for almost a decade. But a new concern has emerged alongside them—the growth of populism and protectionism as significant political forces. The global order that businesses have come to take for granted is essentially the one that emerged after World War II. The United States and its allies were determined to build a more open international economy that would not be a fixed pie and thus a zero-sum game. They were haunted by the period after World War I in which protectionism and beggar-thy-neighbor trading policies had led to the Great Depression. This time free trade and comparative advantage among nations would lead to growth. The Bretton Woods institutions—the International Monetary Fund, the World Bank, and then the General Agreement on Tariffs and Trade (now the World Trade Organization)—were the vehicles to support an open economy. It took some time, and the collapse of the Soviet Union and the opening of China, but globalization took root thoroughly and comprehensively. The global company with operations, manufacturing, and labor forces all over the world is a direct result of those key decisions.

But nativism, populism, protectionism, and isolationism are making a comeback. Globalization lifted millions of people out of poverty and benefited millions of others through macroeconomic growth. Still, there were losers—people who lacked the skills to compete in the modern economy and those for whom a call center in India, servicing American customers, became a symbol of threat, not an opportunity.

The Brexit vote in 2016 and the election of Donald Trump in the United States—the first time that the country elevated someone with absolutely no government experience to the presidency—stemmed in part from these reactions to globalization. And while it is not clear that populists will continue to win elections, it is obvious that all politicians are responding to the "Do you hear me now?"

message from those who feel cheated by globalization. It is telling that in the American election, not one of the candidates—Trump or Bernie Sanders or even the former secretary of state, Hillary Clinton—defended free trade. It is also telling that politicians tread very lightly in Europe and America on the issue of immigration, careful to highlight their toughness on the issue.

What is a global business to do when politicians in the United States talk openly of buying, hiring, and producing goods only in America, and politicians in the United Kingdom talk openly about promoting industrial policy? It is likely that economic realities will temper these protectionist impulses—after all, globalization is a state of being, not a policy. That said, the risks to a system that for several decades has moved in the direction of openness and freer trade should not be underestimated, by citizens or businesses alike.

At this point you may be asking yourselves, "If political risk matters now more than ever, what can companies be doing to help mitigate and manage their vulnerability to it? Is there any hope?" The short answer is yes. Understanding and managing political risk is notoriously difficult for companies, which may explain why studies repeatedly show that they do not focus on political risk, and if they do, they do it badly. But good political risk management mostly comes down to focus. In the next chapter, we take a closer look at why political risk management is so hard, and then we turn to solutions, laying out in the second half of the book a framework that companies of all sizes, operating in all industries and all geographies, can use to better manage this complex landscape.

KEY TAKEAWAYS: HOW WE GOT HERE

- ☐ Megatrends in business, technology, and politics have created a best-of-times/worst-of-times moment: Businesses face more global opportunities but also more political risks.

- ☐ Supply chains have grown leaner, longer, and more far-flung. Innovations have reduced costs and increased product customization.

- ☐ However, the search for margin puts supply chains in higher-risk locations, and extended supply chains expose companies to cumulative risks that are often hard to see.

- ☐ The spread of cell phones, the Internet, and social media is empowering small groups in big ways. Connective technologies lower the cost of collective action, making it easier for like-minded people to find one another and join in common causes, even across vast distances.

- ☐ Social activism is not just for activists anymore. In a hyperconnected world, bystanders can post cell phone videos and participate in spontaneous "Twitter mobs." Governments and businesses must contend with events that "go viral" with little warning.

- ☐ Changes in politics have made borders more porous and economic issues more centrally intertwined with international security.

- ☐ The Cold War brought an end to the separation of Western capitalist economies from the Soviet bloc and ushered in a period of globalization.

- ☐ Since then, four shocks have affected the political and business worlds. The attacks of September 11, 2001, revealed that the ability to do great harm no longer resided only in states with great power. The 2008 financial crisis prompted greater government intervention and rising populism. The Arab Spring and the subsequent unrest have stressed the state system in the Middle East. And China's rise and Russia's reemergence are challenging the international order at a moment when America is turning inward.

4

Mind Games and Groupthink: Why Good Political Risk Management Is So Hard

Jack Welch, the legendary CEO of General Electric, was not used to losing, but in June 2001 he lost big when regulators from the European Union rejected GE's $42 billion acquisition of Honeywell International. The deal at first looked like classic Welch: big, bold, and brilliant. GE, which is one of the world's

AFP PHOTO/Doug Kanter

leading manufacturers of airplane engines, had long been interested in Honeywell, which makes advanced aviation electronics. In the fall of 2000, Welch heard that a rival American airplane engine manufacturer, United Technologies, was set to acquire Honeywell. Welch sprang into action, outbidding United Technologies within forty-eight hours and nabbing the deal. The GE-Honeywell acquisition was poised to be the largest merger between two American industrial companies in history. Welch was so confident the transaction would be successful, he called it "the cleanest deal you'll ever see," and delayed his own retirement to see it through.[1] The proposed merger sailed through the U.S. Justice Department.

But the deal also had to be approved by the European Commission, the executive authority of the European Union.[2] American and European competitors, including Rolls-Royce and United Technologies (still stinging from losing Honeywell to GE), took their concerns to Brussels. They had a ready audience: The recently appointed head of the EU's competition authority, Mario Monti, was reportedly looking for a chance to show the EU's independence from the United States. The United States and the EU also approached merger decisions with different philosophies and processes. While American antitrust policy aimed to protect customers through market efficiencies providing lower prices, EU antitrust policy focused on protecting competitors and whether the proposed merger increased market dominance of the new conglomerate. As for process, the European system gave competitors greater opportunities to voice objections in private testimony, and voice objections they did.[3] Welch said he felt "profound regret" that eight months of effort came to nothing.[4]

In the end, Jack Welch moved so fast and was so focused on the economics of the deal that he did not fully consider the political factors at play. "We haven't touched every base," he said when the proposed merger was announced and he was asked whether GE and Honeywell had contacted regulators in the United States and Europe.[5] GE apparently did not have a good system in place to ensure that he did; Welch and Honeywell's CEO, Michael Bonsignore, were so eager to close the deal, they reportedly never consulted with their Brussels lawyers specializing in European competition concerns.[6] When the European Commission announced conditions that spelled the end of the road, Welch declared that "you are never too old to get surprised."[7]

Jack Welch's EU experience raises an important question: Why is managing political risk so hard? That's the puzzle we tackle in this chapter.

Studies repeatedly find that companies know they are not as good as they should be at political risk management. Although World Bank surveys find that companies believe political risks rank among the most important constraints on investing in emerging markets, many still do not integrate political risk analysis into their overall risk management.[8] In 2015, Aon's Global Risk Management Survey of fourteen hundred executives from public and private companies found that cyber risks were top of mind in C-suites around the world, but 58 percent of companies reported that they had never completed a cyber risk assessment. (It turns out that countries aren't well prepared for cyber threats, either. A 2017 United Nations report found that only half of all nations in the world have a cyber security strategy or are in the process of developing one.)[9] In another survey, only 19 percent of executives gave their own company an "A" grade for reputation risk management.[10] We have been teaching a combined total of more than four decades, and we have never come across a group of students who would give themselves such low grades.

Peter Thiel, a cofounder of PayPal and one of Silicon Valley's most successful investors, told us that assessing political risk is both essential and frequently elusive. "Luck and risk are ambiguous words and they can mean something about the metaphysical nature of the universe—that things are just random or lucky," he said. "But it can also be a statement about our laziness where we don't want to think about it. I'm open to the idea that there is such a thing as risk and randomness. But morally, when you encounter risk, you want to respond and ask what's really going on, what's going to happen, and avoid an excuse for laziness. When you're investing, say, a million dollars in a company, it might be a lottery ticket, but it's likely that if you thought about it more you'd get to a much clearer answer."

Thinking hard to get a clearer answer sounded very familiar. It's a lot like the work that analysts in the CIA and other agencies of the American intelligence community do every day. Amy has spent a long time studying barriers to effective intelligence analysis. Condi has spent a long time living with them. And it turns out that since 9/11, there has been a convergence between the intelligence and the business worlds: Many businesses have been creating their own mini-CIAs, political risk units whose mission is to identify political risks and opportunities and to work hand in hand with business unit leaders to mitigate losses and seize new opportunities. And not just within a certain industry. Political risk units have been arising and expanding in hotel chains, cruise lines, chemical companies, law firms, consumer products companies, oil and gas companies, banks, tech companies, and venture capital firms, among others. So on the one hand, most companies in surveys were admitting they were not doing enough to manage political risks. Yet on the other hand, we knew that some leading companies were innovating, and doing, a great deal. *Managing political risk was elusive for many but considered essential by everyone.*

In this chapter, we take a closer look at this capability gap and where it comes from. Drawing on psychology, our research and experience in intelligence, and real-world examples from business and international security, we highlight the most significant barriers to developing effective political risk management, even for Fortune 500 companies with legendary CEOs. We call them the "Five Hards."

The "Five Hards" of Political Risk Management

1. Hard to reward
2. Hard to understand
3. Hard to measure
4. Hard to update
5. Hard to communicate

1. Hard to reward: "Nobody gets credit for fixing problems that never happened."

Managing political risk often means raising questions about a business decision that otherwise looks attractive. Saying, "No, you might not want to do that," or "Hold on a minute, have you thought about this potential downside?" can be unwelcome news to the C-suite or board, particularly if the immediate economic case looks promising and the political risk may be longer-term or harder to see.

Nobody likes to be the bearer of unwelcome news. This challenge is one major reason why the role of chief information officer is less attractive today than it used to be, despite a fast-rising need for talented cyber security leaders. CIOs "end up being the wet blankets of the technology field," notes Thomas H. Davenport, who has been teaching information technology and management in universities for over twenty years. "They have to tell the Chief Marketing Officer that he can't buy his own server and cool software for automated ad creation. For years they had to tell executives that they must use BlackBerrys rather than iPhones. It's their job to ensure that company employees will have less powerful and desirable technologies than the employees' teenage children."[11]

CIOs are not alone. Managing political risk takes leadership and time to ensure that alternative points of view are heard and rewarded. As one risk manager from a major international oil and gas company told us, "We have to take risks. That's the business we're in. Our measure of success as a political risk unit is whether we have a seat at the table, whether business units are making informed decisions based on our professional expertise. The chairman is very enlightened about political risk. There was buy-in from him almost from the beginning and we see him quarterly. Analysts are as close to the business units as possible. That's a major key to our success."

Organizations that do not reward good political risk analysis are unlikely to get it. Our dear Stanford colleague Bill Perry, who was one of Silicon Valley's early successful business entrepreneurs and who served as the nineteenth secretary of defense, has studied what makes some defense secretaries more successful than others. He found that some failed for just one reason, no matter how smart they were: They would not accept opposing points of view, and when they heard one, they would come down very hard on the person providing it. "Once that happens a few times, the message gets out and they don't get opposing points of view anymore," Perry recounted, "and they make big mistakes because of it."[12]

FedEx's legendary founder Fred Smith is a big believer in the Perry philosophy. "You have to surround yourself with people who will tell you the truth," he says. "If you don't, as your organization gets bigger, you'll fall out of touch with what's going on."[13] Smith, who built FedEx from a small business in an abandoned Memphis hangar to a $44.6 billion global giant, says the man who most influenced his views on leadership was one of Condi's heroes: George Marshall. Marshall is known for securing the Allies' victory in World War II and for his tenure as secretary of state, where he conceived of the economic plan bearing his name that rebuilt Western Europe and saved it from communism. For Smith, one of Marshall's most important and inspiring qualities was that he "wasn't afraid to call it the way it was." As Smith recounts:

> In World War I, when Marshall was the number two man in some regiment, General John Pershing paid a visit and chewed out Marshall's superior. Everybody just stood around, but Marshall said, "General, with all due respect, you're wrong, and this is why you're wrong." Of course, everybody was astounded that he did that. But later Pershing called Marshall and said, "Look, I want you to be my chief of staff." And that's an important lesson that I've tried to follow.[14]

Risk management is also a cost center, which compounds the problem. Cyber protection measures, legal teams, risk officers—these functions produce no revenues and incur costs that go straight to the bottom line.

Marriott International is one of the world's leading companies when it comes to managing global political risk. Marriott believes that superior security can be a competitive advantage in a post-9/11 terrorist threat environment. But it does not own any hotels worldwide, it just operates them. As Marriott's vice president for global safety and security, Alan Orlob, told us, sometimes it takes work to convince a hotel owner that the security investments Marriott wants are worth it.

In 2009, Orlob was meeting with the owner of a new hotel that would soon be opening in Southeast Asia. "I'm out of money," the owner told Orlob. "I've gone to the bank but they won't lend any more to me, so I cannot put in the security measures you're requesting." Orlob didn't mince words: "Let me tell you, if you don't put in these security procedures at this hotel, you're going to be just another hotel in the city. I can guarantee you that if you spend the money, if you put these physical security measures in that we're asking, then we can use that to drive business to your hotel. People will stay there because it's safer than other hotels in the city. You'll see a return on your investment." The owner found the money and followed Orlob's guidance.

A year later, a significant terror threat was issued for the city. A large group staying at a competitor hotel next door moved to the Marriott-operated hotel because it had better security. "To me, that validated what I'd been trying to tell that owner," Orlob reflected.

Those validating moments are rare. More often, business leaders have a hard time knowing whether all these costs are "worth it"; political risk management often entails anticipating bad things and taking action so those bad things never actually occur.

In early 2011, for example, a number of major cruise lines, including Disney and Holland America, pulled out of the Mexican port city of Mazatlán, rerouting ships to other destinations. Their principal concern: Reports of rising drug-related violence suggested increasing risks that passengers on shore excursions could become victims of wrong-place/wrong-time crime. Did these companies' decisions actually prevent dangerous incidents involving their customers? Nobody will ever know for sure.

Similarly, in 2015, Universal Studios announced a multibillion-dollar joint venture deal with a Chinese state-owned consortium to open a Hollywood theme park in Beijing.[15] Even though Universal owned a minority stake in the joint venture, the company ensured that it would have complete control over the compliance system required by the U.S. Foreign Corrupt Practices Act. Universal's position was about prevention—ensuring that American lawyers and American executives had clear responsibility and authority for managing compliance with a far-reaching set of legal requirements from the get-go.[16] Was this decision a worthwhile measure that prevented the occurrence of violations, or was it an unnecessarily cautious and overly costly move? Time probably will not tell.

The trouble with nonevents is that it is often impossible to know what caused them not to occur. Intelligence agencies are all too familiar with this challenge. Suppose one country's intelligence agency warns the president that another country appears to be readying for a surprise attack. The president hears this message and takes some sort of action—maybe he begins to mobilize troops, or he sends a back-channel diplomatic message to the adversary. No attack occurs. Does this mean the intelligence warning was successful, prompting action that prevented an attack? Maybe. Or perhaps the adversary had no intention of attacking in the first place. Maybe they were bluffing to gain leverage in a negotiation. Or they were simply conducting a military exercise, in which case the intelligence warning of a surprise attack was just a false alarm all along.

This actually happened back in 1983, when the United States conducted a large NATO nuclear exercise called Able Archer that the Soviets mistakenly interpreted to be preparations for a surprise nuclear strike, triggering a series of responses that could have spiraled into war. Recently declassified documents reveal that this was a hair-trigger moment, the closest the two superpowers had come to nuclear war since the Cuban Missile Crisis of 1962.[17]

The point here is that in the anticipation business, whether it's about cruise ships in Mexico or cruise missiles in Europe, success can be difficult to discern. Warnings can be harmless false alarms. They can be harmful false alarms that inadvertently lead both sides tumbling into bad outcomes. Or they can be true alarms that prod action forestalling disaster. In retrospect, we may never know which is the case.

For all of these reasons—our natural aversion to hearing bad news and the need for senior-level leadership to overcome it within organizations, the fact that political risk entails costs without measurable profits, and the difficulty of knowing whether any political risk analysis was "worth it"—rewarding good political risk management is hard. As one executive told us, "Nobody gets credit for fixing problems that never happened."

2. Hard to understand

Humans are terrible when it comes to probabilities. Americans are far more afraid of dying in a shark attack than in a car accident, even though fatal car crashes are about sixty thousand times more likely.[18] In fact, many things are more likely causes of death than shark attacks, including being trampled in a Black Friday sale or falling off a ladder.[19]

A large part of this tendency to miscalculate probabilities is caused by common mental shortcuts, called heuristics, that often make decision-making easier and more efficient but can lead to serious errors. Psychologists Amos Tversky and Daniel Kahneman (who later won the Nobel Prize in Economics) were pioneers in this field. One of their most important findings was called the "availability heuristic." The idea is that people tend to judge the frequency of an event based on how many similar instances they can readily recall. Horrifying events that stick in one's mind are easier to remember than mundane ones. That's why people fear airplane crashes more than automobile accidents and Ebola more than influenza—even though airplanes are estimated to be seventy times safer than cars; and the worst Ebola outbreak killed about eleven thousand people worldwide from 2014 to 2016, while influenza, the common flu, killed between half a million and a million people during the same period.[20] The availability heuristic explains why we tend to attribute higher probabilities to events we hear about in the news—like shark attacks—than to more likely events like cardiac arrest or car crashes.[21]

The most controversial and best-known experiment that Kahneman and Tversky did together to show how human processing shortcuts can short-circuit accurate probability calculations was called the "Linda experiment." Participants were told about an imaginary woman named Linda. She was described this way:

> Linda is 31 years old, single, outspoken and very bright. She majored in philosophy. As a student, she was deeply concerned with the issue of discrimination and social justice, and also participated in antinuclear demonstrations.

Participants were then asked which was more probable:

(1) Linda is a bank teller; or
(2) Linda is a bank teller and is active in the feminist movement.[22]

Between 85 and 90 percent of participants in the Linda experiment chose (2). In Kahneman's words, this outcome was totally "contrary to logic."[23] Because every feminist bank teller is a bank teller, (1) always has a higher probability of being true.

Or consider the "birthday trick," which is a fan favorite in math circles and even stumped Johnny Carson when he was hosting *The Tonight Show*.[24] The birthday trick asks: How many people would it take to make the odds that any two people share a birthday 50/50? The answer is that it takes just twenty-three people. Really. The human mind is bad with matching numbers to feelings about likelihood.

For decades, psychologists have found "desirability" or "optimism" bias in everything from business investments to sports contests to political events and calculations of personal risk.[25] People tend to expect that their investments will perform better than average;[26] that good future events will happen more to themselves than to others;[27] that their favorite sports team has a higher chance of winning than it actually does;[28] and that their preferred presidential candidate will win an election even when the polls suggest otherwise.[29] In the 1932 presidential election, for example, 93 percent of Roosevelt supporters predicted Roosevelt would win, while 73 percent of Hoover supporters thought Hoover would win.[30] A few years ago, Wharton professors Joseph Simmons and Cade Massey conducted an experiment with National Football League fans to see if this bias would persist even if individuals were given financial incentives to predict more accurately. They asked participants to predict the winner of a single NFL game. Half of the participants predicted a game involving their favorite team. The other half predicted a game involving two neutral teams. Even when participants were offered up to $50 to correctly predict the winner, fans still overpredicted victories and underpredicted losses involving their favorite teams. Simmons and Massey found that optimism bias persisted even "in the face of large incentives to be accurate."[31]

Condi fully understands this because she experiences optimism bias at the start of every NFL football season. The Cleveland Browns haven't won a championship since she was nine. But every year, she believes that they've turned things around. She'll even utter the words, "I'll only go to that game if the Browns are in the play-offs."

Optimism bias helps explain why financial markets, political leaders, and so many experts were all stunned by the United Kingdom's June 23, 2016, vote to leave the European Union. For weeks before the "Brexit" referendum, polls consistently showed a very tight contest. Of the thirty-five polls conducted in the weeks before the referendum, seventeen showed the "Leave" campaign ahead, and fifteen showed the "Remain" side ahead.[32] Based on the *Huffington Post*'s polling average, the Remain side had just a 0.5-point lead. Take a look at this Bloomberg screenshot of aggregated polls that Amy captured a week after the vote. Bloomberg notes that right

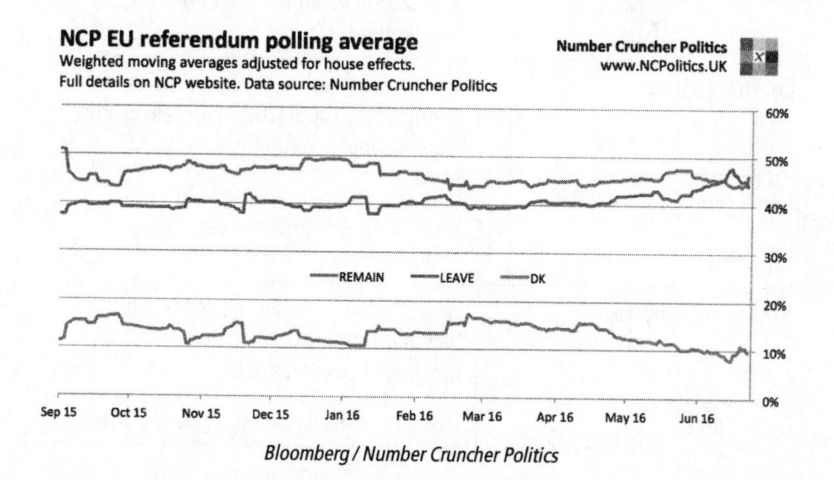

Bloomberg / Number Cruncher Politics

up to the end, it was "still too close to call." The average polls on June 21 in fact showed the Leave campaign with a slight edge, with 10 percent of voters still undecided.

Brexit was never actually a long shot. But many, it seems, were hoping that the U.K. would never really leave Europe, and looked only at the bright side of the numbers they saw. The betting markets put "Remain" at 88 percent just hours before the vote. Optimism bias made Brexit seem like a low-probability event even though it wasn't.

Finally, political risks are susceptible to being considered in isolation, making them appear to have lower probabilities than they actually do over the longer term or in the bigger picture. In the last chapter, we talked about *cumulative risk* to supply chains, noting that the risk of disruption in any one node of a supply chain may be low, but the cumulative risk of disruption across the entire supply chain for a company over time is much, much higher. This is also true of political risks more generally.

Let's take another look at our political risk list.

Ten Types of Political Risk

Geopolitics	Interstate wars, great power shifts, multilateral economic sanctions and interventions
Internal conflict	Social unrest, ethnic violence, migration, nationalism, separatism, federalism, civil wars, coups, revolutions
Laws, regulations, policies	Changes in foreign ownership rules, taxation, environmental regulations, national laws
Breaches of contract	Government reneging on contracts, including expropriations and politically motivated credit defaults
Corruption	Discriminatory taxation, systemic bribery

Extraterritorial reach	Unilateral sanctions, criminal investigations and prosecutions
Natural resource manipulation	Politically motivated changes in supply of energy, rare earth minerals
Social activism	Events or opinions that "go viral," facilitating collective action
Terrorism	Politically motivated threats or use of violence against persons, property
Cyber threats	Theft or destruction of intellectual property, espionage, extortion, massive disruption of companies, industries, governments, societies

We know that many of these political risks seem like low-probability events. Considered in isolation, many of them are. The chance that an American will be killed by a foreign-born terrorist is about 1 in 45,808—more remote than the odds that they will die from a heat wave or by choking on food.[33] No EU member state has experienced a revolution or coup in thirty-five years. But here's the thing: While the probability that a *single* political risk will affect Company A's business in a particular city tomorrow may be low, the overall probability that *some* political risk will significantly affect Company A's business in any one of its key locations over some period of time is surprisingly high. Add up a string of rare events and you will find that the overall incidence is not so rare after all.

Yossi Sheffi, a professor at the Massachusetts Institute of Technology, zeroed in on the importance of cumulative risk in his book *The Resilient Enterprise*. Sheffi describes how General Motors executives came to a startling realization when they took a closer look at disruptions to the company's supply chain from both natural disasters and man-made ones. In 2003, GM's enterprise risk management team compiled a list of rare events that could disrupt the supply chain and then systematically asked managers how many of these events had actually occurred during the previous twelve months. The answer: quite a lot. "We went through the list and checked off, 'Yeah, we've had that one' and 'Yeah, we've had that one, too,'" said GM's Debra Elkins, senior research engineer in manufacturing systems research. One GM plant was even hit by a tornado. As Sheffi notes, "While the likelihood for any one event that would have an impact on any one facility or supplier is small, the collective chance that some part of the supply chain will face some type of disruption is high."[34]

"While the likelihood for any one event that would have an impact on any one facility or supplier is small, the collective chance that some part of the supply chain will face some type of disruption is high."

—Yossi Sheffi, *The Resilient Enterprise*

When it comes to political risks, this is particularly true, because of the availability heuristic. News headlines tell us what's happening now, not patterns over time, so patterns over time can go unrecognized until it's too late. In chapter 2, we mentioned credit defaults and how Greece suddenly defaulted when Prime Minister Alexis Tsipras came to office in 2015. The default seemed to be a shocking bolt from the blue. It shouldn't have been. Mike Tomz and Mark L. J. Wright found that in the 1980s, about fifty countries, making up 40 percent of all nations owing money to foreign creditors at the time, failed to pay them fully, on schedule. Looking at defaults from 1820 to 2004, Tomz and Wright found that new defaults arose every decade. Since the end of the Napoleonic Wars, 106 countries have defaulted a total of 250 times. And a handful of countries have been serial defaulters. Ecuador and Honduras have defaulted a total of 120 times since the 1820s.[35] Defaults surprise investors more often than they should.

Terrorism is also not nearly as geographically isolated as you might think from following the news. According to the global terrorism database, in 2014 terrorists waged more than sixteen thousand attacks worldwide. The vast majority occurred in Iraq, Syria, Afghanistan, and Israel. That's not a surprise. But this probably is: Ukraine, Somalia, and India each reported *more than eight hundred* terrorist attacks that year; the United Kingdom was home to more than one hundred terrorist attacks by various groups; and forty-seven countries (including China, the United States, South Africa, and Germany) experienced ten or more terrorist attacks in 2014. That's nearly a quarter of all the countries in the world.[36]

The first step toward good political risk management is being brutally honest about the political risks your business confronts. Understanding risks requires overcoming blind spots. Mistaking easily recalled events for likely ones, believing desirable outcomes are more probable than they are, confusing low probability and zero probability, and overlooking cumulative risks are big ones.

3. Hard to measure

We have just discussed how political risks are hard to understand even when they are measured and depicted clearly, in quantitative terms, like Brexit polls. This is the best-case scenario. Many political risks are hard to measure quantitatively at all. Where financial risk can be more easily modeled and assessed using metrics like GDP per capita, labor supply, demographics, interest rates, and exchange rates, political risk is qualitative. It's squishy. It requires a sense of the corruption, regime stability, policy stability, social cleavages, the national mood, cultural norms, geopolitics, domestic politics, and the motives and capabilities of everyone from national leaders to neighborhood associations to nongovernmental organizations and transnational groups. (Sure, there are fragile state indices and other tools that attempt to provide quantitative baselines and trends for some of these key factors. But as we note later, these tools should be used with care, since they tend to record national measures while a great deal of political risk arises at the local level, and they provide snapshots in time that can mask important trends.)

Perhaps the squishiest of these squishy qualitative factors involves political intentions. Intelligence officials have long known that assessing the intentions of others is the toughest kind of information to get right. Sherman Kent, a Yale professor and one of the founding fathers of the Central Intelligence Agency's analytic branch, famously wrote in 1964 that there are three types of information for intelligence analysis. The first is indisputable facts, information that is knowable and known by the organization. A modern-day example is the number of aircraft carriers China currently operates (the answer is two). The second category consists of information that is knowable but happens to be unknown to the organization. So, for example, the CIA may know that China operates an aircraft carrier called the *Liaoning*, but no American has ever captained that ship, so the *Liaoning*'s performance characteristics under various conditions can be estimated but not known with certainty. The third category is information that is not knowable to anyone. This is the realm of intentions and decisions that have not yet been taken. An example here would be how long the Chinese Communist Party will remain in power.[37]

This third category, the unknowable realm of intentions and future decisions, is where the rubber meets the road for businesses managing political risk. The cruise lines we mentioned earlier in the chapter had to consider whether drug violence in Mexico would rise or decline, and whether it would affect passengers onshore. For Universal Studios, the big question was whether Chinese partners had the will and capability to comply fully with American antibribery laws on their own. More generally, political risk considerations for companies often hinge on assessing intentions: Will Burma's political liberalization continue? Will Iran cheat on the nuclear deal, triggering snapback multilateral sanctions? Will Colombia's historic peace deal with the Revolutionary Armed Forces of Colombia (FARC) hold, sustaining an end to half a century of violence there? These are questions that the principal political actors themselves are probably not able to answer. And even if they could, they may very well be wrong. People often assess their own intentions incorrectly. They call off weddings, cancel vacations, switch jobs, vote for different presidential candidates than they had originally planned to—because their views and interests change, their options shift, and events intervene. Assessing others' intentions is even more difficult than assessing your own. And remember that in international politics, leaders have an interest in deceiving others about what their true intentions are.[38]

Political risk is also hard to measure because it often entails anticipating events that may have a low probability of occurring but that would involve major consequences for the business if they ever did occur.

Risk always has two components: the likelihood that an event will transpire and the expected impact if it does.

> Risk has two components: *likelihood* and *impact*.

Risk assessments that focus on one without the other aren't worth much. Cyber threats, for example, are everywhere. Companies know that if they have not been breached already, they will be. It is only a matter of time. Yet few companies have a good idea of what the impact of a breach could be. And as we noted earlier, even fewer have stress tested their systems and policies to illuminate vulnerabilities and develop robust defense and response capabilities. The probability of cyber threats is known. The impact is not. Conversely, Brexit was clearly a high-impact event. The probability of its occurrence proved harder for analysts to gauge.

Low-probability/high-impact events are especially tricky. It is always harder to anticipate unusual events than typical ones. Weather forecasting, diagnosing medical diseases, analyzing intelligence, assessing political risks to businesses—these endeavors are particularly prone to outlier mistakes because they are geared toward tracking the most likely outcomes, not the most consequential ones. Judgment hinges, either explicitly or implicitly, on historical data. Professionals assess a specific case by examining accumulated evidence of what happened in similar instances in the past. The average temperature of a given city comes from tracking daily temperatures over many years. Medical diagnoses require linking an individual patient's symptoms with the most common illnesses that tend to produce them. In intelligence, analysts typically judge an adversary's future behavior based on its past behavior. Businesses assess whether the regulatory environment tomorrow will resemble the regulatory environment today. The process ensures that evidence, not wild guessing, informs judgment. But it also leads the analyst away from outliers. A weather forecaster will predict typical temperatures with ease, but is likely to miss predicting an unseasonably cold spell. Even the best doctors often miss rare diseases. "Investors should be skeptical of history-based models," Warren Buffett wrote to his Berkshire Hathaway shareholders after the 2008 financial crisis. After the company posted its worst performance in four decades, Buffett offered unsparing criticism, reflection, and some golden advice: "Beware of geeks bearing formulas."[39]

> "Beware of geeks bearing formulas."
> —Warren Buffett, CEO of Berkshire Hathaway

Predicting sunshine in Los Angeles is no great achievement. Predicting L.A.'s once-a-decade snowfall, however, would be impressive. The more frequently something occurs, the more likely you will accurately predict its occurrence in the future. It's the outliers that get you into trouble. The same is true for medicine. Because most patients most of the time with a certain set of symptoms suffer from the same illness, good doctors are trained to look for statistically likely diagnoses. Rare cases are the most difficult and often the most dangerous. Statistical realities naturally steer the estimator to look for the most frequent occurrences. Outliers, by definition, lie at the tail end of a distribution curve.

In politics, outliers are especially problematic because often there just isn't the information to judge what a "typical" or likely outcome might be. Doctors can diagnose the flu easily because there is a rich store of historical data that show if a patient has certain symptoms, she probably has the flu. But imagine that instead of diagnosing the flu, you're running a company that is investing in Iran and you want to know what the likelihood is that Iran will cheat on the 2016 nuclear deal, subjecting your investment to renewed sanctions. What can historical data tell us about the likely behavior of nuclear aspirants under these circumstances? Almost nothing. Only nine countries in the world have nuclear weapons.[40] Five got the bomb so long ago that nobody had yet landed on the moon. North Korea is the most recent nuclear power, but the Hermit Kingdom is not a generalizable model for anything. The only country that ever developed a nuclear arsenal and then voluntarily dismantled it is South Africa[41]—in large part because apartheid was crumbling and the outgoing white regime feared putting the bomb in the hands of a black government. A few other countries explored elements of a nuclear program but never developed a weapon, for a host of reasons that included American security guarantees, strong U.S. pressure, and domestic regime change.[42] Weather forecasting or medical diagnosis this isn't. Major political events occur so infrequently that the evidence base for predicting the future based on the past is thin.

These kinds of events are known as "black swans." Nassim Taleb popularized the term in his 2007 book of the same name. Black swans are consequential events for which the underlying probability distribution is simply not known, or at least not known with any degree of certainty or reliability. In Taleb's words, "Nothing in the past can convincingly point to [a black swan's] possibility."[43] Most of us just think of black swans as major events we never saw coming, like earthquakes. Calling something a black swan has become shorthand for saying, "It's totally unpredictable. We can't do anything about it."

This conventional wisdom about black swans is important to bear in mind, but it is equally important to put into perspective. Political risks often do not have the historical data required for good probability assessments. But many do have three things going for them that make them easier to anticipate than earthquakes or other "throw up your hands, it's a black swan, nothing can be done" pure bolts from the blue: (1) Political events are man-made, not acts of God; (2) political events require people acting in some sort of concert, and this can leave telltale signs for those who are paying attention before major events arise; and (3) with political events, anticipating directionality is often enough.[44] Companies, for example, do not have to pinpoint Vladimir Putin's departure date to know that Russian authoritarianism is likely to continue for the next several years. Similarly, CEOs do not need to be able to predict the exact time, place, manner, and perpetrator behind the next cyber attack to realize that cyber threats are growing more prevalent and serious, and that they require serious C-suite attention.

So while some black swans are political risk events, let's not get too carried away. Squishiness, intentions, and black swans all make political risk hard to measure but not impossible to handle.

4. Hard to update

It is one thing to assess political risk at the time a company is making its initial decision to move into a foreign market. It's quite another to update that assessment so that management stays ahead of the curve. Ian Bremmer, president and founder of the political risk consultancy Eurasia Group, found that while 69 percent of firms analyzed political risks for a new investment, only 27 percent monitored political risk once the investment had been made.[45] A business analyst from a major private equity fund told us the same thing. Examining investments over a period of several years, he was stunned when he could not find a single instance where the firm had updated its political risk analysis after making an initial investment. Companies often fail to ask, "What's changed?" before it's too late. "People assume things will continue this way forever, but frequently the consensus is wrong," notes J. Tomilson Hill, president and CEO of Blackstone Alternative Asset Management, one of the most successful hedge funds in the world. Blackstone ensures that its political risk analysis is updated by including views that challenge the status quo. "We always include a contrarian view in our scenarios, looking at what can go wrong," Hill told us.

While most companies do not update enough, there is also the risk of updating too much, which can desensitize leaders. Dubbed the "cry wolf" syndrome by intelligence scholars and the "normalization of deviance" by sociologists, the basic idea is that humans frequently take false comfort in false alarms.[46] The more often prior warnings turn out to be nothing, the more current warnings are dismissed.

For several months preceding Japan's December 7, 1941, surprise attack on Pearl Harbor, American military officials, including those at the Hawaii base, were warned that Japan might launch a surprise attack. But the more warnings they received, the less they paid attention. The Army commander in Hawaii received word on November 27, 1941, that Japanese officials in Honolulu were burning their secret codes. He had received many similar reports over the year, and this one did not seem especially serious. Admiral Kimmel and his staff were so tired of checking out false reports of Japanese submarines near Pearl Harbor that Admiral Stark stopped sending new reports to them.[47]

The cry wolf syndrome explains why NASA engineers disregarded warning signs that the space shuttle's O-rings were cracking in cold weather conditions, a design weakness that ultimately caused the *Challenger* disaster in 1986.[48] And it explains why seventeen years later, NASA again assumed away indicators of looming disaster. NASA officials concluded that foam debris shedding from the external fuel tank during launch probably would not be a problem for STS-107, since shedding during liftoff happened so frequently. It wasn't supposed to happen at all. This time, a piece of debris knocked heat shield tiles off the leading edge of the shuttle wing, causing *Columbia* to explode on reentry, killing all seven passengers on board.[49]

The cry wolf syndrome is common. Ever hear a funny noise in your car? The first time, it seems alarming. After living with it for a few days, however, you think it must not be so serious after all. You tell yourself the car seems to be running just fine. You grow accustomed to the noise. After a while you don't notice it anymore. And maybe the car really is fine. Or maybe the funny noise is an indication that the car is about to experience a major malfunction. Which is exactly what happened to Amy when she ignored a strange sound in her car for several weeks until it broke down on the 405 highway in Los Angeles, at night, "without warning."

Like military leaders, NASA engineers, and everyday drivers, CEOs have to work hard to address the cry wolf syndrome. Risk updates have to strike the balance between too little warning and too much.

5. Hard to communicate

Even if political risk management is rewarded, even if it is well understood, and even if it is measured and updated well, conveying risk to others is still fraught with challenges. Political risk is hard to communicate.

We use the following mini-exercise in class every year to send this point home: Imagine we offered you a pill that would enable you to look your very best for the rest of your life. Picture your ideal weight, your favorite age, your best haircut. If you took our pill once, you could keep that look for the rest of your life. The pill is guaranteed to be 99.9 percent safe, with no side effects. How many of you would take it?

In class, every hand usually shoots up except for one or two perennial skeptics.

Now imagine that we told you the pill has a 1-in-1,000 chance of causing instant death. If you take it, 1 in 1,000 of you will drop dead, right here, right now. The other 999 will look your best for as long as you live. How many of you would agree to take the pill now?

Only a few hands go up.

Statistically speaking, 99.9 percent safe and 1-in-1,000 risk of death are exactly the same. But 99.9 percent safe sure sounds a lot better than having a 1-in-1,000 chance of instant death.

The beauty pill exercise underscores just how important risk communication is, even among Stanford MBAs with exceptional math skills. The same person will make a very different call depending on how a risk is presented.

Now imagine communicating risk between two people who may come at political risk from different jobs, vantage points, risk appetites, cultures, or expectations about the future.[50] In the 1990s, an American naval officer and a Chinese naval officer were discussing China's aspiration to acquire an aircraft carrier. The Chinese admiral said he thought China would get a carrier "in the near future." The American admiral then asked, "When exactly?" The Chinese admiral replied, "Sometime before 2050." Near future for the American officer was not anything close to near future for the Chinese admiral.

Condi remembers a moment when the same information was viewed quite differently by two individual American intelligence agencies, with potentially grave consequences for international security. It was December 2001, just a few months after the September 11 attacks. Condi, who was national security adviser at the time, and the rest of President Bush's foreign policy team were facing another international crisis, this time unfolding on the Indian subcontinent. On December 13, five men carrying AK-47s and grenades led an attack on the Indian Parliament House in New Delhi, killing nine people. The Indian government suspected that the attack came from Lashkar-e-Taiba, one of the largest terrorist organizations operating in South Asia and believed to receive support from the ISI, Pakistan's main intelligence agency. Under enormous pressure from the United States and Britain, Pakistani president Pervez Musharraf condemned the attacks and sent a letter of condolence to the Indian government. But Musharraf also issued a warning to India to not take any escalatory actions or else they would face "very serious repercussions." The warning did not sit well with New Delhi, and within a few days, military preparations were under way in the region. It was a mobilization effort that would eventually result in nearly a million troops facing off across the border between two nuclear nations with deep-seated animosity, a war-torn history, and nuclear arsenals held in a near-constant state of alert.

Condi recalls that the National Security Council (NSC) meeting held in the Situation Room in the wake of the attack felt extremely tense, perhaps more so than on any other day since the 9/11 terrorist attacks in New York, Washington, and Pennsylvania. Pakistan and India, both nuclear powers, appeared on the brink of war.[51] The NSC called on the Pentagon and the Central Intelligence Agency to assess the likelihood. Looking at the exact same events unfolding on the ground, the Pentagon and the CIA offered different answers. The Defense Department—which was largely relying on reporting and analysis from the Defense Intelligence Agency—saw the military mobilization at the border as what any country, including the United States, would do under the same circumstances: Pentagon intelligence analysts saw the buildup as routine and not necessarily an indication of anything more serious.[52]

The CIA, on the other hand, believed that armed conflict was unavoidable. It assessed that India had already decided to "punish" Pakistan, and that Islamabad probably felt the same way. The CIA had become reliant on Pakistani sources in its efforts to fight the

Taliban and al-Qaeda in neighboring Afghanistan, and this deeper understanding of the Pakistani mind-set may have informed the CIA's assessment of Pakistan's unfolding conflict with India.[53]

Looking back on the situation now, Condi recalls that the president and other NSC principals were frustrated by the wide gap between the two agencies' assessments. It was clear that where you stood depended on where you sat. Despite the fact that both agencies were looking at the same events, the Defense Department approached the conflict through a military lens. On the other hand, the CIA was informed by the relationships it had fostered with Pakistani intelligence sources in the few months since 9/11. The gap in the assessments showed that even when two groups are looking at identical events, the meaning of those events is colored through organizational lenses. While the CIA and the Pentagon were using some of their own sources of intelligence, senior leaders were attending the same meetings and seeing all available intelligence—yet coming to different conclusions. The same information at the same moment can mean different things to different people even when the stakes are high and everyone shares a fervent desire to "get it right." Communicating risk is hard.[54]

KEY TAKEAWAYS: WHY GOOD POLITICAL RISK MANAGEMENT IS SO HARD

☐ Surveys find that executives consider political risk management essential but elusive.

☐ The "Five Hards" explain why. Political risk is hard to reward, hard to understand, hard to measure, hard to update, and hard to communicate.

☐ Nobody gets credit for fixing problems that never happened.

- ☐ Humans are susceptible to cognitive biases that distort their probability calculations. Brexit, for example, was not a long-shot event, but most observers believed that it was.

- ☐ Political risk often involves hard-to-measure qualitative factors like social cleavages and leaders' intentions.

- ☐ Many companies do not update political risk assessments once an investment decision is made.

- ☐ The same data can mean very different things to different people.

5

Moving Beyond Intuition: Our Political Risk Framework

We now turn from examining political risk to managing it. In the first half of the book, we surveyed twenty-first-century political risks; the megatrends in business, technology, and politics driving them; and the cognitive and organizational barriers that make political risk management so challenging. In this half of the book, we offer a step-by-step framework to overcome these barriers and institute effective risk management. No one model fits all. Risks are always context-specific. Extractive industries like oil and gas companies must contend with large long-tail investments that last thirty years or more and cannot be moved or removed easily. By contrast, consumer-facing industries like hotel chains, cruise lines, and theme parks are particularly susceptible to reputational risks and typically have lower risk appetites as a result. Risk tools come in many varieties, too. As we will see, some companies like Paychex systematically examine political risk across the senior levels of the company in a highly structured process they call the "Tournament of Risk." A prominent investment firm conveys fundamentals to employees in a simple way that is easy to remember. Every investor in every decision is trained to ask: "What if we are wrong?" Some companies hire outside risk consultants to provide analysis and advice when they need it. Others rely largely on in-house units. Many employ a hybrid approach.

Our goal is to provide you with a way of thinking about political risk—an overarching framework to improve political risk management no matter what market you may be considering, what industry you may be in, or what size company you may be operating. The framework is intended to be broad enough to be generalizable but specific enough to be actionable. Companies can acquire an edge if they get the basics right. The basics come down to four core competencies: *understanding* risks, *analyzing* risks, *mitigating* the residual risks that cannot be eliminated, and then putting in place a *response* capability that enables effective crisis management and continuous learning.

Political Risk Framework

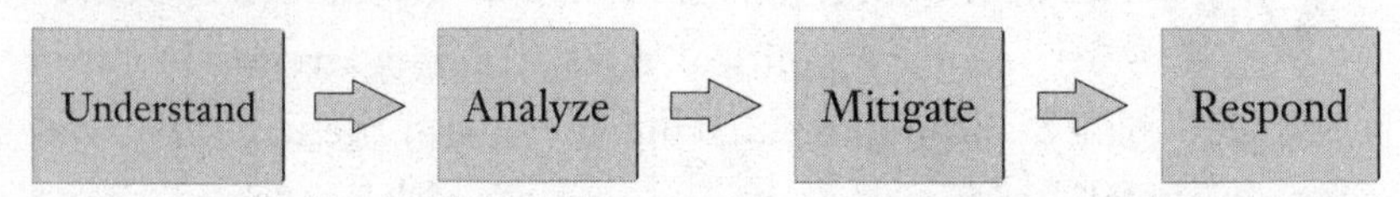

Effective political risk management takes work. It takes a team. It takes practice. It takes time. It takes commitment from the top. And it takes self-awareness to know what your organization's strategy is, how political risk and opportunity fit into it, what your organization does well, what it doesn't, and how to narrow the gap.

For each step in the framework, we provide three guiding questions that everyone in the organization should ask. Good risk management starts with asking the right questions. Not a million questions. Not a hundred. Not even twenty. Just three at each step. These questions do not cover everything, but they cover the most important things.

In each of the next chapters, we take one part of the risk framework and dive more deeply into its guiding questions, with examples of organizations that performed these risk management steps well and some that did not.

Guiding Questions for Effective Risk Management

Understand	Analyze	Mitigate	Respond
1. What is my organization's political risk appetite?	1. How can we get good information about the political risks we face?	1. How can we reduce exposure to the risks we have identified?	1. Are we capitalizing on near misses?
2. Is there a shared understanding of our risk appetite? If not, how can we foster one?	2. How can we ensure rigorous analysis?	2. Do we have a good system in place for timely warning and action?	2. Are we reacting effectively to crises?
3. How can we reduce blind spots?	3. How can we integrate political risk analysis into business decisions?	3. How can we limit the damage when something bad happens?	3. Are we developing mechanisms for continuous learning?

All organizations want to manage political risks. The ones that do it well work hard to see risks coming; they're alert. They deploy resources against priorities—whether it's talent, capital, or mind-share at the top. And they know what to do when bad things happen because they have already stress tested their response systems, incentivized the right people and actions, and created feedback loops for continuous learning.

To get us started with an overview of how all of these steps fit together, let's take a closer look at SeaWorld's *Blackfish* crisis, which we introduced in chapter 1, and compare it to another company's crisis—Royal Caribbean International cruise line's decision to send ships to Haiti immediately after a devastating earthquake there.[1]

At first glance, both companies looked like they were in trouble. Events surprised executives and both companies were lambasted in the press as callous corporations profiting off the misery of others. Royal Caribbean International and SeaWorld faced attacks that "went viral" on the Internet. Things seemed to be spinning out of control. But as we will see, Royal Caribbean International quickly recovered while SeaWorld did not. Differences in political risk management help explain why.

Royal Caribbean International and the 2010 Haiti Earthquake

On January 12, 2010, a 7.0 magnitude earthquake hit the impoverished Caribbean nation of Haiti, killing an estimated 200,000 people, injuring another 250,000, and leaving more than a million homeless.[2] Three days later, a Royal Caribbean International cruise

Melanie Stetson Freeman/Christian Science Monitor *via Getty Images*

Marcelo Casal Jr./ABr.

ship named *Independence of the Seas* landed in the Haitian port of Labadee, sending 3,000 passengers to swim and bask on a beautiful private beach there, just eighty-five miles from the hard-hit capital of Port-au-Prince. It was the first of four Royal Caribbean International cruise ships to dock in Labadee within the next few days, stops that had all been planned before the earthquake struck.[3]

Public reaction was immediate and blistering. News headlines and blogs excoriated the cruise line for vacationing next to (and profiting from) such suffering. While passengers saw gorgeous sand beaches and turquoise coves, news organizations posted pictures of makeshift tents and squalid conditions. The tabloid *New York Post*'s headline screamed "Ship of Ghouls" and noted that passengers were jet skiing and sipping rum "a mere 60 miles south of the earthquake's epicenter—where mountains of decaying bodies foul the air and traumatized residents scrounge for food."[4]

Adam Goldstein is the president and chief operating officer of Royal Caribbean International's parent company, Royal Caribbean Cruises, Ltd.[5] The parent company is the world's second-largest cruise line operator, serving more than fifty million customers a year in 490 destinations with more than forty ships representing six cruise line brands, including the flagship Royal Caribbean International line.[6] Goldstein remembers vividly what it was like when the earthquake hit. "There was some remarkable hostility that we encountered," he told us. "I remember driving home one night, doing a rush-hour radio interview with the Canadian Broadcasting Corporation, and they could not comprehend that we would be willing to send our ships to Haiti. They were simply dumbfounded. It's the most hostility I've ever encountered in an interview."

But the tide soon turned. Within days, National Public Radio and ABC News ran stories highlighting how the company was in fact docking at the request of the Haitian government, bringing desperately needed humanitarian relief and economic development.[7] *Newsweek* reported that despite the controversy, "most passengers and cruise enthusiasts seem to support Royal Caribbean's decisions: A company representative said that 85 percent of guests who docked at Labadee ultimately went ashore."[8] Goldstein remembers that one news source sent a reporter on one of the company's Haiti-bound cruise ships to investigate. "The journalist talked to one of the workers on our site," Goldstein recalled, "and the guy said, 'If the ship doesn't come then we don't eat.' And the journalist published that comment. That was the end of it. When that worker said, 'If the ship doesn't come then we don't eat,' people understood the economic aspect was so dependent on our ships. They understood that for us to withdraw would amplify the poverty of people in the north and potentially create a hunger situation there while people in the south were dealing with a calamity—and that would be a really bad idea." Around the same time, a survey of forty-seven hundred people conducted by the website Cruise Critic found that two-thirds of respondents agreed with the company's decision to proceed with scheduled cruises."[9] Leslie Gaines-Ross, a leading reputation strategist, found that in the end, "Royal Caribbean's decision not to halt cruises in the area soon began to be seen less as a callous action and more as a brave, well-considered attempt to help."[10]

How did Royal Caribbean International weather the reputational storm of continuing its luxury vacation business in a poverty-stricken destination facing a grave natural disaster? This was not simply a matter of following well-crafted talking points and providing some humanitarian assistance. The company did much more than execute a crisis response plan well. It took political risk management seriously years before the earthquake struck. And because Royal Caribbean International had developed the core competencies to handle man-made political risks in Haiti, it was well positioned to deal with a natural disaster there, too.

Haiti was hardly an ideal tourist destination to begin with. For decades, the country had been shaken by political violence, instability, and poverty. The Duvalier era, which lasted from 1957 to 1986, was marked by corruption and widespread human rights abuses. Haiti has struggled to transition to democracy ever since, with coups in 1991 and 2004, and more recently with stalled progress toward democratic elections in 2015 and 2016.[11]

In addition to political turmoil, Haiti has suffered endemic poverty. Even before the earthquake, it was the poorest nation in the Western Hemisphere and ranked among the poorest in the world. In 2005, about 70 percent of Haitians lived on less than two dollars per day. Half the population was classified as malnourished, and one-third of children were not enrolled in school. In the capital of Port-au-Prince, the vast majority of residents lived in slum conditions: Half the city's population lacked access to bathroom facilities and a third had no access to running water.[12]

In short, sending vacationing tourists to a country racked by political instability, repression, corruption, violence, and extreme deprivation posed reputational risks to Royal Caribbean International even without a natural disaster.[13] As Jean Cyril Pressoir, a Haiti tour operator, put it, "For a long time, tourism was almost taboo in Haiti."[14]

Nevertheless, starting in the 1980s, Royal Caribbean International began a long-term relationship with Haiti to develop a private, gated luxury beach destination there. The decision was originally driven by geography: Royal Caribbean Cruises founder and president Edwin "Ed" Stephan wanted to develop an "out island" destination along a seven-night cruise route from Miami to Puerto Rico, Saint Thomas, and back. "He was the real motivating factor," recalls Peter Whelpton, a Royal Caribbean International executive who spent thirty years in the company and was the key player in the development of Labadee. "Ed dreamed the dream and I was the guy that went into the woods and made it a reality." Whelpton looked all over the Caribbean for a suitable location. "There really was nothing," he recalled. "There were lots of islands but they didn't fit our needs. The ones that fit our needs, the owners didn't want to sell." Then Pierre Chauvet, a Haitian friend of Whelpton's who had been integrally involved in the country's tourism industry, suggested Labadee. At first Whelpton was skeptical. "I said, 'Come on. Haiti? It's the poorest nation in the world.' But Pierre said he wouldn't lead me astray. So I went and took a look."

What Whelpton found was an idyllic beach that was so inaccessible by road at the time, he had to borrow a helicopter from the Haitian government and bring along a military general to get there. The good news was that the poorly maintained mountain road to Labadee meant it was far from the turmoil in Port-au-Prince. The bad news was that Labadee was a mess. "There were cinder blocks piled to the roof, rusted and abandoned trucks, a thousand toilets, cows roaming around eating grass," Whelpton recalled. There was no running water, no electricity. They would have to develop Stephan's "out island" from scratch. "If you could overlook the mess, it was beautiful," said Whelpton.

At first, local residents were concerned that the development would drive farmers and fishermen off the land and feared the company would reap all of the economic benefits, leaving few jobs or economic gains for Haitian residents.[15] Labadee, in fact, was designed to be a tropical oasis that would seem worlds away from the impoverished country. Eventually it grew to include a roller coaster, zip line, aqua park, eight-hundred-foot pier, and cabanas lining a pristine beach where passengers could vacation in style in an enclave billed as a "private paradise."[16] Passengers often did not realize Labadee was in Haiti at all. For a time, Royal Caribbean International billed Labadee as being on "Hispaniola" (the island that includes Haiti and the Dominican Republic), until the Haitian government complained.

Still, Royal Caribbean International was committed to Haiti, believing the country once called the "Jewel of the Antilles" in the 1800s could be a valuable business opportunity. Whelpton and his team met local concerns early on. Pierre Chauvet helped organize a meeting with Whelpton and local residents in a church. At first, residents were skeptical, even hostile. "My God, they came after me," recalled Whelpton. "They said that we were taking the best beaches in Haiti and stealing them for some cruise ship. But Pierre was there. He spoke Patois and he said, 'Listen to Peter because he will bring you some things you haven't thought of.'" Whelpton explained as politely as he could that they were too remote for a major tourist hotel—and in fact a hotel deal there had just failed. Labadee had no major airport nearby, and building one would take a decade. But Labadee would be ideal for cruise ships. "And then I said the magic words: As part of the development, we would build a place for Haitian merchants to sell their goods." Whelpton promised jobs for local villagers and a per-guest tax paid to the government. "The lynch mob mentality turned into a love fest," Whelpton recalled. Once Labadee opened, and the promised jobs materialized, local residents became quite protective of Labadee.[17]

Royal Caribbean International became one of Haiti's largest foreign investors, contributing $55 million to the nation's economic development in Labadee in addition to jobs and the tourist tax per passenger.[18] Throughout the process, management took relationship building—with Haitian officials, NGOs, think tanks, and United Nations organizations—seriously.

As a result, when the 2010 earthquake struck, the company had a deep reservoir of trust and relationships with key stakeholders to draw upon. Executives consulted with the government and decided to continue previously planned stops to Haiti. "We actually felt it was a pretty easy decision once we realized that the physical site at our property at Labadee was unaffected by the earthquake and second after the Haitian government made it clear that they wanted to continue to have our ships visit, both for the economic benefit that they normally bring as well as the humanitarian aspect of delivering relief supplies," noted Goldstein in a National Public Radio interview.[19]

The company also launched a well-organized communications plan as soon as the earthquake occurred. It immediately announced it was donating $1 million in aid, bringing hundreds of pallets of relief supplies on its cruise ships, and donating all Haiti shore excursion proceeds to earthquake relief. Goldstein became the human face of the company, using his personal blog to post frequent updates on everything from how the company made its decisions, to daily meeting notes, responses to media reports, and photos of relief supplies. Company spokespeople stayed on message, expressing their empathy and their commitment to contributing to Haiti's recovery. The company announced that it would be partnering with charitable organizations—such as Food for the Poor, the Pan American Development Foundation, and the Solano Foundation, the company's foundation in Haiti—to provide additional assistance to the people of Haiti. Finally, independent advocates and experts came to Royal Caribbean's defense, including the founding director of the Burn Advocates Network, a senior official from the United Nations World Tourism Organization, an official from Sustainable Travel International, and a professor from Duke University's Kenan Institute for Ethics. Leslie Voltaire, Haitian special envoy to the United Nations, declared in a company press release on January 15, "Given the terrible economic and social challenges we now face in Haiti, we welcome the continuation of the positive economic benefits that the cruise ship calls to Labadee contribute to our country."[20] This outside advocacy was golden.

Just as Royal Caribbean International did not suddenly begin managing political risk when the earthquake hit, it did not stop once the immediate press furor died down. Six months after the earthquake, the company announced that it was building a new school in Haiti, establishing a strategic partnership with three other companies to build facilities to provide construction materials for housing and critical infrastructure, and launching "voluntourism" excursion options for passengers to engage in community service projects while stopping in some of its locations, including Labadee.[21] Political risk remains: In 2016, Royal Caribbean had to turn away ships when the Haitian presidential election was postponed and anti-tourism unrest grew. But thanks to effective political risk management, Haiti has proven a valuable destination for Royal Caribbean, and Royal Caribbean International has proven a valuable development partner for Haiti for more than thirty years.

SeaWorld's *Blackfish* Crisis

Royal Caribbean International's earthquake experience in Haiti stands in stark contrast to SeaWorld's *Blackfish* crisis. When the movie was released in July 2013, celebrities and animal rights activists rushed to attack the company's treatment of orcas.[22] The documentary tracked the life of one whale in particular named Tilikum who had been captured in the wild in 1983 as a calf, separated from his mother, and placed in captivity for more than twenty-five years in different amusement parks. The movie suggested that inhumane treatment in captivity turned Tilikum into a homicidal whale: The orca was known to be responsible for the deaths of three people, including veteran SeaWorld trainer Dawn Brancheau. As *Variety* noted in its review of *Blackfish*, "The impression the film leaves is of a deep-pocketed institution that, for all its claims of humane and professional treatment, tolerates practices that are fundamentally at odds with the animals' well-being and refuses to accept any portion of responsibility."[23]

Before Brancheau's death, SeaWorld routinely cautioned trainers about working with Tilikum, giving new employees a special "Tili Talk" about his aggressive behavior, refusing to allow activities in water knee-deep or more with the whale, and informing trainers of previous human deaths involving him.[24] Yet tragedy still followed. On February 24, 2010, at the end of a "Dine with Shamu show" in Orlando, Brancheau reclined on a platform that sat just a few inches below the surface of the water. She was performing something called a "lay out mimic," where both trainer and whale lie on their backs in parallel next to each other. But Tilikum did not roll onto his back. While horrified audience members watched, he grabbed Brancheau off the platform, dragged her into the pool, and started swinging her around underwater—severing her spinal cord, fracturing her jaw and ribs, and eventually drowning her. The ordeal lasted for forty-five minutes while SeaWorld park employees desperately tried to corral the whale and save Brancheau.[25]

The film and the outrage it sparked among animal rights activists went viral. After premiering at the Sundance Film Festival, *Blackfish* aired on CNN, then was distributed by Netflix. Twitter was abuzz with anti-SeaWorld tweets from celebrities. Popular music groups canceled concerts at SeaWorld parks. Corporate sponsors cut ties. Attendance declined and the parent company's share price plummeted. Three years after the release of *Blackfish*, SeaWorld's share price was still 60 percent lower than it was before the movie.

The "*Blackfish* effect" caught on in large part because SeaWorld never built a reservoir of trust with animal rights activists, researchers, political leaders, or others who could have come to the company's defense and stopped the crisis from getting worse when the movie was released. As a result, the political risks kept multiplying. In April 2014, SeaWorld lost its long-standing legal battle to keep human trainers performing in pools with orcas. California state lawmakers and federal legislators started sponsoring bills to ban orcas in captivity. In October 2015, the California Coastal Commission went further, banning domestic breeding of orcas at SeaWorld in California and mandating that no orcas captured in the wild could be housed there as a condition for SeaWorld's expansion of its mammal tanks in the San Diego theme park.[26] New regulations are almost always easier to block than pass. SeaWorld still ended up on the receiving end of new regulation because the company had not spent enough political capital before the crisis building relationships or its reputation. When *Blackfish* depicted the company as mistreating the animals, misleading the public, and putting human trainers' lives at risk, the public mood shifted. And SeaWorld quickly found itself alone.

While Royal Caribbean International's third-party supporters defused the Haiti crisis and helped the company show an empathetic side, SeaWorld was left trying to repair the *Blackfish* damage by itself. In the spring of 2015, the company launched a national reputation campaign that included television and online advertising to showcase the company's concern for and treatment of animals. The centerpiece was a website, AskSeaWorld.com, and a social media campaign under the hashtag #AskSeaWorld.[27] "The campaign emphasized SeaWorld's 50-year commitment to continuous evolution while setting the record straight on false accusations by activists who oppose whales and other animals in zoological settings," said Fred Jacobs, SeaWorld's vice president of communications.[28]

It backfired. Animal rights activists "brandjacked" SeaWorld, jumping on board the Twitter discussion. Tweets included, "@SeaWorld are your tanks filled with Orca tears?" Others tweeted, "If you were a killer whale, would you rather live in the ocean with your family, or in one of your tanks alone? #askseaworld," and "Why do you keep breeding whales when you barely have enough room for one? #askseaworld."[29]

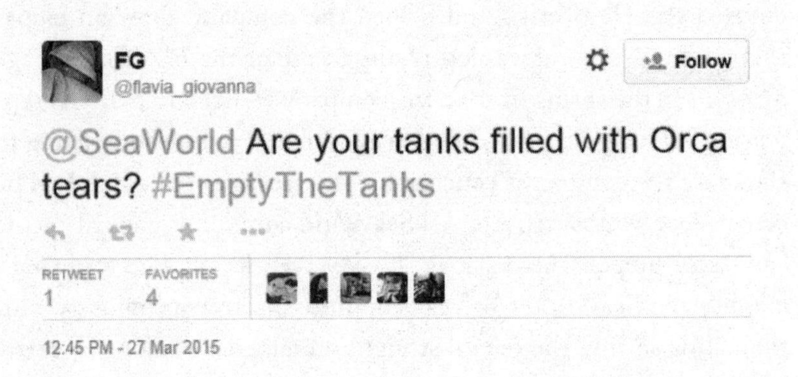

The company's first crisis erupted in large part because executives did not foresee the power of social media or the new reputational risks this technology raised. Now it was happening all over again.

After three years of crisis, and under the leadership of new CEO Joel Manby, SeaWorld finally started turning the page. In a *Los Angeles Times* op-ed, Manby announced that SeaWorld was ending all of its orca breeding programs across the United States, phasing out its theatrical orca shows,[30] and dedicating $50 million to a new partnership with the Humane Society of the United States to create educational programs, rescue animals, and combat commercial whale and seal fishing. The op-ed garnered the first positive reaction since *Blackfish* and was hailed by animal rights groups as a move in the right direction. SeaWorld also continued discounting admission prices, built roller coasters and other new rides to reduce its parks' reliance on animal shows, and embarked on another advertising campaign.[31] Initially, SeaWorld share prices jumped 25 percent after Manby's op-ed.[32] As former SeaWorld marketing executive Joe Couceiro noted, the move enabled the company "to talk about the wonders of SeaWorld as opposed to more of a defense posture."[33] But by August 2016, declining Florida tourism and other factors sent the stock back down, with Manby telling analysts that SeaWorld was in "an environment where we haven't proven that we've hit the absolute bottom."[34]

Blackfish undoubtedly dealt a serious blow to the company, but the crisis lingered and worsened for three long years because SeaWorld did not manage political risks well. In both cases, sudden events struck and companies were pummeled with criticism that quickly spread through mass media and the Internet. One company rebounded. The other continues to struggle.

What Royal Caribbean International Did and SeaWorld Didn't

In global business, sometimes even the best-prepared companies get caught in the maw of political events or natural disasters that no one ever saw coming. But Royal Caribbean International did not just get lucky, it got to work. Without good risk management in place, the cruise line's reputational crisis during the 2010 earthquake, and its future operations in Haiti, could have taken a very different turn. Royal Caribbean International effectively implemented the political risk framework—understanding risks, analyzing them, mitigating the risks that remained, and responding to crisis.

Royal Caribbean International *understood* Haiti's political risks early on, *analyzed* them, and concluded that they were significant enough to warrant serious action and sustained attention. The cruise line instituted a number of risk *mitigation* efforts before the first ship ever docked in Haiti. These included building relationships at the local level to reassure the communities near Labadee and becoming a trusted economic development partner of the Haitian national government. The company also earned the support of international NGOs, the United Nations, and national experts focused on ethics and development. It physically separated the compound at Labadee from other parts of Haiti with fences and security guards to lower the chances that violence and wrong-place/wrong-time crime would affect passengers.[35] Executives made sure to diversify the business: Labadee was just one of more than 250 ports of call at the time, and the cruise line began developing a Labadee-like private destination in CocoCay, Bahamas, just four years after it entered Haiti. Over time, risk mitigation also entailed embracing a corporate philosophy of "destination stewardship" that encouraged working with a wide range of stakeholders to maintain the local cultural, environmental, economic, and social integrity of their destinations. And it included maintaining close relationships over a long period of time. As Adam Goldstein told us, "The relationships we had built before the earthquake paid off during the crisis. I had been involved very personally going back to 1997. It was already thirteen years of knowing the prime ministers, touring Labadee, talking about what we wanted to do there before the earthquake." For Goldstein, that personal trust was essential.

"The relationships we had built before the earthquake paid off during the crisis. I had been involved very personally going back to 1997. It was already thirteen years of knowing the prime ministers, touring Labadee, talking about what we wanted to do there before the earthquake."

—Adam Goldstein, president and COO, Royal Caribbean Cruises, Ltd.

Finally, Royal Caribbean International's *response* plan was well considered and well executed, with clear leadership from the top. Goldstein made a deliberate call to land in Labadee. Haitian officials wanted the company, and the company wanted to help, both by providing badly needed relief supplies and with economic development. Royal Caribbean International's actions were not misconstrued for long: Goldstein quickly and clearly communicated what mattered to him and why. He put a human face on this human tragedy, explaining in media interviews and on his own blog what exactly the cruise ships were doing in Haiti and why it mattered. Haitian government officials, NGOs, and experts that Royal Caribbean had known for years rallied to the company's defense. When the earthquake suddenly hit, all the hard work that Royal Caribbean International had done to understand, analyze, mitigate, and respond to political risk paid off.

Thanks to good political risk management, Royal Caribbean was able to assist in earthquake relief efforts in Haiti and continue its business operations there successfully.

By contrast, SeaWorld struggled at every step of risk management. Although SeaWorld *understood* the safety risks posed by human–killer whale interaction early on and took steps to address them, the company apparently never *analyzed* that the risk of trainer injury or death could jeopardize its core business. SeaWorld's incident reporting system, which was supposed to improve training by reporting whenever a whale did not act as predicted or trained, was voluntary and incomplete: Brancheau's death and a second SeaWorld death caused by Tilikum were never included as incidents.[36] In addition, the company allowed trainers to lie on slide-out platforms inches below the surface of the pool, but considered interaction with Tilikum in water below knee-depth to be too dangerous—an arbitrary distinction that eventually led to an OSHA ruling, a fine, and a Labor Department requirement that trainers be barred from engaging in close contact with orcas during shows unless they were protected by a physical barrier. The incident reporting system, moreover, was undercut by management practice and culture, which strongly encouraged trainers to keep their shows going and keep audiences happy.[37] In 1999, for example, one whale's erratic and dangerous behavior caused two trainers to stop a show. Instead of receiving support or praise, they were criticized in the form of a strongly worded memo from Michael Scarpuzzi, vice president of animal training. "The show did not need to be cut short," Scarpuzzi wrote, adding, "We have reiterated our existing policy to utilize any and all resources before canceling a show."[38] In short, safety issues were identified, but not assessed to be serious enough to warrant more strenuous measures or systematic safety procedures either before or after Brancheau's death.

SeaWorld was also flat-footed when it came to *understanding* and *analyzing* the risks posed by animal rights groups, or the impending release of the *Blackfish* documentary. *Blackfish* was not a surprise. Gabriela Cowperthwaite had asked SeaWorld executives to be interviewed for the film, but the company had refused. Similarly, animal rights groups had been criticizing the theme park for years. Although they had not garnered widespread support before *Blackfish*, they provided a ready-made infrastructure to galvanize sustained public action once the movie was released.[39] As American University social change expert Caty Borum Chattoo noted, "The film wasn't released into an issue or activism vacuum. It fell into a prime spot with a social-change infrastructure ready to leverage a strategic distribution strategy and well-produced story."[40]

Because SeaWorld did not *understand* or *analyze* these risks sufficiently, it did not take adequate steps to *mitigate* them by diversifying its revenue sources or attractions, dramatically improving safety, or aggressively pursuing a strategy to build goodwill among external stakeholders—all steps the company began to take after the crisis hit. Dawn Brancheau died in 2010. Yet in 2013, when *Blackfish* was released, six of the eleven theme parks operated by the parent company, SeaWorld Entertainment, were either SeaWorld parks or companion parks that extended the SeaWorld brand and experience.[41] The company's top theme park by attendance and revenue was SeaWorld Orlando, where Brancheau died. And all three SeaWorld theme parks still relied heavily on the famed "Shamu" orca shows to draw visitors. Named after SeaWorld's first orca, the Shamu shows were so central to SeaWorld's value proposition that the logo for SeaWorld parks was an image of a killer whale, and every SeaWorld park featured a "Shamu Stadium."[42] Meanwhile,

SeaWorld's good deeds went largely unnoticed. The company's rescue and rehabilitation program had saved more than twenty-three thousand injured, abandoned, or orphaned animals. Its foundation had awarded millions of dollars for animal research, conservation, and education over the years. Yet it seemed unable to get the word out.[43] Instead, Shamu was literally and figuratively the face of SeaWorld to the public, the image most associated with the brand and the SeaWorld park experience. And that's precisely why *Blackfish*'s criticism went straight to the company's bottom line. Where Royal Caribbean International took concerted steps to lower the probability and impact that something would go horribly wrong in Haiti, affecting its business, SeaWorld continued to bet big that nothing would go horribly wrong with Shamu.

Finally, SeaWorld's *crisis response* was not knowledgeably executed. As we discuss in chapter 9, the best crisis response organizations learn from near misses. They plan for failure instead of assuming continued success. They reward truth-telling and institute feedback loops for continuous learning *before* disaster strikes to lower the odds that it will happen and to improve the odds that when it does, everyone will be better prepared. And in the face of crisis, they are quick to communicate their values, tell their stories, and take serious steps to earn back the trust of their customers.

SeaWorld had plenty of near misses to learn from. In fact, it bought Tilikum in 1992 from a Canadian company called Sealand of the Pacific that had gone out of business after Tilikum had killed a trainer in full view of horrified spectators. In 2006, a San Diego SeaWorld orca bit the foot of experienced trainer Ken Peters, repeatedly submerging and thrashing him underwater and nearly drowning him during a performance. In 2009, one of SeaWorld's leased whales killed a trainer at a Spanish theme park company. SeaWorld modified its shows and safety procedures over time. What it did not do was adequately prepare for the possibility that killer whales killing humans at its fun-filled family amusement parks might someday create a public relations and business crisis.[44] The company's voluntary incident reporting system and trainer confidentiality agreements did not encourage or reward truth-telling about safety concerns. Management signaled that canceling performances was highly discouraged. The operating assumption was that Shamu shows would always be prized assets; nobody was well prepared when *Blackfish* made them toxic assets instead.

The company's response to *Blackfish* did not help. Before *Blackfish* was released, SeaWorld mounted an aggressive, preemptive public relations campaign attacking the veracity of Cowperthwaite's claims in a critique sent to fifty potential film reviewers—a move that many believe garnered wide attention to what would otherwise have been a small, little-seen documentary. Eamonn Bowles, president of Magnolia Entertainment, which released the film, called SeaWorld's letter to reviewers "the gift that keeps on giving," adding, "Frankly, I've never seen anything like it."[45]

Not until 2016 did the new SeaWorld CEO and board appear to be aggressively dealing with the crisis, cleaning house among senior executives, announcing a phased end to orca shows, and making a proactive public message about SeaWorld's next steps to improve the treatment of animals and the protection of its human trainers.

The moral of the Royal Caribbean International and SeaWorld stories is this: Political risk management really can make a difference. Royal Caribbean International has not always had smooth sailing in Haiti, canceling visits to Labadee during moments of unrest in the 1990s, in 2004, and most recently in 2016.[46] But the company has carefully positioned itself to operate in a challenging political environment. SeaWorld, by contrast, is learning the lessons of political risk the hard way, in the shadow of crisis, amid growing pressure and declining profits. To be sure, the Haitian earthquake affected a small part of Royal Caribbean International's business while *Blackfish* struck at the heart of SeaWorld's. But it did not have to be that way. Royal Caribbean International could have fared much worse and SeaWorld could have fared much better. In the pages that follow, we walk you through our risk framework so that you can better manage political risks early and well.

KEY TAKEAWAYS: MOVING BEYOND INTUITION

- ☐ Political risks are context-specific, but there are four basics to get right: understanding, analyzing, mitigating, and responding to risks.

- ☐ Royal Caribbean International and SeaWorld both confronted sudden crises that went viral. Political risk management helps explain why one recovered quickly and the other did not.

- ☐ Royal Caribbean's decision to send cruise ships to Haiti after a devastating earthquake initially sparked outrage. But because the company had spent years understanding and analyzing political risks in Haiti, it was well prepared for a natural disaster, too. Royal Caribbean had deep stakeholder relationships, mitigation strategies, and a response plan in place.

- ☐ SeaWorld did not appreciate how a safety incident involving one of its killer whales could jeopardize the core business or how easily animal rights groups could amplify the *Blackfish* effect, turning a $76,000 film into major losses. Because SeaWorld did not understand or analyze risks effectively, it failed to mitigate them by diversifying the business, improving safety, aggressively building goodwill with stakeholders, or responding to the crisis with contrition, commitment, and authenticity.

6

The Art of Boat Spotting: Understanding Political Risks

Hans Læssøe was not sure where to begin, so he Googled "strategic risk management." An engineer by training, Læssøe was a twenty-five-year veteran of the Lego Group, the privately owned Danish company best known for its Lego brick toys. It was 2006 and the Lego Group was in trouble. Global sales had plummeted and the company had narrowly avoided bankruptcy just two years earlier. Part of the problem was that executives had no systematic process for understanding, assessing, or managing strategic risks in an industry dependent on the rapidly changing tastes of kids and expansion into emerging markets. The Lego Group was understanding risks, all right, but they were operational risks like what to do if a machine broke down, a facility caught on fire, or the company's legal team found trademark violations. A new chief financial officer began working with Læssøe to build a strategic risk management capability—including political risks—from scratch. They had no playbook, so Læssøe created one as he went along.[1]

He started by gathering two dozen of the most creative thinkers he knew in the company across functions. Then he and his team brainstormed with key people from support functions such as product design, logistics, marketing, and compliance so that they could understand how risks interacted with different aspects of the value delivery chain. Læssøe's group conducted its own half-day risk identification brainstorming session, then narrowed down the top risks to about a hundred. In addition to financial and economic risks, the group identified a number of political and strategic risks, including the start of a trade war between the United States and China; a physical threat to its vital factory in Monterrey, Mexico; and a regulatory change that would prevent the company from using certain materials to make its toys.[2]

Next he involved two veteran Lego Group executives with a broad view of the company to spend several days with him carefully and systematically estimating both the likelihood and the potential financial impact of each risk. "We asked ourselves: What is the likely revenue impact given a certain scenario? Why do we think so? How did we get to that number?" said Læssøe. They used mini-scenarios for each risk and developed a simple 5-by-5 scale to measure the probability and impact for each. Læssøe used numbers that he thought would be easier for most people to distinguish: A very high likelihood had a 90 percent chance of occurring, high likelihood meant 30 percent, medium likelihood was 10 percent, low was 3, and very low was 1 percent. Finally, Læssøe's team went back to senior managers who needed to "own" each risk to get their feedback, ideas, and buy-in about risk identification, prioritization, and mitigation strategies. Læssøe believed strongly that risk leaders had to develop the risk strategy to own the risk. He saw his role as partnering with business managers in their effort to identify and mitigate risks, not serving as a compliance check on them.[3]

Ultimately, Læssøe's initiative created a database of strategic risks—including political risks like what would happen if regulations suddenly banned the use of certain materials or if the United States and China engaged in a trade war—and a systematic, continuous process to engage every important business leader, including the board, in setting the risk appetite, understanding and identifying risks, and integrating risk assessment and mitigation into business planning.[4]

Rather than making the company more risk-averse, the process helped the Lego Group seize opportunities more aggressively,[5] which contributed to a stunning turnaround. In 2015, Lego posted revenue increases of 25 percent, to more than $5 billion; net profits rose 31 percent to $1.3 billion; and with 350 new product launches, the company saw double-digit sales growth in nearly all of its markets.[6] The Lego Group began thriving again thanks in large part to Læssøe's innovations in risk management.

How can companies more clearly see political risks? There is no one process or tool that guarantees success. But there are many steps companies can take to get better at what Læssøe calls "boat spotting"—identifying big emerging challenges before you miss the boat.[7]

The most important one is realizing that understanding risks is not just about looking outside your office, at the risks "out there" in the world. It's about looking inside your company—developing the core competencies and organizational culture for good boat spotting. As we'll see, companies that understand risks well develop a common language for seeing and discussing risk systematically. They evangelize the importance of setting the risk appetite and owning risk across the company. And they work to harness creativity, perspective, and truth-telling to reduce blind spots.

The Lego Group

There is seeing, and then there is seeing. Risks are out there, but unless they are internalized and prioritized, companies are unlikely to take concerted action to manage them effectively.

It's much like how many of us treat news about healthy living habits. We all know we should exercise regularly, sleep well, and eat fruits and leafy green vegetables instead of fried and processed foods. But few of us actually do these things. (Condi is one of them, exercising every morning even as secretary of state, and trying to get seven hours of sleep each night. "You don't want me making decisions on behalf of the United States of America on four hours of sleep," she told her staff.) Many people do not take the actions they know they should because the risk is general—and their life is specific. It often takes a wake-up call—a high cholesterol test, a back injury, or something worse that translates the general risk into a very personal one—to prompt concerted action.

The same is true for companies. Knowing or listing risks is the easy part. Internalizing and prioritizing the management of those risks is much harder. Asking these three questions—explicitly and often—can help turn knowledge of the risks "out there" into concerted action "in here," where it can make a difference.

Understanding Political Risk: Three Key Questions

1. What is my organization's political risk appetite?
2. Is there a shared understanding of our risk appetite? If not, how can we foster one?
3. How can we reduce blind spots?

1. What is my organization's political risk appetite?

Companies that manage political risk well start with a grounded general understanding of what risks they are willing to accept and what risks they are not. Their risk appetite is explicit, updated, widely known, and closely tied to business strategy.

As we noted in chapter 1, political risk always rides shotgun with reward. Weighing the risk and reward of a business decision depends on many factors. These include:

- **Time horizon**—How long will it take for an investment to pay off? Oil companies operate with very long time horizons. Retailers, less so. For Vinod Khosla, the founding CEO of Sun Microsystems and a leading Silicon Valley entrepreneur and investor, timing is essential. Khosla's firm, Khosla Ventures, focuses on both for-profit and social impact investments. He recalled to us one particular technology start-up investment. His team assessed that there were substantial political risks that the start-up's intellectual property would eventually be taken if it entered a foreign market. The question was how long before that happened. Khosla estimated that the start-up probably had a ten-year window to make profits, which provided sufficient returns to move forward. As Khosla Ventures notes prominently on its website, "Every plan has risks, and we both understand and cherish risk."
- **Alternatives**—What other investment options is the company considering to put capital to work? One reason why oil companies end up in unstable places is that there is only so much good geology in the world.
- **Ease of exit**—If political risks become acute, is it possible to exit the market easily, by, for example, selling a foreign plant or investment to a local owner? How constrained are exit options by the type of investment at stake?
- **Visibility to customers**—How might political risks become reputational risks for your company's brand that damage relationships with key clients?

Risk appetite also often varies in some systematic ways by industry type and firm size.

Some industries are naturally more accepting of risk than others. Consider manned spaceflight versus commercial aviation. In its thirty-year history, the space shuttle program fleet flew 135 missions with 833 total crew members.[8] Two missions ended in tragedy—the 1986 *Challenger* accident and the 2003 *Columbia* accident, which together killed 14 astronauts.[9] That's a crash rate of 1.48 percent. If U.S. commercial airlines had the same accident rate as the space shuttle, there would be about three hundred fatal plane crashes every day.[10] Fatal accidents are always tragic, but they are more expected in spaceflight than they are in commercial aviation because space is seen, correctly, as inherently risky. Astronauts understand that. Their risk appetite is large, and they are considered heroes precisely because everyone is well aware of just how dangerous the job is. Before he became the first astronaut to orbit Earth in February 1962, John Glenn saw the November 1961 explosion of an Atlas rocket with a monkey on board. When asked how he felt about his space mission aboard the same kind of rocket, Glenn joked, "How would you feel sitting on top of a machine with a million parts all made by the lowest government bidder?"[11] Commercial airlines would never stay in business with a risk appetite like NASA's.

Consumer-facing companies like cruise lines, restaurants, and amusement parks confront public reputational risks that other industries (like extractive industries or business-to-business firms such as Oracle, Salesforce, or Dow Chemical) do not. Manufacturing companies tend to face greater political risks involving labor shortages, stoppages, and disputes. Apparel companies face particular corporate social responsibility risks involving working conditions and human rights in overseas facilities. Oil and gas companies are accustomed to operating in politically challenging environments where the "aboveground" risks of political crackdowns, corruption, instability, asset seizure, and violence are often persistent and substantial. Their investments can be driven largely by "belowground" geological factors instead of aboveground ones in part because consumers do not choose a local gas station based on where its unleaded fuel is sourced. By contrast, family-oriented entertainment companies like the Walt Disney Company are hyperaware of where and how they operate. Disney would never open theme parks in places like Nigeria, Libya, Venezuela, or Iraq. In fact, Disney has one of the lowest political risk appetites of any major firm in the world because executives have long recognized that the company's brand is its most valuable asset.

Frequently named one of the most powerful global brands,[12] Disney has become synonymous with safe and magical family entertainment, whether through its theme parks, cruise lines, movies, or cable television channels. Customers admire, trust, and adore Mickey Mouse, and the company wants to keep it that way. That means aggressively monitoring and mitigating any political developments—from terrorist attacks to inhumane overseas labor practices in the manufacturing of Disney-branded apparel—that could negatively impact the reputation of the "happiest place on earth." Disney was one of the first in a wave of companies after the September 11, 2001, terrorist attacks to develop a political risk unit, and has been a leader in political risk management ever since. As one Disney security executive told us, "Nothing hurts the mouse. It's a zero-risk threshold across all lines of the business."

"Nothing hurts the mouse. It's a zero-risk threshold across all lines of the business."
—Disney security executive

Perhaps the most important source of variation in risk appetite—and one that companies do not consider enough—is personal. Anyone who has ever watched kids in a playground knows that risk tolerance varies greatly by individual. When Amy's two sons were young, they would go to a weekly preschool gym class that included obstacle courses. One son raced through, climbing, diving, and running as fast as he could. The other son never tried a single course. Instead, he would sit on the side, safely watching everyone else, memorizing how the different patterns of courses changed from week to week. Research has found that these differences in risk tolerance tend to be innate and lasting. One study compared the penchant for risk-taking among identical and fraternal twins and found that genetics explains as much as 55 percent of the difference between people's willingness to take risks.[13] Researchers have identified several genes, such as the "worrier" gene (*COMT*) and the "impulsiveness" gene (*DRD2*), that are associated with the tendency to take risks.[14] (Beyond genetics, many factors, including geography, gender, age, religion, birth order, friends, and family, have been found to influence one's risk tolerance.) Risk tolerance is not just about physical risks. Claudia Sahm, an economist at the Federal Reserve Board, surveyed twelve thousand respondents over a ten-year period about a series of hypothetical gambles of lifetime income. She found that risk tolerance differed greatly across individuals but was relatively stable for a particular person.[15]

Every year, we run a simulation in our political risk class in which five different Stanford MBA teams deal with the same political risks for the same hypothetical company, an American cruise line named Triton. The students receive detailed backgrounders on the fake company (including personnel and financial performance), the cruise industry, and key political risk considerations. Here is a short summary of the scenario:

Triton Cruise Line in the Mexican Riviera

Triton is a premier cruise line, operating seventeen ships and offering more than a hundred itineraries to 350 destinations around the globe. Triton's seasonal cruises along Mexico's west coast constitute 8 percent of the business and make it the regional cruise leader. In recent years, increasing drug-related violence in Mexico, including "wrong-place/wrong-time" crime against twenty-two Carnival cruise line passengers in Puerto Vallarta during a shore excursion there in 2012 and rising security concerns in Acapulco, have prompted several competitors to leave the Mexican market. Triton has been hearing from Mexican tourism officials that the press stories are overblown, and other data suggest that tourist destinations in the Mexican Riviera actually have lower crime rates for Americans than many American cities. Nevertheless, it is clear that since the downfall of Colombia's Cali and Medellín cartels in the 1990s, Mexican drug cartels have assumed much greater control over the wholesale illicit drug market, and since 2006, successive Mexican presidential administrations have been combating the deteriorating security situation there with varying degrees of success. Triton's board of directors has asked for a strategic review of the company's Mexican business to determine whether the company should reposition ships to other Mexican cities, keep its existing itineraries (with possible changes to shore excursions and security), or withdraw from the Mexican Riviera entirely.

In class, each team develops recommendations, presents its analysis, and fields rapid-fire questions from Triton's board of directors (played by Amy, Condi, and class research and teaching assistants).

We have run this simulation for five years, involving 25 teams and 125 students. The results are pretty wide-ranging. About a third of the teams opt to remain in all existing Mexican ports of call but add various modifications to onshore excursions. About half the teams elect to shift itineraries across Mexican destinations (spending more time in Cabo, for example). And about one team every year or two decides to leave the Mexican market entirely. That's a substantial amount of variance. Remember, all five teams each year have identical background information, and the students are part of the same business school community, taking the same core first-year courses. What's more, this variance is not especially lumpy; we see a spread of different strategies each year. What best explains these outcomes? To be sure, this is hardly a scientific study, but we believe the answer lies in differences in the personal risk appetites of the team "CEOs" who are selected at random. Two moments drove this point home for us.

In 2016, two student teams took the exact same piece of data as justification for completely opposite decisions. The first noted that Mexico was "just 8 percent" of Triton's business, so the company could afford to exit the Mexican market. The very next team started by noting that "Mexico is important to us, 8 percent of our business, and that could grow." For one team, 8 percent was low. For another, it was high. The same information analyzed through different risk lenses led to different decisions.

Another time, in 2012, we were down to the last of our five team presentations. The four previous teams had all advocated strategies that involved remaining in Mexico, though some wanted to shift itineraries within the riviera while others wanted to beef up security and oversight of onshore excursions. Then Team 5 gathered in front of the room. The team CEO, Jessica Renier, was confident and adamant: Triton would pull out of Mexico immediately. You could feel the other students in the room suddenly growing uncomfortable: The herd had moved in the opposite direction. Jess and her team were alone, in front of their peers as well as the "board." What exactly were they thinking? And why?

Condi and Amy remember pressing Jess. "What's the business loss to the company for this sudden move?" Amy asked. "This is a big decision. How will you communicate this to your customers?" Condi queried. Jess stood firm. "Triton cruise lines has a zero-tolerance policy when it comes to safety and security issues involving our passengers. And we mean what we say. I'm the CEO. It's my call, I stand behind it, and I want everyone to know that this is who we are as a company. I'll take the short-term hit to my balance sheet. The risk of one passenger being harmed is exponential, and you can't ever anticipate how bad that will be." The room was abuzz. It was a bold and commanding presentation. And it stemmed entirely from Jess's deep-seated views about what risks she was and was not willing to accept as the leader of her hypothetical company. Before the board presentation, we had observed all of the team deliberations and we knew that Jess's team was evenly split about what to do. The decision was hers.

Later, Jess offered these reflections:

- I remember thinking that it came down to my call. Whatever it is, in my opinion, with political risk you have to make a bold call. You can't "split the baby." By trying to compromise, you open yourself to both risks. Which is the worst decision instead of just calling it one way or the other. I made the decision and just told the team, "This is the decision that I am going to make."

- Evaluating the risk, we looked at general business trends. Tourism in the area was going down. You generally want to look for growth markets. I remember other teams arguing that we should stay because if everyone else leaves, then we can dominate the market. If the degree of risk is so bad that everyone is leaving and you are the one that stays, that's not a reason to stay. It's not a reason you want to be known for owning the whole market share.

- Stats only get you so far. That's true in all political risk situations. When evaluating risk, you get inundated with stats and information, and the first thing you have to do is immediately cut out the stuff that doesn't apply. Or else it can cloud your decision.

There was no right answer to the simulation. The point of the exercise was to explore how and why different groups of people come to different judgments about political risk when facing the same situation. Jessica Renier made a call that most of her classmates did not because she had an innate view about what the company's risk appetite should be and what role the CEO should play.

Companies, like individuals, often see the same risks differently. They develop with specific cultures, identities, and ways of viewing the world that filter data in different ways. Yes, risk appetite does vary systematically across industries, as we noted above. Disney and Chevron are unlikely to accept the same levels of political risk to their businesses. But that does not mean firms should make the same political risk calls just because they are within the same industry. In Iraq, for example, both ExxonMobil and Royal Dutch Shell originally made a strong play to sign exploration and production contracts with the Kurdish regional government during 2011. Both companies were well aware that they faced substantial political risks operating in northern Iraq at the time. These included a decades-long independence movement by Iraqi Kurds, disputed territorial claims between the central government and the Kurdish regional government over the oil-rich lands involved in the contracts, unresolved legal conflicts over the management and distribution of oil revenues across Iraq, and a fledgling Iraqi democratic government struggling to contain sectarian violence. When Baghdad learned that the Kurdish regional government had signed an oil deal with ExxonMobil, the first industry "supermajor" to do so, the central government in Baghdad threatened to cancel Exxon's contract to develop a major oil field in the southern part of Iraq. The threat was significant: Southern Iraq offered some of the largest potential oil reserves in the world. Despite the threat, Exxon held firm, betting that Baghdad would let both deals go through. Shell, however, was not willing to take that chance. It called off its talks with the Kurds to preserve its contracts in the south. Two supermajors faced the same choice at the same time in the same industry. Neither one was wrong. Each made the best call they could based on a clear understanding of their own risk appetites.

The most important thing about risk appetite is that you know what it is. This sounds obvious. It isn't. In many organizations, risk appetite is assumed. It's implicit. Everyone thinks they understand it. But it is much better to make the risk appetite as explicit as possible, for three reasons. First, as we noted in chapter 4, human cognition is a tricky thing; even when we have the same concrete facts, we can and do interpret them differently. The second is turnover: New people are always entering an organization, and they may walk in the door with a very different understanding of what the company's risk appetite is or what it should be. Third, risk is dynamic. It is always changing, and a company's risk appetite may shift with it. As Royal Caribbean president and COO Adam Goldstein told us, "To be successful in managing political risk is very much an ongoing undertaking. It's not episodic." If everyone thinks they know what the risk appetite is but nobody ever discusses it, misunderstanding is more likely. Making hidden assumptions less hidden improves decision-making, whether it is for economic modeling, intelligence analysis, or corporate strategy. Companies that explicitly set their risk appetite are more likely to develop a coordinated, effective, and nimble approach to risk management.

There are many ways to establish the risk appetite. At Suncorp Limited, a leading insurance and financial services firm in Australia, the firm's risk appetite is developed deliberately each year. "We formally set the risk appetite annually, and that's tied into our strategic planning cycle and process," says Clayton Herbert, Suncorp's chief risk officer. The process "sets the boundaries within which strategies are built."[16] At Canadian electricity company Hydro One, chief risk officer John Fraser facilitates a handful of workshops each year where he asks employees from all levels and departments to identify and rank the foremost risks they feel the company faces. Employees use an anonymous voting system to rate each risk on a scale of 1 to 5 based on its impact, the likelihood of occurrence, and the strength of existing controls. Fraser then uses the rankings for discussion at workshops, and employees are given the opportunity to share and debate their risk perceptions. Based on the discussion, the group develops a company-wide consensus that is recorded on a visual risk map, recommends action plans, and designates an "owner" for each major risk.[17] The specifics vary by company, but the best practice is the same: Start by asking what your organization's risk appetite is. If you do, the business will be better positioned to make good decisions about what risks to accept, and why.

2. Is there a shared understanding of our risk appetite? If not, how can we foster one?

The second question every business leader should ask is closely tied to the first: Is there a shared understanding of the company's risk appetite? It is not enough for a CEO, a chairman of the board, or a senior executive team to know the company's risk appetite. *Everyone* needs to know it. Shared understanding across the organization is crucial. If political risk management is the responsibility of just the "risk people," you'll be in trouble. The best companies ensure that political risk is everyone's business, from the boardroom to the sales floor, and spend a great deal of effort evangelizing so that everyone shares a *common language* for discussing risk, a *consistent and repeated process* for identifying risk, and a *sense of ownership* about risk.

At Disney, the shared understanding about "not hurting the mouse" pervades the company. As a Disney security executive told us, "It's weirdly inculcated in every business leader." Disney "is one of the greatest places" to do political risk management, said the executive, "because everyone accepts that what you've got is going to be valuable. You're not bugging anyone when you give them bad news. I don't know how that got transmitted, but it's there."

Many leaders in political risk management develop formalized processes for identifying and evangelizing risk, raising both awareness and understanding across business units. Paychex has one of the most creative. A public company with more than a hundred offices serving more than half a million small and medium businesses, Paychex has been providing payroll, human resources, and benefits services since its founding in 1971. Each year Paychex's risk management team holds what they call the "Tournament of Risk," modeled after the NCAA men's basketball March Madness tournament. About two hundred top leaders, from every business group and functional unit (including IT, finance, marketing, and sales), meet to collectively review sixty-four top risks identified by the risk team based on estimated impact, likelihood, speed, and other factors. During the tournament, risks such as credit risk, regulatory risk, and data security "compete" against one another in brackets where all two hundred business leaders get to vote electronically. The winning risk with the most votes in each head-to-head match then advances to the next round of "play." One year, for example, pricing took the top prize. Frank Fiorille, Paychex's senior director of risk management, emphasizes that the final risk scores don't particularly matter. "The ultimate goal for the Tournament of Risk is to gain collective feedback from senior leadership," he said. "It is one way to get executives engaged and interested in risk."[18]

The Mexican company Cemex is one of the world's leading building materials companies, with forty-three thousand global employees, trade relationships with more than a hundred countries, and $15 billion in annual sales.[19] At Cemex, the chief risk officer and his team prepare a global risk agenda for the company two times a year—more often if events warrant it. The global risk agenda includes both country- and corporate-level issues, and engages all top managers to identify risks and suggest ways to mitigate them. The results are presented to the executive committee of the board, "so they are always aware of the issues that we'll be facing," notes

Enrique Alanis, Cemex's chief risk officer. Alanis views communication, or, in his words, "evangelizing about risks and our preparedness," as an integral part of his job.[20]

At the Lego Group, identifying political and other strategic risks is now integrated into the business strategic planning process.[21] Over the past decade, Hans Læssøe designed the risk management function to develop a common understanding of risk appetite, a shared language for discussing risk, and clear ownership of risk throughout the company. All project managers at Lego must be trained in risk management. Probability and impact of risks are rated along consistent quantifiable metrics. And the risk team calculates a "net earnings at risk" each year that management and the board use to set Lego's risk appetite and estimate its risk exposure.[22]

What Disney, Paychex, Cemex, and the Lego Group have in common is buy-in from the top about the importance of understanding and managing political risk, practices that create shared knowledge of the company's risk appetite, and a system that ensures there is focused responsibility for owning specific risks. In all of these companies, the risk appetite is clear, widely held, and updated. There is enough guesswork in the political risk business as it is. Knowing your own company's risk appetite should not be part of it.

3. How can we reduce blind spots?

Every person and organization has blind spots. The trick is figuring out ways to reduce them so you can see emerging risks before it's too late. Paychex's Fiorille is particularly concerned with what he calls "risks around the corner," whether they are market trends or changing political conditions. "I always think that it's the bus that you don't see coming is the one that runs you over," said Fiorille. "The emerging risk piece is the key."[23]

Vivek Karve, chief financial officer of Marico, a leading Indian consumer goods company, is especially concerned about risks that *arise gradually* around the corner. "Some aspects of how any business is conducted can be slow killers," he notes.[24] One such risk is consumer activism in India. "Inability to deliver quality goods to consumers is one of our top reputation risks. Marico has invested significantly in ensuring that top quality products are delivered to its consumers," he told Deloitte in its 2014 annual reputation risk survey.[25] Another slow-killing political risk is environmentalism. "Companies that disregard the environment in pursuit of profits may well find that this could come back to bite them," notes Karve. Marico is so concerned about rising environmentalism that it has already started going green, shifting to PVC-free packaging and using renewable energy for 90 percent of its needs.[26]

There are three ways that organizations—from toy companies to spy agencies—reduce blind spots and better see risks around the corner: imagination, walking in the shoes of others, and processes that prevent groupthink at the top.

Imagination: Lessons from Star Trek

The *Star Trek* brand, which started with a television series in 1966 and has generated a television and movie franchise in the fifty years since, features two lead characters who provide a nice way of thinking about the role of imagination. Captain Kirk is the dashing, maverick captain of the starship *Enterprise*. Kirk is creative, unorthodox, and emotional, a man who flouts convention and has a sky-high appetite for risk. Lieutenant Commander Spock, Kirk's second in command, is the opposite. He is half Vulcan, a people who are devoid of human emotions and operate solely on the basis of logical reasoning. Though Spock's human half occasionally surfaces, he is notoriously data-driven, logical, and focused on following established procedures and conventions. Kirk and Spock are each flawed characters who would surely fail alone. But together, they have a yin and yang of imagination and analysis, action and thought, rule-flouting and rule-following that always wins the day.

This make-believe dynamic duo conveys a real-world message: Kirk and Spock are far more effective together than they are apart. The same is true with risk identification and analysis.

Risk analysis, which we turn to in the next chapter, is Spock—it is about hard-nosed, unsentimental analysis of facts. Risk imagination is much more Kirk. It is about creativity, emotion, and thinking about what could be, not just what is. Pure analysis without imagination can fail to see when history curves, when trends emerge that make discontinuous change more likely. Pure imagination without analysis can also lead to failure by focusing on futures that will never happen instead of realities that are already here. It takes imagination to understand risks. It takes structured thinking to analyze them. Like Spock and Kirk, imagination and analysis are better together.

Understanding risks as a first step is an exercise in imagination. J. Tomilson "Tom" Hill serves as the vice chairman of the Blackstone Group and president and chief executive officer of Blackstone Alternative Asset Management, the largest discretionary investor in hedge funds in the world, with $69 billion in assets under management as of July 2016. Blackstone also has skin in the game, with $1.8 billion of the firm's and employees' assets under management. Thinking about risks of all types is core to everything Hill does. "Our institutional investors," he says, "expect us to protect their capital in every different scenario."[27] Hill and his team start with imagination. They are always thinking about what could change in the world that would affect Blackstone's investments. "Frequently the consensus is wrong," Hill told us. "People assume things will continue this way forever... The biggest mistake is believing the future will look like the present. It almost never does."

> "The biggest mistake is believing the future will look like the present. It almost never does."
>
> —Tom Hill, president and CEO, Blackstone Alternative Asset Management

At FedEx, founder and CEO Fred Smith has long treated risk identification and management as a board-level and senior management issue, not just an operational one. Chapter 8 examines how FedEx mitigates risks operationally at its Global Operations Control Center in Memphis. But as Smith told us, "We look at [political risk] more at the senior management level as one of the most important things we have to manage."

In the 1990s, Smith was serving on board audit committees of other companies when he noticed something important: The audit committees were talking increasingly about information technology issues, not just budget issues. So he decided that his FedEx board should focus more on IT issues, too. They set up a board information technology and oversight committee. And over time, FedEx recruited new board members with IT and cyber security expertise such as Judith Estrin, who served as Cisco's chief technology officer and Silicon Valley technology pioneer, and John "Chris" Inglis, former deputy director of the National Security Agency. Ten years ago, Smith also elevated the chief information security officer and began working with cyber security companies like Mandiant to improve FedEx's defenses. Smith was able to move faster than many companies because he first noticed trends while serving on other boards, and he made sure that his own board would have the expertise to understand and manage what he calls the "looming cyber risks."

Companies also use an array of specific tools to help spot emerging risks. The Lego Group uses Google Trends, which shows word searches by region over time going back more than a decade, to try to see trends that could present risks or opportunities for company products.[28] Paychex's "Tournament of Risk" uses "gamification"—turning an analytic exercise into something competitive and fun—to get creative juices flowing. Many organizations, from Blackstone Alternative Asset Management to Shell, the Lego Group, the U.S. National Intelligence Council,[29] the World Economic Forum, and the University of California, Berkeley's Center for Long-Term

Cybersecurity, use scenario planning.[30] To keep it interesting, the Lego Group even gave its early scenarios fun names like "Murphy's Surprise" for its scenario on trade protectionism and lack of resources, and "Brave New World" for one on significant growth driven by Asian markets.[31] Eventually, Lego created a half-day workshop process known internally as "Prepare for Uncertainty," where leaders of a strategy defined and named their own scenarios. (We will talk more about scenario planning later. The point here is that it is first and foremost a tool to spark imaginative thinking about risks around the corner.)

War games are also becoming popular tools to identify and understand risks. Used in the U.S. military since 1886, these are exercises designed to provide a better understanding of future possibilities and current weaknesses in thinking and capabilities by simulating an interaction with an adversary and seeing how it unfolds.[32] One of the most frightening results occurred in a 1983 Pentagon war game called Proud Prophet, which was declassified a few years ago. The game ran around the clock for two weeks, included actual U.S. officials, including the sitting secretary of defense and chairman of the Joint Chiefs of Staff, and used real U.S. top-secret war plans. Yale professor Paul Bracken, who advised the war game, writes that it was "the most realistic exercise involving nuclear weapons ever played by the U.S. government during the Cold War."[33]

Proud Prophet revealed that many of the core ideas that American military planners and policymakers were employing to deal with the Soviet Union were, in Bracken's words, "either irresponsible or totally incompatible with current U.S. capabilities."[34] Among them was the strategy of limited nuclear war—the idea that a few, smaller nuclear strikes against the Soviet Union would lead the Soviets to accept a cease-fire rather than engage in a total nuclear war with devastating consequences for the planet. In Proud Prophet, the "Soviets" (played by American officials) did not show restraint once the United States launched a limited nuclear attack. Instead, the Soviets viewed the "limited strikes" as an attack on their homeland

and their national honor, and consequently responded with a massive nuclear retaliatory attack against the United States. The United States then reciprocated, and in the end half a billion people died, NATO was no more, and large swaths of the planet were rendered uninhabitable by radiation.[35] Proud Prophet showed that the theory of escalation control could be wrong and reckless. U.S. war planners assumed limited nuclear war would reduce catastrophic risks. Proud Prophet revealed that limited nuclear war might very well magnify them.

War gaming in recent years has spread outside the Pentagon. Procter & Gamble, Cadbury, Pratt & Whitney, Mars, and market leaders in more than fifty industries worldwide have all used them. Amy's former employer, McKinsey & Company, in 2012 wrote an essay advocating the value and use of war games by companies seeking to better deal with cyber threats. The McKinsey essay noted that one cyber war game enabled a public institution to discover that its risk identification was way off: The organization's security processes were focused on online fraud when the greater risk was a loss of confidence in the aftermath of a breach.[36]

Like scenario planning, there are better and worse ways to conduct effective war gaming, and there is a large literature about how to do it well.[37] Here, our aim is to give you a glimpse of the wide range of tools that are already being used to foster imagination and reduce blind spots.

Walking in the Shoes of Others: Lessons from Labadee

Risks are often hard to see because businesses do not anticipate the concerns, interests, values, and incentives of others. Trying to imagine any particular risk or situation from another stakeholder's perspective can help uncover hidden risks before they become a problem.

In the last chapter, we recounted that first, difficult meeting in the Haitian church between Royal Caribbean's Peter Whelpton and local residents who were deeply worried about the cruise line's plans to establish a private resort in Labadee. "My God, they came after me," Whelpton reflected. He thought the entire deal might go down before it ever got started. Whelpton had the critical support of his Haitian friend Pierre Chauvet, who knew the residents, spoke Creole, and urged them to listen. But that was not enough. Whelpton knew he had to look at the situation from the residents' perspective, acknowledge their concerns, and address them. The local community was skeptical. They were worried that the land would be destroyed and jobs would not be forthcoming. They lived in abject poverty and political turmoil. They had no relationship with Whelpton or the company. They had no reason to trust them and no idea what benefits might ever come to Labadee. "I tried to put myself in their shoes," Whelpton told us. "How are they going to look at what I'm doing? Am I doing it for them? Am I doing this with them? Am I doing this to them? You don't want to do it to them." For every project, he told us, he tried to think about how others might view it. "I'm saying to myself, 'I'm Haitian. I've never seen a project like this before. I'm suspicious.' Once you can do that, then you know how to go at it and you get a lot farther that way... Start from that point and work your way to build friends." What began as a tense meeting ended in a productive discussion about what the local residents hoped for and feared. Whelpton left with a better understanding of what he needed to do to bring them on board, including providing jobs and running water, and genuinely committing to the community.

The shooting down of a Malaysian airliner over eastern Ukraine during Russia's invasion and resulting civil war in 2014 showed how walking in the shoes of others, even if you may not agree with or follow their decisions, can still uncover hidden risks. The Dutch Safety Board investigation found that the airliner was hit by a missile while it was traveling from Amsterdam to Kuala Lumpur. (Many believe the missile was fired by Russian-backed separatists in

Ukraine who mistakenly thought the civilian airliner was a Ukrainian military plane.) The report faults the Ukrainian government for not closing its airspace sooner, noting that two days before the Malaysian airliner was hit, two Ukrainian military planes were also hit while flying at commercial airliner altitudes. There was good reason to close the airspace, the report finds, but Ukrainian authorities resisted. Why? The report offers no answers, but a risk officer with experience in commercial aviation does.[38] "There are reasons governments don't want to close their airspace," he told us. Chief among them are overflight fees and, perhaps more important, sovereignty. For the Ukrainian government to have closed its airspace, he said, "would have acknowledged that they had limited control over their territory. It would acknowledge that they did not have control over their airspace, that they were in a civil war and didn't have sovereign control." To identify risks well, he told us, risk managers in airlines have to walk in the shoes of government officials and understand why their overflight decisions might come too late—and why airlines need to be more proactive. Some airlines, in fact, were proactive: Australia's Qantas and Korean Air both stopped flying over Ukraine several months earlier amid concerns about increasing tensions on the ground and implications for overflight safety in the air.[39]

Preventing Groupthink: Lessons from the Secretary of State

Processes that encourage truth-telling and dissent within the organization can also reduce blind spots. We have talked a lot about the importance of developing a shared understanding of the risk appetite across your organization. But it is also important to create strong channels for dissenting views, new information, difficult feedback, and unconventional thinking to get to the top. Those who use these channels also need to be rewarded: Just because you build it does not mean they will come. The dark side of shared understanding is developing a siege mentality where everyone believes the same things, uses the same lenses, and dismisses alternative perspectives.

Psychologists have a name for the organizational pressures that cause groups to come to a uniform view even when they shouldn't. It's called groupthink.

Earlier, we shared the study that our colleague Bill Perry conducted about what makes some secretaries of defense more effective than others. It is a subject of high personal interest: Perry served as Bill Clinton's secretary of defense. He found that the secret sauce for success was not sheer intelligence. The key was their ability to prevent groupthink. Secretaries of defense who did not welcome opposing points of view rarely got them—and, as Perry recounted, "they [made] big mistakes because of it."

When Condi became secretary of state for President George W. Bush, preventing groupthink was very much on her mind. Inside the State Department, the secretary is referred to as "S." It was amazing, she recalls, how people would walk around Foggy Bottom saying, "S thinks this," or "S wants that." This was all very well-meaning. State Department foreign service officers, civil servants, and appointees were not trying to lie or hide the ball. They were trying to fix problems before they ever got to the secretary's desk. But that sometimes meant that by the time problems did arrive on Condi's desk, they had become even more difficult to fix.

That's exactly what happened in 2007, when Congress passed the Western Hemisphere Traveler Improvement Act, mandating that anyone traveling between the United States and Canada had to have government-issued identification. It was an effort to improve border security, and it meant that Americans who had been traveling to Canada without any documentation now would need travel documents. "When most people hear they need government ID for travel, they think they need passports," Condi thought. "And passports is me." Envisioning Americans in Buffalo or Detroit traveling to Canada to watch hockey games, she suspected that the State Department would face a spike in demand for U.S. passports as a result of the new law. She gathered her team and asked, "Will we be able to meet increased demand for passports?" The answer was yes. Some weeks later, while doing her early morning workout, Condi happened to see on television the lead local news story: A woman who had spent her life's savings on a trip to the Caribbean could not get her passport in time to take the trip. "So I go into the office," she recalls, "knowing that Congress would be all over this by 10 a.m." She called another meeting with all the key personnel in charge of passports and asked if there was a problem. "We're a little behind," they admitted. "How far behind?" she asked. "Six months." It was April. Summertime travel was fast approaching. "And so we went on red alert," she recalled. "I dedicated resources. We mobilized interns. We brought in retired officers. We brought in anybody who could process passports so that we could catch up."

In the midst of the crisis, Condi had dinner with her cousin Lativia. "This demand for passports is crazy," Condi said. Her cousin replied, "Yeah, I went ahead and got mine renewed because it was about to expire." Condi asked, "Oh, when does it expire?" Lativia answered, "In a year." That moment crystallized what was happening: It wasn't just Americans traveling to Canada who wanted passports. Expectations of delay were causing even more people to get their passports renewed, making matters worse.

By the time hockey season rolled around that winter, the six-month delay had been cut to two months, but it was still too long. "I had identified the problem but I did not stay on top of it," Condi later reflected, "so by the time it got to me, it had become a crisis." Looking back, she wished she had directed someone to stay on top of the passport process every couple of weeks after the law was first passed. "You know, you're the secretary of state. You're doing Middle East peace. But passports become a crisis. And you think, 'Passports? Really?' It's a systems issue. People don't pay enough attention to systems. I wish the people who had run the passport office had told me they were behind. I could have gotten more resources on it earlier to help solve the problem."

While the passport backlog did not work out as she had hoped, Condi took deliberate steps to create truth-telling mechanisms so that she could get information from the ground, and honest advice, early and often. She did this by hiring in special roles three people she had known for years: Steve Krasner, Philip Zelikow, and later Eliot Cohen. Steve, an international relations expert, had been a faculty colleague of Condi's at Stanford for more than twenty years and was brought in as the director of policy planning, the secretary's think tank. Philip, a historian who had taught at the University of Virginia and Harvard, had coauthored a book with Condi about German reunification and served as her counselor. He was succeeded by Eliot Cohen, an academic colleague of Condi's for many years. All three advisers played invaluable roles in giving her information and counsel that she otherwise would not have heard. "Steve Krasner, Philip Zelikow, and Eliot Cohen would always tell me what they really thought," she reflected. "And as secretary, you really need that. You need to have someone who can close the door and tell you what you might not want to hear."

The process generally worked very well. In Iraq in 2005, for example, state-building efforts were faltering. A major part of the problem was poor coordination between the State Department and Defense Department efforts on the ground. So Condi sent Zelikow and Ray Odierno, her military liaison, to Iraq to get a better understanding on the ground of the challenges and to recommend some new approaches. "We had to a have a different system," Condi recalls. "And they came up with PRTs," provincial reconstruction teams. PRTs started in Afghanistan but had been used for a different purpose: extending the central government into the highly decentralized country. In Iraq, PRTs would prove highly successful with the strategy of "clear, hold, and build" to combat al-Qaeda and its associates and allow economic and political institutions to take hold. Sending two trusted advisers outside the normal channels proved critical in adapting an approach from Afghanistan to the very different conditions of Iraq.

The lesson from Condi's experience is to find ways for truth-tellers to reach the top of your organization and build systems that keep information and honest perspectives flowing. For many companies, including the Lego Group, this means ensuring that the senior executive in political risk reports directly to the CEO or CFO. For others, like Cemex, it means political risk falls within the purview of the broader board of directors, not just the audit committee, which tends to look at issues from a compliance perspective. The most important thing to remember is not to isolate political risk from the senior levels of the organization. Do not put political risk in a corner. Make sure your political risk team has a seat at the senior table.

Organizations cannot identify every risk all the time. But reducing blind spots through imagination, walking in the shoes of others, and truth-telling can help master the art of boat spotting.

KEY TAKEAWAYS: THE ART OF BOAT SPOTTING

- ☐ Know your risk appetite: Managing risks "out there" starts by understanding priorities "in here."
- ☐ It is not enough for senior leaders to know the risk appetite. Everyone in the organization needs a shared understanding.
- ☐ Reduce blind spots through creativity, understanding stakeholder perspectives, and truth-telling.

7

Analyzing Risks Like a Physicist

The following scenario involves a fictional Japanese telecommunications company operating in Burma:

> Imagine it is August 12, 2014. You are the president of Kiku Telecom, a large Japanese company with operations in the United States, Japan, and Asian emerging markets.[1] As you peer out the window of your Tokyo office, you see a crowd of reporters gathering on the street below. The crisis is escalating quickly.
>
> An hour ago, you received an urgent phone call from the head of your Burma office reporting that peaceful labor protests by your Muslim workers in the western region known as the Rakhine State have erupted in violence. Several workers have been critically wounded, at least a dozen others have been arrested. Much is still unclear, but it appears the incident was the result of premeditated ethnic violence perpetrated by the Burmese army, which is also your telecom joint venture partner. A shaky cell phone video has already gone viral. It shows the arrival of a group of radical Buddhist monks and military personnel. As verbal confrontation between Kiku's Muslim workers and the Buddhist monks escalates to rock throwing, the military charges into the crowd, leaving the

monks alone but assaulting and arresting the workers. The BBC World News is running a continuous loop of the video under the headline "Military Beats Muslims at Japanese Telco Site." The Asia Director of Human Rights Watch has launched a fast-growing Twitter campaign, #brutalitypaysKiku. Meanwhile, the Burmese government has shut down your telecom network indefinitely for what it claims are "national security reasons." Your telephone calls to Burmese officials have not been returned.

A year ago, entering the Burmese telecom market seemed like a big win. You brokered a $2 billion partnership deal with the state-owned, army-backed Myanmar Posts and Telecommunications (MPT), the nation's monopoly telecom services provider. Securing the coveted foreign contract license committed Kiku to building infrastructure over the next ten years in exchange for splitting earnings 50/50 with MPT. The deal was a chance to enter one of the world's most promising emerging markets, with only 5 to 10 percent mobile phone penetration and a government trying to transition to a capitalist-oriented democracy. Now you are wondering: How can we contain the damage and ensure returns on our investment? Was entering Burma a mistake?

Although we made up this crisis scenario for our course several years ago, the general conditions in Burma are real. The country has been riven by ethnic conflict, corruption, and authoritarian rule for decades. Starting in 2010, however, Burma began opening to the outside world. The military junta was replaced, national elections were held, and Nobel Peace Prize winner Aung San Suu Kyi was released from house arrest. In response, the United States and the European Union lifted a number of sanctions, opening new opportunities for foreign investment.

In 2017, Burma's military, its security forces, and others launched a brutal crackdown against the country's Muslim Rohingya minority, making our hypothetical scenario tragically realistic.

We use this case to walk students through the nuts and bolts of analyzing political risks in a challenging new market. The full case includes information about Burma's history, sanctions regimes, human rights concerns, and telecommunications industry dynamics. As in our Mexican cruise industry case, there is no right answer. But there are three important lessons about analytic pitfalls and how to avoid them.

The first lesson is about what constitutes useful data. Each year, when our MBA students discuss whether entering Burma was a good idea, they seize on national-level data in the case materials such as literacy rates, GDP, and cell phone penetration. These figures are quantifiable, available, and useful for assessing the business opportunity. But they do not say much about political risks. Instead, as we note in chapter 4, political risk data are often localized and hard to quantify. What are the prospects for democratization in Burma? Where is ethnic conflict most severe and likely? Answering these questions requires more specific and qualitative data.

We write the case deliberately so that Kiku Telecom begins its Burma operations in a western region called the Rakhine State. In real life, this is one of the worst locations from a political risk perspective. While central Burma is populated by an ethnic Bamar majority and is under firm control of the state, it is surrounded by a horseshoe of ethnic and separatist conflict involving nearly two dozen groups. The Rakhine State is wracked by poverty and conflict between Buddhists and Rohingya Muslims, a group described by the United Nations as one of the most persecuted minorities in the world.[2] Although we include this information about ethnic conflict in the case materials, it tends to be overlooked. Why? Because for many, "data" means numbers, not words. People find hard numbers alluring and reassuring.

The "aha" moment in class usually comes when we point to the paragraph discussing the Rakhine State and ask, "So why did the company start here, of all places?" Students realize that they overlooked a major risk. Investing in Burma is one thing. Making your investment beachhead in one of the most conflict-prone areas of the country is quite another. The location and phase of the investment increased the probability of an adverse event and narrowed risk mitigation options from the start.

The second lesson is that political risk analysis should not stop once an investment begins. In our Burma case, fictitious company executives assess political risks before signing the joint venture deal but do not conduct ongoing analysis afterward. That's surprisingly common in the real world, too. Ian Bremmer, CEO and founder of the Eurasia Group, notes that most businesses analyze political risks for new investments but few continue to assess political risks once the investment is made.[3] A survey conducted by Bremmer's firm and PricewaterhouseCoopers in 2006 found that only 24 percent of respondents reported on political risk on a biannual or more frequent basis.[4] Ten years later, a McKinsey global survey of executives found that only a quarter had integrated risk analysis into a formal process rather than conducting ad hoc analyses as events arose.[5]

View from the White House: Keeping Up with the Cold War's End

Governments are designed to monitor global politics constantly, but even policymakers sometimes cannot keep pace with events. Condi experienced one ill-fated review when she served on the George H. W. Bush National Security Council staff.

The administration came to office in 1989, and immediately conducted an assessment of Soviet, Eastern European, and European policy given the rise of Gorbachev. Those reviews assessed that Gorbachev would not radically reform the Soviet Union, and that the United States needed to institute a more robust containment approach. The ink had not dried on the documents before events raced ahead and the Soviet Union soon collapsed.

Especially in today's environment, political conditions change, sometimes quickly. Good political risk analysis is not a one-shot deal, it is a continuous endeavor.

The third lesson is to beware of optimism bias. Most students walk into class enthusiastic about Burma, seeing a rare opening and a historic business opportunity.[6] After three hours of political risk discussion, they reach a more sober assessment of the trade-offs. Although many say they would enter Burma anyway, nearly all say they would enter differently. Once they focus on political risks, students come up with all sorts of mitigation ideas—from starting construction in central Burma to building relationships with human rights groups to insisting on legislation that limits the government's ability to cut transmissions. Every year, we find that optimism bias keeps students from seeing risks and ways to reduce them.

Integrating political risk analysis into business decision-making helps guard against optimism bias. Not enough companies do this. SeaWorld executives saw profits, not exposure, in the company's dependence on orcas for theme park attendance and brand reputation. Jack Welch got so excited about the business potential of the GE-Honeywell merger that he did not take seriously enough the risk that the European Commission would nix the deal. Boeing executives were so buoyed by demand for the 787 Dreamliner that they did not see the slow-motion supply chain disruption coming when the fastener industry contracted after 9/11. By contrast, companies that manage political risks well make risk analysis a core part of the business. They bake political risk in. They do not bolt it on. And importantly, they see political risk as helping the business. The "risk folks" are not the voice of doom. As Pat Donovan, Chevron's director for global security, told us, "We have to speak to people in a way that we aren't trying to prevent them from doing their job, but showing them the best way to go about doing it—politely, diplomatically, but candidly. No doesn't work. Ninety-nine percent, yes, we will find a solution, does."

These takeaways from our Burma case raise three questions that every organization should ask to analyze political risks.

Analyzing Political Risks: Three Key Questions

1. How can we get good information about the political risks we face?
2. How can we ensure rigorous analysis?
3. How can we integrate political risk analysis into business decisions?

1. How can we get good information about the political risks we face?

General Michael Hayden, who ran the NSA and the CIA, has a knack for explaining complex ideas in colorful ways. At his 2006 confirmation hearing, Hayden described the perils of analysis. "I have three great kids," he told the Senate Intelligence Committee, "but if you tell me, 'Go out and find all the bad things they've done, Hayden,' I can build you a pretty good dossier, and you'd think they were pretty bad people, because that was what I was looking for and that's what I'd build up. That would be very wrong. That would be inaccurate. That would be misleading."[7] Hayden's message was: Be careful. Good information is not so objective. Context matters. What you find depends on what you seek.

Companies analyzing political risks confront many of the same challenges the CIA does. Information often seems straightforward when it isn't. The story of Hayden's kids reminds us that context is crucial. Even cold, hard facts can tell different stories. Is the drug-related violence in Mexico increasing or decreasing? It depends on when you start counting and what cities you use for comparison. Where should Kiku Telecom begin its operations in Burma? If you are looking to start where cell phone penetration is lowest, the Rakhine State is a good bet. If you are looking to mitigate political risks, not so much. Identifying what constitutes "good information" is itself an act of judgment. What you find depends on what you seek.

Three rules of thumb are useful.

Rule 1: Good information is specific, not generic.

Good information does more than indicate the political risks of operating in Country X. It helps answer the question, "What are the political risks to my organization from this place at this particular time?"

Note the words "my organization." Political risk information should be tailored to your company, its risk appetite, alternatives, strategy, and strengths. Recall that in Iraq, ExxonMobil was willing to assume far greater political risk in pursuing oil exploration and production contracts with Iraqi Kurds than Royal Dutch Shell was. That's because even in the same industry and location, the two companies had different risk appetites and strategies.

For this reason, off-the-shelf products are likely to be off the mark. Country reports, corruption indices, global industry analyses, and other generic products are fine places to start analyzing risks, but poor places to end. For example, Transparency International conducts an annual poll assessing perceptions of corruption by country. The poll is a valuable indicator of national-level corruption over time, but not of how corruption varies *within* a country. Research finds that within-country variations in corruption are significant even among EU member states such as Belgium, Bulgaria, Portugal, Romania, and Spain.[8]

Similarly, industry-based information about political risks in a particular market tends to rely on assessments at a single point in time. With today's pace of change, the lag between assessment and reality can be substantial. Argentina is the poster child for just how fast a nation's economic policies and political circumstances can shift. In October 2015, Argentina was poised to continue its leftist rule of heavy government subsidies and interventionist economic policies. Populism was so deeply rooted, no center-right candidate had led the nation since democracy was restored in 1983. Daniel Scioli, the ruling-party candidate, was expected to win. Instead, Mauricio Macri, a millionaire conservative businessman and the mayor of Buenos Aires, pulled an upset victory. Suddenly, Argentina appeared poised for transformation. "Today is a historic day," Macri declared in his victory speech. "We need to build an Argentina with zero poverty. A marvelous phase is beginning for Argentina."[9] He moved with lightning speed, dismantling subsidies and lifting currency controls on the peso to spur foreign investment. In March 2016, he negotiated an end to the country's debt dispute with holdout creditors, clearing the way for Argentina to access global credit markets.[10] Later that month, he restored relations with the United States, hosting President Obama, the first visit by an American president in two decades. "Argentina is back," then finance minister Alfonso Prat-Gay proclaimed.[11] But by summer, Argentina's political situation was changing yet again. With a shrinking economy and surging inflation and unemployment, Macri faced rising popular discontent. In July, angry citizens reacted to rising utility prices by banging pots and pans in the streets.[12] In August, more protests erupted, with tens of thousands gathering outside the presidential palace. In September, pilots halted flights of Argentina's airline to demand higher wages. Macri's approval plummeted. While economic analysts praised his efforts to reform the nation's economy and urged patience, political uncertainties grew about whether he would suffer the same fate as so many Argentine leaders ousted by popular economic discontent. All of these developments—the predicted continuation of Cristina Kirchner's socialist policies, the surprise election of a pro-business conservative president, the breakneck pace of economic reforms followed by political backlash, social unrest, and rising uncertainty about whether Macri would even finish his term—transpired in less than a year.

In short, generic products are likely to be incomplete and quickly outdated. Companies need to develop the capability to drill down into national data, gathering additional information that is more localized, contextual, and dynamic about the risks that matter most for them.

Doing this well does not require hiring an army of doctoral students or regional experts. Marriott International, one of the pioneers in global political risk management, has a full-time team of just two professional intelligence analysts, one in Hong Kong, one in Washington, D.C., so that someone is assessing intelligence all the time. Because Marriott operates properties around the world, including in some high-threat terrorist locations, Vice President for Global Safety and Security Alan Orlob is continuously assessing whether to move a hotel up or down a five-tiered color-coded alert system. He and his team do this by taking the intelligence they receive and analyzing its implications for specific properties. "We're very careful about not spreading threat levels across a country," Orlob told us. "For example we don't say, 'All of India is at our highest level.' We look at it city by city, product by product (what kind of hotel it is), and we look at it by history."

Management by walking around goes a long way, too. The best information about political risks in the field often comes from visiting the field. Consider Royal Caribbean International's assessment of the political risk of developing its port destination in Labadee, Haiti, during the 1980s. As the crow flies, Labadee is located just eighty-five miles from the violence-ridden capital of Port-au-Prince, a seemingly poor choice from a political risk perspective. But when executive Peter Whelpton visited, he found that

Labadee was actually much farther, since there was only one poorly maintained road that took several hours to traverse.[13] "People say, 'Oh, there's insurrection in Haiti; my God, there's shooting in the street,'" Whelpton told us. "But Labadee is way, way, way from Port-au-Prince."

Back to the question, "What are the political risks to my organization from this place at this particular time?" We use the phrase "*from* this place," not "*in* this place." As we noted earlier, political risks in one location or time often produce effects elsewhere. They cascade, thanks to connective technologies, global supply chains, and politics. In our hypothetical Burma case, for example, one of the issues we discuss is how human rights abuses by the Burmese military, which is Kiku Telecom's joint venture partner, could generate corporate social responsibility concerns among Kiku's Japanese and American customers. Political risks in Burma may not stay in Burma.

In the real world, examples of cascade effects abound. The outbreak of unrest in Yemen hurt tea farmers in Kenya. Progress against the illegal drug trade in Colombia shifted trafficking to Mexico, which in turn contributed to rising drug-related violence there. During the Arab Spring, the self-immolation of a fruit seller in Tunisia ended up bringing down the Mubarak regime in Egypt. In 2014, China moved an offshore oil rig close to Vietnam, sparking local Vietnamese protests, factory shutdowns, and clothing stock-outs in American cities.

Corruption is the most obvious cascading political risk that global companies face. As we note in chapter 2, the extraterritorial reach of U.S. and U.K. antibribery laws is extensive, covering activities anywhere in the world for companies that have some portion of their business operations in the United States or the United Kingdom. These laws also cover the activities of third-party contractors. "The middleman did it" is no defense. Small bribery requests in faraway places may pose no serious political risk where they occur, but they present substantial political risks of fines and prosecution in the United States and the United Kingdom.

When we asked Royal Caribbean executive Adam Goldstein to identify the hardest political risks his company faces, he immediately brought up the Foreign Corrupt Practices Act, sharing an incident that highlights the challenge. A few years ago, the company was charged a fee at one of its ports of call that appeared suspicious. Executives tried to get a justification from the host government, but as the ship neared the port, no answer came. "In the end, we were never provided with the proper documentation to justify the charge and they never backed off insisting on the charge," said Goldstein. "And so we did not call on the port. The restitution to our guests for missing that port of call for a reason that was not an act of God was $1 million to avoid a $5,000 bribe." Goldstein and his team knew the political risk was *from* the foreign port of call but was not confined there. The real risk was back home, in the potential to expose the company to violations of the Foreign Corrupt Practices Act.

Rule 2: Good information includes perception and emotion.

Good information also provides insight about perception and emotion. Perception and emotion are tightly intertwined drivers of human behavior, whether it's consumers in department stores, protesters on streets, or lawmakers in Congress.

Perhaps no episode in Condi's government service illustrates the power of perception and emotion better than the Dubai Ports World controversy. She taught this case to all incoming MBA students for several years. Here's what happened.[14]

In 2006, Dubai Ports World, an award-winning port management company owned by the government of the United Arab Emirates, acquired the London-based Peninsular and Oriental Steam Navigation Company (P&O), one of the world's oldest and largest port operators. The $6.8 billion deal made Dubai Ports World the fourth-largest container port operator (by throughput) in the world, with terminals in the Middle East, Europe, Asia, Australia, Latin America, and the United States. Because the acquisition gave Dubai

Ports World control over operating container terminals in six U.S. ports (Baltimore, Miami, New Orleans, New York, New Jersey, and Philadelphia), it needed to be approved by the Committee on Foreign Investment in the United States (CFIUS), a federal interagency panel charged with reviewing the national security implications of transactions granting foreign control over U.S. businesses. At the time, twelve government agencies were represented on CFIUS, including the National Security Council and the Departments of Defense, Homeland Security, State, and Justice.

The approval process began smoothly. Foreign operation of shipping terminals in the United States was in fact common: Seventy-five percent of shipping at the time passed through terminals leased by foreign companies.[15] Security at American ports was the primary responsibility of the Coast Guard, not terminal operators. What's more, the CFIUS review found no specific cause for concern. The Department of Homeland Security found Dubai Ports World to be fully cooperative with the mission of protecting American ports and American ships in foreign ports. The UAE was a longtime American ally and partner in the war on terror. In fact, UAE ports hosted more U.S. Navy ships than any port outside the United States. In addition, the UAE was providing valuable assistance to American missions in both Iraq and Afghanistan, and the government had played an instrumental role in arresting Abd al-Rahim al-Nashiri, the suspected mastermind of the USS *Cole* bombing (which killed seventeen American sailors) and the 1998 U.S. embassy bombings in Kenya and Tanzania.

On paper, everything looked good. CFIUS unanimously approved the deal.

But perception and emotion were quite another matter. Just four years after 9/11, fears of terrorist attacks on the U.S. homeland remained acute. The prospect of allowing an Arab government to operate shipping terminals in American ports sparked concern and outrage in Congress. The UAE was an Arab country, one of only three nations that recognized the Taliban regime in Afghanistan before

9/11, home to two of the 9/11 hijackers, and the place where financial transactions supporting the attack appeared to have occurred.[16] The Dubai Ports World deal quickly came under fire. Opposition was visceral, bipartisan, and widespread. Democratic senator Chuck Schumer declared, "Foreign control of our ports, which are vital to homeland security, is a risky proposition. Riskier yet is that we are turning it over to a country that has been linked to terrorism previously."[17] Republican representative Sue Myrick wrote a one-sentence letter to President Bush that read, "Dear Mr. President: In regards to selling American ports to the United Arab Emirates, not just NO but HELL NO!"[18] A Gallup poll found that 66 percent of the American public opposed the deal, and 45 percent opposed it strongly. On March 8, the House Appropriations Committee voted 62–2 to block the transaction. Although the White House wanted the deal to go through, it had little room to maneuver. On March 9, one day after the House committee vote, Dubai Ports World announced that it would transfer its shipping terminal operations to an American entity.

Condi was secretary of state at the time. She remembers thinking that the facts showed there was no security risk in the deal. No agency in the U.S. government, including the Departments of Defense and Homeland Security, believed that having a UAE company operating shipping terminals in American ports posed a threat to national security. Especially in the aftermath of 9/11, every department and agency was hypervigilant about potential homeland security vulnerabilities. But none of that mattered. The timing and ownership of the company were political killers. As Condi later reflected, "Americans heard 'Arabs, ports, and 9/11,' and those three things just couldn't go together. In the aftermath of 9/11 there was no way this deal was going to go through."

How can companies avoid a Dubai Ports World moment? For starters, by realizing that good information includes gathering a sense of the heated feelings and passions of key audiences. Think of "perception information" as anything that helps put a finger on the pulse of a group critical to your business, whether it's a segment of customers, a leadership group of government officials, or the political mood of a population. No telepathic powers or pinpoint accuracy is necessary. Perception is about general feel, broad trends, the arc of emotion.

Condi spent a great deal of time in the Middle East as secretary of state, traveling to the region thirty-one times in four years. In 2005, six years before protests erupted in Tahrir Square and brought down the regime of President Hosni Mubarak, she went to Cairo and delivered a speech urging Mubarak to embrace political reform before it was too late. "The Egyptian government must put its faith in its own people," she said, "[and] the day must come when the rule of law replaces emergency decrees." Years later, Amy asked why she gave the Cairo speech long before anyone thought Egypt would experience a major political change, through either evolution or revolution. "I could not tell you when the Arab Spring was going to ignite or exactly how a Tunisian fruit seller would lead to the fall of an Egyptian monarch," Condi reflected, "but I could tell you even then that the Middle East had some brittle regimes, bad demographics, rising social unrest, few outlets for all that pressure, and that time was definitely not on the side of the autocrats." Close contact with the region gave her insight.

Rule 3: Good information comes from asking good questions.

Third, and finally, good data come from asking good questions. How you label a problem can send your team searching in the right direction or in a very wrong one.

On March 11, 2011, a 9.0 magnitude earthquake struck Japan, triggering a catastrophic tsunami that hit the Fukushima Daiichi Nuclear Power Plant. Immediately after the temblor, the plant shut down its nuclear reactors according to emergency protocols. Then the power went out. Because power is essential for cooling nuclear fuel rods, diesel backup generators kicked into action. So far, safety systems were running as planned. But then the tsunami hit. The wave flooded the backup power generators for five of the six reactors, knocking them out. Without sufficient power, the plant suffered partial meltdowns in two reactors. The result was the worst nuclear disaster since Chernobyl. Nearly two hundred thousand residents were forced to evacuate as several hydrogen explosions erupted, radioactive steam and water were released, and officials desperately sought to contain the contamination and prevent a full core meltdown.[19]

The conventional wisdom about Fukushima is that nobody could have seen this disaster coming. The 9.0 magnitude earthquake was one of the most severe ever recorded. The tsunami, too, was a rare event: There had been only three tsunamis in fifty years in Japan. Fukushima seemed like a black swan, so unlikely as to be unpredictable.

But not if you frame the risk differently. Our Stanford colleague Rod Ewing, a leading expert on nuclear waste, has examined what went wrong at Fukushima. He found that while the immediate risk of this specific event might seem remote, the longer-term risk of a major seismic event affecting a Japanese nuclear power reactor was far more likely. "You could ask, 'What if I have a string of reactors along the eastern coast of Japan? What is the risk of a tsunami hitting one of those reactors over their lifetime, say, 100 years?'" said Ewing.[20]

The answer is, pretty high. For starters, Japan has a lot of nuclear reactors—fifty-four in 2011, the third most of any country in the world.[21] Most are located on coasts. Before the disaster, Japan planned to double the number of reactors and expected to rely heavily on nuclear power for hundreds of years. Japan is also located in the Pacific "Ring of Fire," where 90 percent of the world's earthquakes originate. Finally, the fact that major tsunamis had not struck recently gave false comfort: Ten years before Fukushima, some of Japan's leading earth scientists, led by Koji Minoura at Tohoku University, found the interval of major earthquakes and tsunamis to be about a thousand years, with the last one occurring in 869. "From a geologic perspective," Ewing writes, "the earthquake and its great magnitude should not have been a surprise."[22]

Considering long-term seismic risks to nuclear facilities

throughout Japan could have unearthed what turned out to be the critical design failure at Fukushima: the location of backup power generators. All five failing generators were located near the low-lying coast, which is why they flooded so fast. Only backup generator number 6, located on higher ground, kept working. The flooding of five generators was not an accident; it was a design flaw. All of the backup generators could have been located farther from the ocean on higher ground had the risk been framed differently.[23]

Advances in evidence-based medicine also reveal how finding useful data begins with asking the right questions. For years, researchers did not think to conduct experiments gathering data on certain medical procedures because they assumed the outcomes were obviously better than any alternative course of treatment. But the evidence-based medicine movement has shown how doctors' experience and judgment can be wrong—sometimes frighteningly so. David S. Jones, a Harvard Medical School professor, recounts how two of the most common treatments for heart disease, coronary bypass surgery and angioplasty, have been widely used for years because doctors believed—falsely, it turns out—that these procedures would extend life expectancy.[24] Physicians believed that patients suffering from blocked arteries would live longer if the clogs could somehow be removed or circumvented. Bypass surgery did this by grafting veins or arteries from another part of the body into the heart vasculature. Angioplasty involved inserting a balloon into the blocked artery to compress and shrink the blockage, and then inserting a meshlike stent to keep future clots from forming. In 1996, doctors performed a peak of six hundred thousand heart bypass operations. In the 2000s, more than a million angioplasties were performed annually. Yet when randomized clinical trials were finally conducted, results showed that bypass surgery and angioplasty did not extend life expectancy any more than medication and lifestyle changes did except for a few of the sickest patients. And importantly, surgery imposed significant risks of side effects, including brain damage, that medication and lifestyle changes did not. The bottom line was that for most cardiac patients, noninvasive treatment options produced equivalent outcomes at a lower risk of serious complications.

For years, the data about bypass surgery and angioplasty were out there, waiting to be collected. But nobody ever asked: Do these surgical procedures lead to overall better outcomes than less invasive alternatives when we consider possible side effects?[25] Good information remained hidden until doctors began asking good questions.

Harnessing the power of information requires searching for data tailored to your organization's needs and strengths, considering perception and emotion, and asking the right questions to search in the right direction.

2. How can we ensure rigorous analysis?

The first step in good political risk analysis is getting good information. Step 2 is analyzing that information well.

Richard Feynman, one of the world's great physicists, said that analysis is how we try not to fool ourselves.[26] He was onto something. Whether you are analyzing next quarter's prospects in a foreign market or geostrategic trends over the next five years, good political risk analysis challenges assumptions and mental models about how the future could unfold. *The goal of political risk analysis is not to predict the future. Nobody can do that. The goal is to create better decisions for your organization by developing insight about key drivers and possibilities.* Rigorous analysis hinges on traps, tools, and teams—understanding the cognitive traps and group pathologies that lead analysts astray, utilizing analytic tools to overcome these barriers, and enlisting the entire business team.

Traps

Cognitive traps are deadly and they are everywhere. In chapter 4, we discussed how humans are terrible when it comes to statistics and calculating risk. People are more worried about dying in an airplane crash than a car crash even though airplanes are about seventy times safer than cars. All of us suffer from the "availability heuristic," believing that bad events which can be recalled easily (usually because of press coverage) are more likely to occur than they actually are. Optimism bias is also pervasive, explaining why investors believe their investments will perform better than average, why NFL fans overpredict wins for their favorite teams, and why so many were taken by surprise by the "Brexit" vote to leave the European Union in the summer of 2016 even though polls consistently showed the vote was statistically too close to call.

Mental mind-sets are particularly challenging. Everyone uses them. Mind-sets are unconscious analytic frames used to organize information and make sense of complexity.[27] While frequently useful, mind-sets can also distort thinking in hidden ways. To see how, try your hand at the following exercise. It first appeared in Norman Maier's 1930 article "Reasoning in Humans" and for years has been part of Richards Heuer's book on intelligence analysis, a staple in CIA analytic training.[28]

The Nine-Dot Exercise

Instructions: Without lifting your pencil from the paper, draw no more than four straight lines that cross through all nine dots.

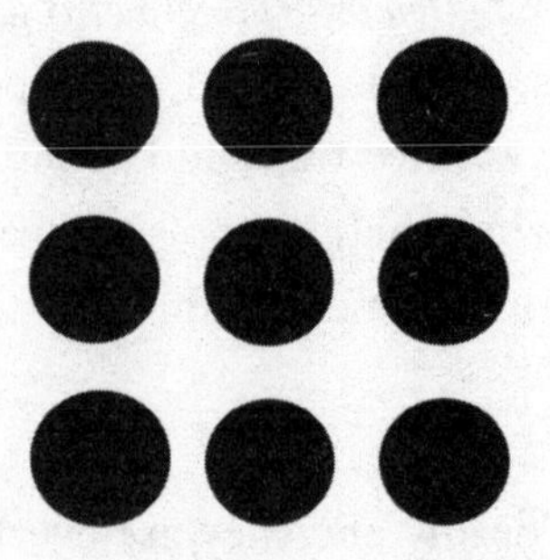

Many people find this puzzle difficult to solve because they assume they are not supposed to let the pencil go outside of an imaginary square drawn around the dots. They try drawing the lines this way:

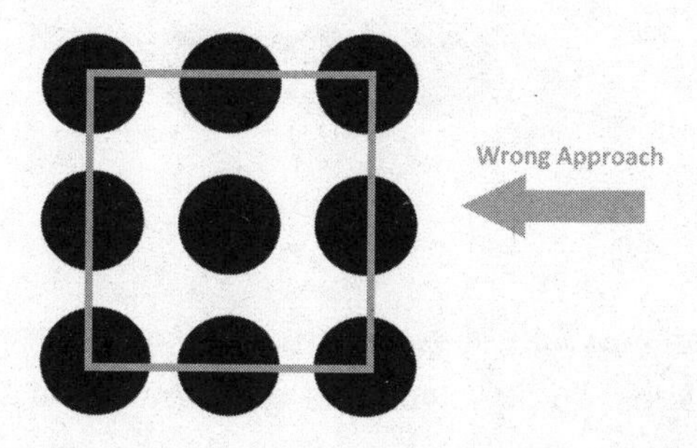

This obviously does not work: Drawing a line around the perimeter omits the center dot. However, once you discard the assumption of equal line length, it should be pretty easy to draw the four-line answer below:

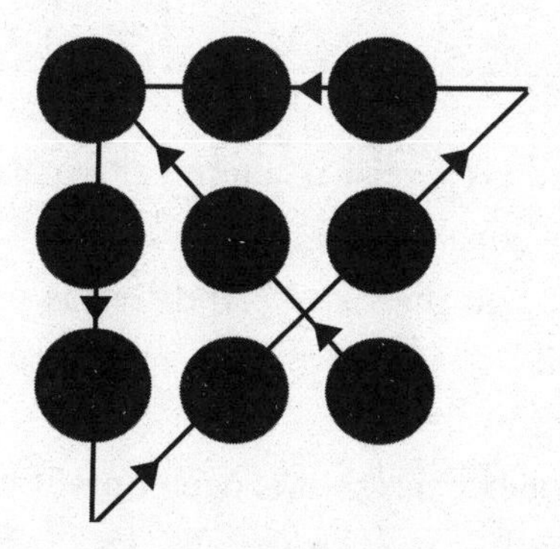

Many also assume that the lines must pass through the center of the dots. This constraint is entirely in the mind of the problem-solver as well. Once this constraint is relaxed, you can reach a solution using only three lines, not four.

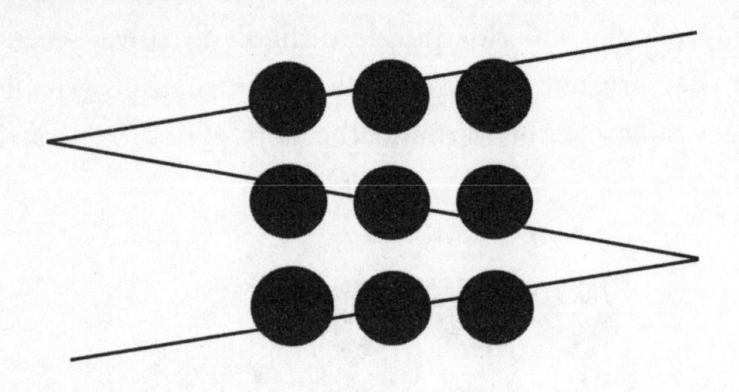

Another answer can be found if you relax the mental mind-set that the puzzle has to be solved in a two-dimensional plane. If you roll the paper into a cylinder, you can draw a single line passing through all nine dots.

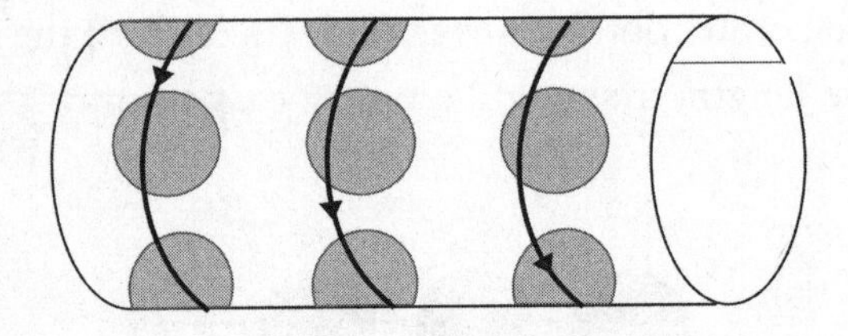

Amy has used this exercise in a number of classes over the years. Each time, students react the same way: "You never told us we could solve the puzzle that way!" And that is precisely the point. Students' own mind-sets impose barriers to analyzing the problem and finding a solution.

As the nine-dot exercise shows, people are routinely constrained by mind-sets they do not even realize exist. These mind-sets are formed by many inputs—past experience, cultural norms, organizational standard operating procedures, situational context, education, and training. Recognizing them is the first step toward overcoming them. The simple act of awareness can unlock a host of possibilities.

In addition to cognitive traps, group dynamics pose analytic challenges. Nobody wants to be seen disagreeing with the boss. Many bosses do not like to hear dissenting views. Hierarchy and status often stifle discussion of vital information without anyone realizing it.

In his bestselling book *The Checklist Manifesto*, physician Atul Gawande finds that one of the reasons surgical complications arise with such frequency has to do with group dynamics: Nurses, doctors, and other operating room staff typically come together in ad hoc teams for each procedure. Often, not all the people in the room even know one another's names. Add to this the natural tendency to defer to the doctor and you get a silent social system where dissenting information is hard to elicit. A 2008 study instituted a checklist at eight hospitals worldwide that included a simple step: Before surgery began, every member of the team had to introduce herself and say what her job was. That simple act of learning the names of the team was found to generate different team dynamics and better patient outcomes. Nobody quite knows how or why, but it's believed that a basic act generating familiarity and camaraderie also generated more valuable dissenting information—a process known as the "activation phenomenon."[29] In one particular case in Jordan, a surgeon inadvertently contaminated his glove while adjusting an overhead light. A nurse noticed and spoke up, requesting that he change his glove to avoid infecting the patient. The surgeon initially brushed it off, but after the nurse told him not to be stupid and demanded that he change it, he obliged.[30]

Research finds that even when dissenting views are encouraged, there are strong psychological pressures toward conformity. Particularly in high-pressure situations, individuals may come to value their membership in a decision-making group more than anything else. Preserving the group's cohesiveness takes precedence over considering alternative views, leading members to adopt a distorted view of reality, unwittingly suppress their own nagging doubts, silence dissent, and strive for unanimity—a process Irving Janis called "groupthink." In his pioneering 1972 study, Janis examined how psychological dynamics in small groups led to foreign policy fiascoes, including the Bay of Pigs invasion and escalation of the war in Vietnam.[31]

Cognitive traps and group dynamics are big challenges. The good news is that there is help; political officials, intelligence professionals, and business leaders have developed and deployed a number of tools to combat cognitive traps, groupthink, and other pitfalls. We discuss some of our favorites below so that you can use them, too.

Scenario Planning

In 1965, Ted Newland was tapped to start a unit called Long-Term Studies at Royal Dutch Shell's London headquarters. "I was placed in a little cubicle on the 18th floor and told to think about the future, with no real indications of what was required of me," Newland later recalled.[32] It was the beginning of Shell's pioneering use of scenario planning for political risk analysis. Soon Newland was joined by Pierre Wack, a former magazine editor who believed in the value of storytelling. In 1971, they began a major scenario planning exercise, looking for events that could affect the price of oil. The task was more radical than it sounds: Because the price of oil had experienced low volatility since the end of World War II, imagining factors that could dramatically affect oil prices was a venture into the unfamiliar. The conventional wisdom at Shell was that stable oil prices would continue.

Wack and Newland found a number of reasons why oil prices might spike at some point down the road. American demand for energy was rising while domestic reserves were dwindling. The Organization of the Petroleum Exporting Countries (OPEC) consisted heavily of Arab countries. While OPEC had not coordinated to boost oil prices yet, their opposition to Western support of Israel during the 1967 Six-Day War might give them reason to, and there was already a scheduled renegotiation of the Tehran price agreement slated for 1975. In September 1972, Wack and Newland developed two scenarios, a stable price scenario and a drastic price change scenario. The stable price scenario was eventually called "the three miracles" because its occurrence hinged on wildly optimistic exploration and production; all major countries' willing depletion of their hydrocarbon resources to meet consumer demand; and no major supply or demand changes (including regional wars or demand spikes).

Wack and Newland did not know if, when, or specifically why a major price hike might occur. But their scenario planning revealed something essential: The possibility was much more likely than Shell executives had imagined. As Wack later put it, "We wanted to change our managers' view of reality."[33]

Sure enough, in October 1973, about a year later, OPEC did suddenly boost oil prices, triggering an energy crisis. Shell was the only major oil company whose executives were prepared emotionally, strategically, and operationally, thanks to the scenario planning process.[34] Scenario planning has been at Shell ever since. Angela Wilkinson, formerly on Shell's corporate scenario team, and Roland Kupers, a former Shell senior executive, wrote, "For an operation that doesn't contribute directly to the bottom line, and that emphasizes the uncertainty of the future rather than making bold predictions, this is remarkable."[35]

Scenario planning is used more frequently today.[36] Bain & Company's annual survey queries thirteen thousand respondents from more than seventy countries about the use and utility of management tools. In 2014, 18 percent of respondents reported using scenario planning and 60 percent said they expected to use it in 2015.[37]

As with any tool, there is scenario planning and then there is effective scenario planning. Simply spinning out possible futures is unlikely to get attention or action in the C-suite. Pierre Wack and

Peter Schwartz, who worked together at Shell, have each written extensively about what makes for good scenario planning. We summarize their top tips in the box below.[38]

Effective Scenario Planning . . .

- Does not predict the future. Instead, it imagines equally plausible possibilities to stimulate thinking about forces driving the system, their connections, and uncertainties.
- Deals with both facts and perceptions.
- Identifies the underlying technological, business, political, and societal forces driving your business.
- Organizes information into three or four stories of alternative future worlds, each meticulously researched and intended to catalyze "unexpected leaps of understanding."[39]
- Draws on diverse views, including from unconventional sources.
- Connects tightly with business strategy and the concerns of managers.
- Includes opportunities, not just threats.
- Uses narratives and language to get managers' attention, interest, and buy-in.

It is important to underscore that the test of good scenario planning is not whether it pinpoints the future but whether it enables managers to view the future differently—helping them get out of their mental mind-sets. Wack and Schwartz call this "re-perceiving."[40] Scenarios are not prediction tools. They are learning tools. They help managers cross the bridge between their mental mind-set view of the world and future realities that may be far different.

Red Teams, Devil's Advocates, Thinking Backwards, and Other Tools

Scenario planning is probably the best-known tool but certainly not the only one to illuminate "risks around the corner." Organizations ranging from military units to start-up companies use many other mechanisms and processes to help managers "re-perceive" the world, step out of their mental mind-sets, and overcome team barriers like groupthink.

The Lego Group, for example, uses both scenario planning and Monte Carlo computer-based simulations, which employ mathematical equations to quantify the likelihood of possible outcomes, to get a better handle on the quantification of various risks. Paychex employs a "Tournament of Risk" that is modeled after the NCAA men's basketball tournament where managers vote on risks in head-to-head competition to flesh out ideas. When Carmen Medina ran the Central Intelligence Agency's analytic directorate, she asked a handful of top analysts to create graphic designs of threat landscapes. The end product had to fit on a single page, and it had to use images to depict the drivers of conflict and their interconnections. For analysts accustomed to writing reports in prose, it was a creative, powerful way to unpack hidden assumptions about the evolving threat environment. U.S. Strategic Command, the combatant command that oversees U.S. nuclear forces and has to think long and hard about conflict escalation, has a dedicated war-gaming unit that designs and role-plays realistic future conflicts to stress test assumptions about how interactions might unfold. At STRATCOM headquarters in Nebraska, there is even a special war game room with a Hollywood-like center stage whose floor is a map of the world. We use role-playing simulations extensively in all of our Stanford courses as well as in our cyber "boot camps" for policymakers and have found them to be invaluable tools for breaking mind-sets and generating fresh insight.

"Call the Russians": Putting Training into Practice

Condi was a veteran of crisis simulations during her various tours in government service. Several times she was a part of a team that was sent out to an undisclosed location to practice responses to a nuclear attack on the United States. The idea was that some form of government had to survive so that the United States would not cease to function. Nuclear war—thank God—didn't happen. But September 11 did. Her participation in those Cold War simulations provided essential training for that moment.

"When I reached the bunker after the attacks two thoughts immediately occurred to me," she remembered. "One was that I had to reach the Russians right away. Our forces were going up on alert, raising the DEFCON, or Defense Condition, level of our military around the world. The Russians through multiple sources—electronic and likely human—would see that and might raise their DEFCON levels in response. That could set off a 'spiral of alerts' with the two countries' militaries spiraling toward a showdown."

Condi asked to speak to President Putin, who was already trying to reach President Bush. "Mr. President," she said, "President Bush is trying to get to a safe location. But I want you to know that our forces are going up on alert." Before she could say, "Please don't respond," Putin replied, "Don't worry, we are canceling all exercises. Our defense condition will remain as it is." Condi was stunned. "The Cold War really is over," she thought. It had been the simulations of nuclear attack that taught her about the spiral of alerts and caused her to make that call.

Similarly, the exercises had always emphasized that it was important that the United States communicate to its allies—and its foes—that it was still functioning. Remembering this lesson, Condi asked her deputy, Steve Hadley, to call the deputy secretary of state, Rich Armitage. "Get a cable out to all posts—have every ambassador go in and tell foreign officials that the United States has not been decapitated," she said, using the language of nuclear war. She knew that the president wouldn't be able to speak for some time. The world would see only images of planes flying into buildings and the ruins of the Pentagon and the World Trade Center. "Our friends needed to know that we were okay. Our foes needed to know, too, just in case someone might want to take advantage of us at that moment," she recalled thinking.

These were reflexive responses, and it was not until days later that she realized it wasn't instinct—it was training and practice.

The Intel Corporation, Goldman Sachs, the Central Intelligence Agency, the New York Police Department, and many others use "red teams," people assigned to assume the role of competitors or adversaries.[41] Some red teams conduct cyber hacks of the companies' own systems to expose hidden technical and human vulnerabilities.[42] Some pretend to be terrorists smuggling weapons through airport security checkpoints to improve Transportation Security Administration performance. Some scrub a potential new business strategy or government policy by exposing it to contrarian thinking. All are designed to push insiders to "think like the enemy."[43]

Jayson E. Street is one of the most colorful and successful cyber red teamers around. "I promise you, I would never try to steal from you, kill you, or ruin you financially unless you pay me first," he declared at a DEF CON hacker conference. "I am just going to F you up the best possible way."[44] He makes his penetration tests as easy as possible, spending no more than two hours conducting reconnaissance on Google and the client's own website. His goal is to show that anyone can get in. Using simple "social engineering" techniques, such as posing as a tech repairman, customer, or job applicant, he convinces employees to help him compromise their own systems. He also deliberately escalates until he gets caught—Street wants to create teachable moments for frontline employees, not just reports for managers.[45] He has conducted red team exercises for financial institutions around the world. In one, the Beirut Bank of Lebanon wanted to know whether an online compromise could come from a physical source. With access to just three branches selected at random, and no advance research or preparation, Street was able to execute a fraudulent wire transfer. It took less than three minutes for him to gain full physical access to the first branch, including the manager's office. Within twenty minutes, he was given an employee's ID card, network password, and smart card for authenticating network access.[46]

Not every tool for political risk analysis involves flying wily penetration testers around the globe, spending half a million dollars on a corporate war game,[47] or building a cool auditorium with a James Bond–like map of the world. Two frugal tools can help analyze political risks from your desk or nearby conference room: *thinking backwards* and *devil's advocates.*

Thinking backwards is an exercise that starts by imagining that a surprising and significant future event has transpired. Your job is then to look back from this future and understand how the event could have come to pass.[48] Like scenario planning, thinking backwards is not designed to predict the future. It is designed to help individuals learn, to challenge mental mind-sets and resist the thinking of the herd.[49]

Devil's advocates can be a "quicker and dirtier" version of red teams. They were first used by the Catholic Church centuries ago to inject more rigor into the saint-making process. In 1587, church authorities created the official position of *Advocatus Diaboli* to serve as an in-house skeptic, arguing against a candidate's saintliness, questioning miracles performed, and exhaustively investigating claims and evidence in a process that could take decades.[50] By the eighteenth century, the term was being used secularly and broadly to describe any in-house dissenter whose job was to challenge the predominant view and defend unpopular views even if they didn't actually believe them. As many have noted, real devils are always better than devil's advocates. Dissenting views carry more weight when they are genuine. And the more dissent becomes a routine process, the greater the danger that it will be dismissed or perceived as simply an exercise in "ritualized compliance."[51] However, devil's advocates, particularly on matters where there is strong consensus, can play a useful role.

The goal of all these analytic tools is the same: opening mental mind-sets and group processes so that information can be assessed from a range of perspectives. The most common analytic mistake organizations make is assuming the future will look like the present. It almost never does.

3. How can we integrate political risk analysis into business decisions?

The team, finally, is critical. Business leaders throughout the organization have to believe that political risk is integral to their jobs or the best information and analysis won't accomplish much. Companies that manage political risk well go out of their way to integrate political risk analysis into the everyday rhythms and decisions of the business.

Here, too, the Lego Group is an innovative leader. Remember that when Hans Læssøe started building Lego's strategic risk management capability in 2006, he literally began by Googling it. He quickly realized that instituting a robust risk analysis process was just half the battle: Ensuring that strategic risks were "owned" across the company was the other half. He divided the practice of strategic risk management into four building blocks. Block number 1 was spreading risk management across the company so that it was genuinely seen as everyone's business.[52] As we mentioned in chapter 6, Læssøe created a systematic, continuous process to engage every important business leader, including the board, in setting the company's risk appetite, understanding risks, and integrating risk assessment and mitigation into business planning.[53] Among his innovations, Læssøe created a database and risk process that every project manager could easily use, and he created training in risk management for them all.[54] In addition, rather than putting risk management in the reporting chain to the general counsel, where it could be seen as another onerous compliance activity, he reported to the chief financial officer and gave himself the title of Lego's "Professional Paranoid." He told the *Wall Street Journal*, "I use the title jokingly whenever I get the chance, because it lets me pose questions that I couldn't have gotten away with as a business controller. It removes some of the defensiveness that managers feel when they are being questioned."[55] Læssøe realized that getting risk analysis embraced by the company's board, executive leaders, nineteen senior vice presidents, and ten thousand employees was an act of persuasion, not authority.

A second building block in Læssøe's plan was creating a standardized decision-making process that incorporated strategic risk analysis. He called it Active Risk and Opportunity Planning, or AROP. As the name suggests, AROP was designed to ensure that managers consider both downside risks and upside opportunities. And while Læssøe utilized a number of risk assessment tools, including Monte Carlo computer simulations, Google Trends word searches, and scenario planning, keeping business leaders engaged was always top of mind. The Lego Group's scenarios used attention-getting names like "Cut Throat Competition" and "Murphy's Surprise."[56] As a result of Læssøe's efforts, strategic risk analysis that included political risks became tightly integrated into business decision-making. Making strategic risk everyone's business helped the Lego Group turn the corner after nearly going bankrupt.

We interviewed a number of political risk officers from different industries. All of them emphasized the same lesson that Læssøe learned early on: Their most important job is making political risk useful throughout the company. That starts with developing a deep understanding of the business and the needs of managers. As one political risk officer at a major international airline told us, "You've got to know what's going on and ask, 'So what for my company? Why does this matter?' Political risk analysis has got to be proactive and forward-looking." This risk officer used to work in an organization with many academics. "They had a genuine interest in the issues. They'd sit around and talk about political risks over morning coffee," he said. "But company leaders can't do that. The people who are consuming what you're putting out cannot necessarily have a natural interest in it. It will take them away from running the business, so you'd better be able to say why you're telling them what you're telling them and why it matters."

When Pat Donovan was hired to take over Chevron's global security unit, the first thing he did was embark on a company listening tour. "I needed to figure out what they wanted to know but didn't know yet," he told us. "You have to know the business," he emphasized. "What is it like to have two hundred customers out there? You don't take all your problems to the chairman. You need to go out and learn what the business is and how you can bring value to that." Donovan sees business leaders, including the chairman, regularly, and works hard to ensure that every member of his eight-person global risk team is "forward deployed," working as closely as possible with each business unit. Forward deployment, understanding his "customers," and getting buy-in from the top have been essential for his successful integration of political risk into Chevron's business decision-making. When we asked how he judged success, Donovan answered without hesitation: "Whether the business unit keeps coming back to us and wanting more, and whether they are considering what we say when they make their decisions."

At FedEx, the world's largest express transportation company, natural and man-made disruptions to delivery service are a constant concern—from labor strikes to civil unrest to tropical storms and volcanic eruptions. The company constantly monitors and mitigates risks of all kinds at its Global Operations Control Center in Memphis, Tennessee. As we will see in the next chapter, part of the reason FedEx excels at risk management is its focus on the human factor: Many company leaders, including Paul Tronsor, FedEx's vice president of global operations and service quality assurance, started out as couriers and package handlers. FedEx's "Purple Promise" to make every FedEx experience outstanding is not just a slogan. It is personal. Company leaders, including risk managers, understand firsthand how what they do affects the customer.

Ultimately, integrating political risk analysis into business decisions requires encouraging different perspectives and building trust. In the last chapter, we talked about how understanding political risks requires seeing how others may view the world in ways that could generate challenges and opportunities for your business. Recognizing the incentives, priorities, and perspectives of others does not apply just to external stakeholders, but within companies as well. When it comes to corporate roles, where you stand does depend largely on where you sit. General counsels get paid to focus on legal restrictions. CFOs naturally gravitate to the financial implications of decisions. Sales teams are focused on driving revenues. Strategy shops think about longer-term industry trends, consumer tastes, competitor moves, market opportunities, and company advantages. Political risk officers are hired to assess how political actions could affect business operations and opportunities around the globe. None of these functions work well in isolation. Effectively integrating political risk analysis requires developing mechanisms to see these different perspectives so that political risk can be baked into assessing the trade-offs of a business decision, not considered as an afterthought.

One final example sends this point home. It involves Nike,[57] one of the world's largest suppliers of athletic footwear and apparel and the most valuable brand in sports.[58] In 2013, Nike faced a major decision: Should the company increase its manufacturing relationship with Lyric Industries, a Bangladeshi supplier? Bangladesh was home to a $20 billion garment industry, offering some of the lowest-priced labor in the world, along with notoriously unsafe working conditions. "Our competitors were moving fast into Bangladesh and the pressure was getting bigger and bigger," noted Nike chief operating officer Eric Sprunk. "We needed a strong point of view to say, 'Are we going to increase our source base there or not?' "[59]

While Sprunk and other manufacturing executives believed they could cut costs, improve margins, and put adequate safety conditions in place, Hannah Jones, who headed Nike's sustainable business team, warned that Nike could not ensure safe working conditions in Bangladesh and that the cost advantages would not be worth the risk to its brand of another outsourced labor scandal. Jones's team had hired a consultant to create a country risk index for Nike's global operations, and Bangladesh ranked near the bottom because of its labor practices and unsafe working conditions. "We faced a decision," said Jones. "There was a lot of pressure to say, 'Let's go into Bangladesh like everyone else and get great margins and low costs.' So we went through this discussion and looked at the risk index and said, 'We're not going to do that.' "[60] The issue was especially salient for Nike. The company had come under heavy fire in the 1990s for child labor violations, and despite its devoting tremendous resources and effort to improving working safety and labor conditions in its suppliers since then and serving as a corporate social responsibility leader, challenges remained. In 2006, Nike faced another public crisis when a supplier was found to be using Pakistani children to stitch World Cup soccer balls, forcing Nike to pull $100 million worth of balls from stores just weeks before the World Cup began.[61]

Sprunk and Jones, both of whom reported to the CEO, could not agree about Lyric Industries. So they decided that their teams should go on a field trip together to see conditions on the ground and make a joint decision about what Nike should do. "They had to go together," said Sprunk, "because if Hannah came back and said we couldn't do it there, the manufacturing guys would be unconvinced, and if only Nick [Athanasakos, the vice president of global sourcing and manufacturing] went, there would still be doubts."[62] After visiting the facility and meeting with Lyric managers, employees, and local residents, the joint team decided to cut ties with Lyric and reduce its manufacturing footprint in Bangladesh. Months later, Bangladesh experienced the worst industrial disaster in its history when the Rana Plaza factory collapsed, killing more than a thousand people. The disaster caused some companies, including Disney, to pull manufacturing from Bangladesh, while others stayed and vowed to institute new safety accords and inspection regimes.[63]

For Nike, the political risk perspective and the business perspective suggested different decisions about Bangladesh. But rather than handing political risk analysis off to business leaders and calling it a day, Nike executives realized they needed to bring the two teams together, in the field, to see conditions. Production teams are going to gravitate to the financial implications of a decision. Corporate social responsibility teams are more acutely attuned to the potential NGO reaction and damage to the brand. Spending time together in Bangladesh gave both teams a better feel for conditions and something else that proved just as essential: trust. Nike integrated political risk analysis into the business through shared experience.

KEY TAKEAWAYS: ANALYZING RISKS LIKE A PHYSICIST

- ☐ Collect information that is specific to your needs, includes perceptions and emotions of key stakeholders, and answers the right questions. How you frame the question determines whether insights will emerge or remain hidden.

- ☐ Harness tools such as scenario planning to combat mental mindsets and overcome group decision-making pathologies. Remember, the goal is not to predict the future but to make better decisions by "re-perceiving" potential key drivers and possibilities.

- ☐ Integrate political risk analysis into business decisions through top-level buy-in, effective listening, forward-deploying risk officers, and joint problem-solving.

8

The Nuclear Triad, the Empty Plane, and Other Ways to Mitigate Risks

Each night, an Airbus A300 flies from Denver to Memphis. It carries no passengers and often no cargo. Flight 1311 costs about $30,000 a night and runs 365 nights a year.[1]

This nightly flight is part of the secret sauce behind FedEx Corporation, the world's largest express transportation company, which delivers four million packages to 220 countries and territories each day with 650 planes, 48,000 vehicles, and 165,000 employees.[2]

Flight 1311 is just one component of the company's risk mitigation efforts. FedEx's success depends on delivering packages on time in a world full of surprises—an erupting Icelandic volcano, missile launches in Syria, trucker strikes in France,[3] protests in Venezuela, typhoons in Asia, cyber threats, or a sudden spike in Apple iPad orders. The plane's role: recovering unanticipated cargo. "It's our flying spare, attempting to sweep up anything that our other aircraft don't pick up," explains Marcus Martinez, managing director of FedEx's global operations control.[4]

Martinez's Global Operations Control Center (GOCC) is FedEx's risk mitigation nerve center, employing 220 people and located at the company's "SuperHub" in Memphis. The SuperHub is a city unto itself, stretching across more than 800 acres, with 150 airplanes and nearly 80 miles of conveyer belts that process more than a million packages a day.[5] It has its own hospital,

Mike Brown for the Washington Post *via Getty Images*

Daniel Acker/Bloomberg via Getty Images

fire, and police departments, 20 backup electric power generators, and branch offices of the Department of Homeland Security and other U.S. federal agencies.[6] At peak times, planes are landing every 40 seconds.[7] That's about as fast as combat flight operations on an aircraft carrier.[8]

The GOCC has hundreds of computer screens displaying real-time conditions and locations of FedEx flights worldwide. The place is wired with the latest technology and hums with activity twenty-four hours a day. The team includes fifteen full-time meteorologists; dispatchers and logistics experts coordinating with control centers in Asia and Europe; industrial engineers; scenario and contingency planners; customs compliance experts; crew scheduling specialists who make sure flight crews are where they need to be and that they are complying with regulations about flight hours and mandatory rest; and many more. The center "is kind of like Wikipedia for the FedEx pilot," says captain Steve Zeigler. "Wherever we are in the world, they have the ability to get the answers, which makes our job much easier."[9]

At FedEx, risk mitigation is about people and process, not just technology. Paul Tronsor, who started out as a package handler, ran GOCC for a decade and currently serves as vice president of global operations control and service quality assurance, notes, "One of the things that makes FedEx such a strong and people-oriented company is that many of us in leadership roles started out as handlers or couriers. It makes us understand two things: one, the value of the customer, and two, the value of the team members working at FedEx."[10] That teamwork is personal. Every FedEx airplane is named for an employee's child. (The tradition started when a Falcon aircraft was named Wendy, after the daughter of Fred Smith, FedEx's founder, chairman, and CEO.)[11] When it comes to hiring, FedEx looks for people who are team players, are adept at evaluating large quantities of information, can make fast decisions, and can stay calm under pressure. "We have a saying around here: 'When in control, be in control,'" notes Tronsor.[12]

The GOCC also has well-developed processes. The center conducts regular training to ensure cool, focused action under pressure. Authority is delegated downward so that managers can change flight paths whenever necessary rather than wading through layers of bureaucratic approvals each time. Crisis decision cycles extend over three to four days to limit confusion and improve coordination. "When you're in a situation that's spinning fast, it's tempting to change gears daily. This leads to chaos by pulling your people and systems in different directions," notes Tronsor.[13] Each major crisis ends with a team debrief to share lessons learned.

In addition, the center invests in anticipation. GOCC leaders know the earlier they catch a potential disruption, the more options they have to work around it. Meteorologists forecast weather days in advance. Contingency planning is continuous so there is always a Plan B on the shelf. Routines are designed to facilitate flexibility, not impede it. Each morning begins with a "war room" conference call among FedEx managers to review the previous day's operations and plan for the current day.

FedEx is a model of effective risk mitigation. While most companies do not need a bevy of meteorologists working around the clock or operations running as fast as aircraft carriers in combat, everyone can learn from FedEx's underlying approach. FedEx assumes that political risks can never be eliminated, no matter how hard you work or how good you are at identifying and analyzing them. "The GOCC may not be able to foresee what will cause the next European truck drivers' strike, but they know ground delays will happen at some point, and when it happens, the backup plans are ready to go," the company once said.[14]

In the last two chapters, we discussed how to understand and analyze political risks. This chapter offers a guide for tackling residual risks that inevitably remain. Success requires a multilayered approach that uses three interlocking strategies: *developing mitigation strategies in advance*, *creating warning systems that enable fast action when you need it*, and *building resilience so the entire organization can bend without breaking when bad things happen*.

Mitigating Political Risks: Three Key Questions

1. How can we reduce exposure to the risks we have identified?
2. Do we have a good system in place for timely warning and action?
3. How can we limit the damage when something bad happens?

1. How can we reduce exposure to the risks we have identified?

Organizations can reduce exposure to political risks in many ways, but every strategy should begin by understanding what most needs protecting. No company, nonprofit, or government agency can afford to protect everything from every contingency. Risk mitigation requires trade-offs, and trade-offs require understanding what assets are *most valuable and most vulnerable.*

Understanding Where Asset Value and Vulnerability Converge

At FedEx, asset value and vulnerability are clear: On-time delivery is the company's holy grail. It is the most important part of FedEx's value proposition and also the most vulnerable to man-made and natural events. FedEx has been innovating ways to reduce the risk of delivery delays for nearly half a century. "Since FedEx Express started, there's not been a minute of any day in our 40-year history that the ops control group has not been here overseeing the operation," notes Tronsor.[15] FedEx invests in the GOCC because it must. "You have to put your money where your mouth is," says FedEx chief Fred Smith.[16] "At the end of the day we're essentially selling trust. People give us some of the most important things that they own. There's medical equipment that's going to a surgery this morning or a part that's going to determine whether the new 787 flies."[17] Everyone at FedEx knows that "if we don't get it there, we don't get paid," says Smith.[18] Smith doesn't even think of risk management as risk management. "I wouldn't call this risk management," he told us, "but instead it's our commitment to our customers. It's the purple promise: We will make every FedEx experience outstanding."

A surprising number of firms lack FedEx's visibility into the convergence of asset value and vulnerability. A 2013 survey found that 74 percent of companies had encountered significant supply chain disruptions in the previous two years requiring C-suite attention but still had not developed an effective continuity plan to deal with them. The risk was there but the mitigation game plan wasn't.[19] In a 2015 cyber threat survey, two-thirds of risk management professionals said they did not know the value of the company's critical assets being hacked. Nearly 40 percent said they did not have a clear understanding of what their data assets even were.[20]

SeaWorld and Sony Pictures illustrate why it is so important to know asset value/vulnerability convergence. SeaWorld had long recognized that putting humans in orca tanks was dangerous and that animal rights groups opposed the company's treatment of animals in captivity. What company executives did not realize was just how dependent their brand and core business were on Shamu. When *Blackfish* was released, nearly half of all parks owned by SeaWorld's parent company were SeaWorld theme parks or extensions of the SeaWorld brand. Every SeaWorld park featured its famed "Shamu shows" in "Shamu stadiums." Shamu was the company's logo, its star attraction, and its marketing cornerstone—the image everyone associated with the brand. That's why it did not take much to destroy half of the company's shareholder value.

After SeaWorld's stock price plummeted, management began reaching out to animal rights groups, moving more aggressively into new business lines such as television programming, and creating more ride-based attractions as it phased out orca shows.[21] These steps could have been taken before *Blackfish* if only executives had considered where asset value and vulnerability converged.

Like SeaWorld, Sony Pictures executives did not see the convergence of asset value and vulnerability until it was too late. North Korea's cyber attack over a Seth Rogen comedy was certainly bizarre and hard to imagine. But studio executives should have known that yet-to-be-released movie scripts and contracts with Hollywood stars were among its most valued assets, and that Sony's weak cyber defenses left it exceptionally vulnerable to anyone who wanted them.[22] Sony's parent company had been the victim of more than twenty cyber breaches in the previous three years, including a 2011 attack on its PlayStation network that cost $170 million. Yet efforts to improve cyber security floundered. A new cyber chief abruptly quit in 2014 amid speculation that he was frustrated by insufficient authority and resources. Meanwhile, at Sony Pictures, IT administrator user names and passwords were stored in unprotected files, including one named "Password."[23] The studio's email system did not employ basic protections such as two-factor authentication (where logging in requires two forms of identification, usually a regular password and a randomly generated code sent to a mobile phone). And just weeks before the North Korean breach, a cyber security firm visited the Sony Pictures offices to sell its services. After checking in with security, they walked right into the studio's unlocked information security offices. Nobody was inside. The computers were sitting there, connected and unprotected. "If we were bad guys, we could have done something horrible," said entertainment attorney Mickey Shapiro, who was there.[24] As cyber expert James Lewis noted, Sony "[left] the doors wide open and put out the welcome mat."[25]

Sketching value and vulnerability along a 2-by-2 matrix helps illuminate risk mitigation priorities. Start by asking:

- What assets are most valuable to my organization?
- What assets are most vulnerable to political risk?
- Where do high value and high vulnerability cluster?

In the example matrix below, Sony scripts and contracts and SeaWorld's Shamu brand are in the "High/High" quadrant, making them top-priority assets for risk mitigation. Medium priorities include assets that are of lower value but highly vulnerable to political risks, and assets that are valuable but not so vulnerable. Coca-Cola's Angola bottling plant is an example of a lower-value/higher-vulnerability asset. When Coke decided to build the plant in 2000, Angola was still experiencing civil unrest, with shooting between rebel and government forces not far from the plant. But the value of this site for the company's global operations was relatively low—a $33 million investment in a $20-billion-revenue business. Coke made the value even lower by sharing the investment with partners.[26]

Occidental Petroleum's West Texas drilling operation is an example of a higher-value/lower-vulnerability asset. West Texas oil production accounts for 39 percent of the company's global total, and the capital investment required is substantial. But the risk of expropriation or sudden, severe regulatory change in Texas is extremely low.[27]

Value \ **Vulnerability**	Lower	Higher
Lower	Low priority	Medium priority Coca-Cola bottling plant in Angola (unrest there but small investment shared with others)
Higher	Medium priority Occidental Petroleum West Texas drilling operations (39% of company global production, no risk of expropriation, low risk of state regulatory change)	**Top priority** Sony unreleased move scripts, contracts (valuable IP, weak cyber defenses) SeaWorld's "Shamu" brand (essential to company, vulnerable to activists, trainer safety scandals)

Two Common Mitigation Strategies: Market Avoidance and Timing

Once you have visibility into what needs protecting, you can pursue a number of mitigation strategies. Market avoidance and timing are the most frequently used. It should come as little surprise that investors and companies often make judgments based on general rules of thumb about country conditions. As Silicon Valley entrepreneur and investor Vinod Khosla told us, "We're dealing mostly with small companies, so... we end up worrying mostly about do we even want to be in a country or not... There are places where we don't do business." Other investors told us the same thing. As Marc Andreessen explained, early stage investment is a case where market avoidance can work well. "One of the reasons the U.S. does so well in tech," he told us, "is because we're blessed with such a large and vibrant early adopter market here, so these companies can get to their $100–$200 million in sales by just selling in the U.S."

Timing is another common strategy. Blackstone's Tom Hill includes timing in his definition of risk. "In investing, risk is the probability and magnitude of capital loss over a defined time period," he told us. "Your investment time frame and duration of committed capital truly matters. In private equity, we have capital commitments from our investors which run ten years, with automatic extensions built into LP agreements. In the 2008 financial crisis, as long as we capitalized our investments well, as long as we bought them at the right price and had no financing coming due, we could hold through the crisis, so that we are able to achieve our desired return when markets recovered. Staying power is really important." As we noted in chapter 6, Khosla advised one of his companies to enter a foreign market knowing that its intellectual property would likely be compromised. But because the company was estimated to have a ten-year profit window in that market before that occurred, the entry made sense. Timing helped mitigate the risk.

Beyond these usual suspects, three mitigation strategies can be useful: *dispersing critical assets*, *creating flexible surge capacity*, and *aligning with others*. Or as we like to put it: Build your nuclear triad, fly the empty plane, and band together.

Build Your Nuclear Triad: Dispersing Critical Assets[28]

The strategy of dispersing critical assets has been central to nuclear deterrence. During the Cold War, nuclear planners worried that if a single massive Soviet strike could eliminate all American nuclear forces, the Soviets would be more likely to attack. So they arranged American nuclear forces into a "triad" of hardened intercontinental ballistic missile sites, distributed bombers, and roving, hard-to-find submarines to ensure that no enemy first strike could ever eliminate America's entire arsenal. Dispersing our most powerful nuclear weapons in three different platforms ensured that no matter what happened, the United States could retaliate. Paradoxically, the credible threat of nuclear retaliation lowered the risk of nuclear war. Survivable second-strike forces kept both sides from stepping into the nuclear abyss.

Businesses need to build their equivalent of the nuclear triad to reduce the impact of any single political event on the bottom line. No organization should have its most valuable resources exposed to the same risk at the same time. To be sure, dispersing critical assets is more easily done in some industries than in others—and sometimes may be impossible. For example, in the oil business, refining standards (which vary by state in the United States) make it impossible to easily move production from one refinery to another should a disruption occur. But there are areas—such as data management capabilities—where creating redundancies is a good mitigation tool for any company.

FedEx's equivalent of the nuclear triad is its network of global hubs. The Memphis SuperHub is the company's largest, but it is one of a dozen FedEx hubs around the world, all designed to enable regional flex. Multiple hubs ensure that a bad day in Memphis does not become a bad day everywhere.

The bond and equity trading firm Cantor Fitzgerald is the most searing and incredible example of how dispersing assets can make a difference. On September 11, 2001, terrorists killed 2,977 people in New York, Washington, D.C., and Pennsylvania. Not since the War of 1812, when British troops burned the White House, had an enemy attacked the continental United States so destructively. No company suffered more loss of life that day than Cantor Fitzgerald, whose offices were located on the 101st to 105th floors of the World Trade Center's North Tower. The firm lost 658 employees, nearly two-thirds of its U.S. workforce. And because hiring friends and family was part of the Cantor culture, many lost multiple family members. Cantor CEO Howard W. Lutnick, whose younger brother died in the attack, lived only because he was taking his five-year-old son, Kyle, to his first day of kindergarten and was not yet in the office.

Few thought Cantor could possibly survive. Yet when Treasury markets reopened two days later, Cantor was back in business. In the years since, the firm has not only survived but thrived. How did it manage to hang on in those dark early days? In part because of the extraordinary dedication of Cantor's surviving employees. In part because of Lutnick's determined leadership. In part because other firms, even competitors, came to Cantor's aid. In part because of what Lutnick calls a series of "miracles" like a golf outing and a fishing trip that kept several key executives out of the office that morning.[29]

> "No one ever builds a disaster recovery plan that allows for the destruction of everybody in the office at 8:45 a.m. That is never in any plan."
> —Howard W. Lutnick, CEO, Cantor Fitzgerald

But a large, unheralded part of the story is that before 9/11,

Cantor Fitzgerald had dispersed many of its critical assets. After the 1993 World Trade Center terrorist attack, the company decided to set up a backup disaster recovery site in Rochelle Park, New Jersey, just in case.[30] Cantor's eSpeed online trading subsidiary, which was the backbone of the firm's real-time electronic trading in Treasury markets, had three data centers, so when the main New York data center went down on 9/11, eSpeed did not.[31] When markets opened at 8:00 a.m. on September 13, eSpeed was ready at 7:00.[32] With nearly all of the firm's voice brokers killed, the firm shifted even more to eSpeed to keep trading. Finally, though New York was Cantor's headquarters and largest office, the firm had a seven-hundred-person office in London that worked furiously to perform all the jobs of their lost New York colleagues to keep the company afloat.[33] "No one ever builds a disaster recovery plan that allows for the destruction of everybody in the office at 8:45 a.m. That is never in any plan," Lutnick told listeners in an emotional conference call a month after 9/11.[34] But Cantor had built its nuclear triad. Without a risk mitigation plan that included dispersing key assets, Cantor Fitzgerald probably would not have survived.

Fly the Empty Plane: Creating Flexible Surge Capacity

Dispersing key assets is closely related to a second mitigation strategy: creating excess capacity, whether it's flying FedEx's empty plane, keeping warehouses partly empty, or employing personnel who aren't 100 percent busy 100 percent of the time. In recent years, slack has become synonymous with "waste." Many companies have been trimming margins by reducing slack, moving to just-in-time inventory management. But slack has benefits. Without it, unforeseen events—from terrorist attacks to cyber threats to civil unrest or a surprise referendum result—can take a heavy toll. Earlier we mentioned Boeing's 787 Dreamliner, which suffered unprecedented production delays in part because nobody foresaw that the 9/11 terrorist attacks would lead to a decline in air travel, a contraction in the fastener industry, and a shortage six years later of the nuts and bolts that hold jets together. These special fasteners constituted just 3 percent of the cost of an aircraft, but they became one of the reasons Boeing experienced a three-year production delay.[35]

Though better risk assessment certainly could have helped, it wasn't the only solution to Boeing's Dreamliner nightmare. The company did not need a crystal ball to protect itself from the fastener shortage. It needed more slack. Even if Boeing executives had missed the ripple effects of 9/11, the company could have lessened or prevented the disruption of its fastener supply chain with an inventory policy that required keeping parts on hand for a minimum number of months.[36] Instead, the shortage came as a surprise, without any slack in the system to keep production lines moving. This dramatically delayed six hundred airplane orders. It didn't have to.

Other firms create flexible surge capacity through standardization or last-minute customization. The Intel Corporation, for example, designs all of its semiconductor fabrication plants to be identical so that if one plant cannot function at full capacity, another can quickly step in, decreasing both response time and cost in a crisis.[37]

Band Together: Aligning with Others in Your Industry

Aligning with others in your industry takes two forms: sharing information about risks, and pursuing voluntary collective action to preempt more damaging legal or regulatory changes to the industry.

Alan Orlob's experience at Marriott International highlights the benefits of banding together. Since 9/11, terrorist groups have taken greater aim at luxury hotel chains. As governments have moved to harden parliaments, offices, and military facilities, hotels have become "softer" targets. Western hotel chains are particularly vulnerable because they are seen as symbols of Western values and have a continual stream of people—including guests, third-party vendors, and employees—that make security challenging. Hotels have to strike a careful balance between taking measures to protect guests (like security guards and metal detectors) and creating a warm and inviting atmosphere. Terrorist attacks against hotels included the 2003 and 2004 car bombings of the JW Marriott in Jakarta and the Taba Hilton in the Sinai Peninsula; the 2005 triple suicide bombings of the Grand Hyatt, Radisson SAS, and Days Inn in Amman, Jordan; the storming assaults on the Taj and Oberoi hotels in Mumbai, which killed one hundred in 2008; the double bombing of the JW Marriott and Ritz-Carlton hotels in Jakarta in 2009; and the 2011 Intercontinental hotel attack in Kabul.

Orlob told us that when he first started his job, he thought that security could be Marriott's competitive advantage. "My early philosophy, and I used to espouse it frequently, is that in any city we operated a hotel, we would have more security than any other hotel," he told us. "By doing this we knew it would dissuade terrorist organizations from attacking us because we became in that city the hard target if they were looking for a hotel." Operating hundreds of hotels around the world, including in high-threat cities like Islamabad and Jakarta, Marriott took security seriously. Orlob developed a process for assessing and hardening the hotels according to a risk level that was continuously reviewed and adjusted. He created an in-house intelligence analysis unit to track global events 24/7. And he developed one of the industry's first comprehensive crisis management plans. But after the 2005 Amman attack, when suicide bombers simultaneously hit the Hyatt, Radisson, and Days Inn, killing fifty-seven people, Orlob realized that Marriott's security measures weren't enough: The industry needed to work together. The realization came when he learned that Jordanian police had picked up an Iraqi woman suicide bomber whose vest failed to detonate in that triple bombing. She told investigators that her terror cell had looked at the Amman Marriott but found the security there too robust, which was why they targeted other hotels instead. Even though Marriott was not struck in the attack, its business was. After the bombings, Orlob said, "nobody wanted to come to Amman,

Jordan, and stay in a Western-branded hotel." From a business perspective, an attack on one Western hotel was an attack on them all.

Orlob thought, "Rather than competing in this space, we should be collaborating in this space." So he established a hotel security working group to share information and best practices among security directors from the ten biggest hotel companies and got the State Department's Overseas Security Advisory Council to sponsor it.

Cruise lines, which also confront rising terrorist threats, have embraced "aligning with others" as a risk mitigation strategy, too. Royal Caribbean's Adam Goldstein told us, "In marketing or sales we fight with our competitors like cats and dogs. But when it comes to safety, the environment, and security, we all pitch in because it's in the interests of our customers and the industry to do that."

Aligning with others is not just about improving defenses against suicide bombers. Sometimes industry action can protect companies from reputational risks in tough political situations and preempt regulatory or legal changes. In the 1970s, for example, Reverend Leon Sullivan, an African-American minister and member of General Motors' board of directors, proposed a code of conduct for all American-owned companies operating in apartheid South Africa. At the time, General Motors was the largest employer of blacks in the country. Sullivan's principles included ending segregation of races in the workplace; equal and fair employment practices; equal pay; training programs for nonwhite employees; increasing the number of nonwhites in management and supervisory roles; improving the quality of life for nonwhites outside the work environment; and working to eliminate laws and customs that impeded social, economic, and political justice. Although initially a response to apartheid, the principles eventually gained popularity among companies not operating in South Africa.

The Sullivan Principles were an early version of what has become increasingly commonplace: voluntary corporate social responsibility standards embraced by an industry. American movie studios adopted their own rating standards in 1930 to fend off government regulation.[38] Seventy years later, as international opposition to "conflict diamonds" grew, the diamond industry adopted a set of standards called the Kimberley Process to prevent conflict diamonds from entering the market. After the Rana Plaza factory collapse in Bangladesh killed more than a thousand employees in 2013, more than 150 major clothing companies signed an accord to inspect, fix, and publicly disclose safety violations in Bangladesh's notoriously unsafe factories. Banding together in these cases is a kind of preemptive self-regulation. The goal is to reduce the probability of more serious regulatory and legal changes and to reduce activist and consumer backlash on salient social issues.

2. Do we have a good system in place for timely warning and action?

Reducing exposure to political risks through dispersal, flexible surge capacity, and banding together provides the first layer of risk mitigation. The next is developing a warning system to spot residual risks in time to take action. In the last chapter, we suggested tools like scenario planning and devil's advocates to analyze risks over the horizon. Warning systems, by contrast, are designed to deal with risks knocking on the door.

In the national security world, this is the difference between strategic and tactical intelligence analysis. Strategic intelligence analysis examines over-the-horizon questions, like "What are the prospects for Egyptian democracy in the next ten years?" Tactical intelligence analysis examines questions about the here and now, like "How many improvised explosive devices has ISIS laid in the Sinai this week?" Translated to the business context, strategic political risk assessment involves peering into the future to better see broad trends. Tactical political risk assessment involves penetrating the present to see imminent challenges. Warning systems are all about tactical analysis, conveying real-time information to prevent bad events from occurring or limit the impact if prevention is impossible. Effective warning systems do two things well: *provide situational awareness* and *set tripwires and protocols* so that certain steps are triggered automatically when conditions warrant.

Situational Awareness

Situational awareness is a dynamic understanding of political risks knocking on the door. In our hypothetical Burma case, for example, Kiku Telecom receives word that a peaceful labor protest by its Muslim workers has triggered a violent ethnic crackdown by the Burmese military, which also happens to be Kiku's joint venture partner. Initial reports are that the Burmese government has shut down all telecom service in the region, several Muslim Kiku workers have been injured, and others have been arrested, prompting outcries from human rights groups.

But first reports are almost always incomplete. Getting an accurate understanding of a crisis as it unfolds is essential, difficult, and requires robust information sources and coordination. President John F. Kennedy realized that he lacked situational awareness within his own government during the Bay of Pigs invasion. That's why he created the Situation Room in the White House to serve as a communications and coordination center, which it still does.

In the Burma case, our MBA students like to jump into problem-solving mode even though it's unclear what the problem is. We usually have to slow them down with some basic questions:

- Has the situation at the company's work site stabilized or is there an ongoing risk of protest, violence, and government action?
- Was this a deliberate attack by the military or was it an effort to restore order?
- Has telecom service actually been shut down to the region? If so, by what authority? Who has the power to reverse the

decision? What are the implications for Kiku's operations in Burma if the government is arrogating to itself the right to impose a communications blackout during times of civil unrest?

- What is the reaction to the unfolding incident among key stakeholders such as parliament, the military, Burmese political opposition groups, human rights groups, and the press?
- How is the situation likely to unfold in the next several days?
- How does this event change our assessment of the political risks in Burma, and what additional steps, if any, should we take?

Our student executives struggle to answer these questions because the fictitious company never developed a robust situational awareness capability in the first place. We use the case to show the importance of thinking ahead. The lesson is not to let exciting business opportunities blind you. Companies need to be able to track developments as they unfold with diverse information sources in a coordinated manner. If that capability is not in place before crises hit, you'll regret it.

Today, companies on the front lines of managing global political risk have developed in-house threat assessment units staffed with former intelligence and law enforcement professionals to provide situational awareness about political developments around the world in real time. Royal Caribbean's team is led by a twenty-five-year veteran of the FBI. Disney's senior vice president for global security, Ron Iden, served as the director of the California Office of Homeland Security and spent twenty-five years at the FBI, including leading the Bureau's Los Angeles field office, where he oversaw investigations of terrorism, counterintelligence, and corruption. Marriott's Alan Orlob worked in the U.S. Army special forces for twenty-four years and has been a consultant for the U.S. State Department's Anti-Terrorism Assistance Program. Chevron's eight-person team of global analysts and risk experts has a combined ninety-two years of experience in U.S. and other government security services.

The best in-house risk teams have four core competencies to develop situational awareness:

- An ability to sift through voluminous amounts of information quickly to determine relevant political risks
- A deep understanding of the business to identify quickly what matters most for their bosses
- A forward-leaning entrepreneurial approach to collect and share information that may not be obvious or readily available through standard products
- A healthy skepticism about how incentives might affect what information they receive and when they receive it

Above all, situational awareness needs to be proactive and timely to be useful. Companies that manage political risks well do not sit back waiting for government advisories or quarterly industry reports. They know that warning systems need to be fed continuously and creatively. As Chevron's director of global security, Pat Donovan, told us, "You have to be informed about the world. You have to be reading five newspapers a day. If you want to stay on top of it, you have to be on top of it." Some companies station risk analysts in different regions. Some hire analysts with particular geographic expertise. Some bring in consultants to help the in-house team surge on a particular issue. Many develop customized tools to identify, collect, and analyze information. McDonald's, for example, uses a sophisticated model developed by Northwestern University to gather press reports and other information about groups that might launch boycotts or conduct activities that could disrupt company operations or tarnish the brand.[39] All of the high-functioning political risk units we found are proactive about getting and vetting information from a variety of sources. Informal networks play a vital role. As Nenad Pacek and Daniel Thorniley write, "A manager who relies solely on desk research is like a ship's captain who sees only the top of an iceberg; it is the large chunk below the surface that makes or breaks the business."[40]

In chapter 6, we recounted the shooting down of Malaysia Airlines Flight 17 in July 2014 over Ukraine during conflict between Russian-backed separatists and Ukrainian forces. That same day, 160 other commercial airliners were flying through Ukrainian airspace, despite the fact that it was a war zone. Just two days earlier, two Ukrainian military planes were shot down while flying at commercial altitudes.[41] Still, Ukrainian airspace remained open, and that was good enough for most airlines.

But not every airline was relying on the Ukrainian government to determine whether it was safe to fly. Months before the Malaysia Airlines shootdown, as hostilities on the ground escalated, Australia's Qantas and Korean Air rerouted flights to avoid passing over Ukraine.[42] These two airlines assessed the political risk of Ukrainian overflight differently than many of their competitors because they were not passive recipients of Ukrainian government decisions. Both airlines moved early to mitigate the risks they saw unfolding. Timing proved critical.

Setting Tripwires and Protocols

Situational awareness goes hand in hand with setting tripwires and protocols. Tripwires are systems that identify what information to look for in advance. Protocols make clear what steps should be taken by whom when the tripwire gets crossed. The idea is to reduce decision-making on the fly.

Tripwires and protocols are common in high-risk environments like emergency rooms and aircraft carriers. When a patient comes into a hospital with symptoms of a heart attack, doctors and nurses don't sit around deciding what to do. A flatlined EKG crosses the tripwire, automatically prompting a team to fetch a crash cart and begin CPR. Roles are clear: One member prepares and administers a dose of epinephrine if needed. Another works through the "Hs and Ts," a mnemonic used to identify possible causes of cardiac arrest. One keeps time and records the process on the patient's chart. Everyone understands what data crosses the tripwire and who does what.

The same goes for aircraft carrier operations. Because so many hazards pose lethal risks to the fifty-two hundred sailors on board, tripwires and protocols must be clear, quick to activate, and universally understood. One of those tripwires is physical—it's called the foul line. It's a bright red line painted alongside the length of the flight deck. All personnel who are not on shift must stand behind the foul line during flight operations. There are no exceptions. Anyone crossing the line for any reason is physically moved by a designated safety officer out of harm's way—tackled, if necessary. Crossing the foul line also triggers a host of other prearranged actions. Flight operations are immediately suspended. Red lights flash. There is a system in place for waving off approaching aircraft, rerouting other aircraft that are airborne farther away, and addressing any other safety concerns, like FOD (foreign object damage) or small pocket debris, which can get sucked into jet engines and cause engine failure, resulting in an unsafe or foul deck.

Like emergency rooms and aircraft carriers, companies can develop tripwires that identify specific political risk indicators to watch and protocols that identify specific actions to take when the indicators light up. To be sure, indicators of political risk are much murkier than indicators of a heart attack or a safety problem on a carrier flight deck. But the basic idea is the same: Organizations that identify warning indicators and reaction protocols are better able to mitigate risk than those that don't.

How exactly can a company develop tripwire indicators? For starters, by asking one of Condi's favorite questions: "How do you know it when you see it? What evidence would prove your hypothesis right or wrong?" In our class's Triton cruise line simulation, students grapple with setting tripwires. As you may remember, our fictitious cruise line has to decide how to respond to reports of rising drug-related violence in Mexico that could result in "wrong-place/wrong-time" crimes against passengers.

One key issue we probe during our "board meeting" with Triton executives is Condi's question: How do you know it when you see it? When does drug-related violence cross a threshold warranting a risk review and further action?

As in the real world, we provide the students with accurate but contradictory background information. Here's a sampling:

- In February 2012, twenty-two Carnival Cruise Line passengers were robbed at gunpoint near Puerto Vallarta. In February 2013, masked gunmen attacked and raped a group of Spanish tourists vacationing in Acapulco. In 2014, unrest rocked Acapulco after the disappearance of forty-three student teachers in nearby Iguala.
- In May 2015, the U.S. State Department issued a travel warning for Puerto Vallarta in Jalisco, the twenty-first Mexican state under such a warning.
- Local tourism boards stress that much of the negative press about Mexico coming from the American media is overblown. The Mexican government has made the war on drugs a top priority and devoted significant resources, including forty-five thousand police and military personnel, to enhancing the safety of tourist areas.
- Data show that Mexican tourist destinations are safer for many Americans than their home cities. The Department of State recorded eighty-one American deaths out of more than twenty million Americans who visited Mexico in 2013.[43] That constitutes about 0.4 deaths per 100,000 American tourists, less than a tenth of the national U.S. homicide rate.[44]

- In 2013, Detroit, which registered as America's most dangerous major city, suffered 45 homicides per 100,000 people, well over a hundred times the rate for Americans visiting Mexico that year. America's ten most dangerous cities each had higher murder rates than Mexico's national rate of 19 per 100,000.[45]
- Mexico was considered so safe that in April 2012 the first daughter, Malia Obama, took a spring break trip to Oaxaca.

How can analysts make sense of this information? The short answer is they can't. The best they can do is make an educated guess. As we discussed earlier, educated guesses based on press reports often lead smart people to make cognitive mistakes—by, for example, giving more credence to vivid stories about tourist violence than broad trends about murder rates or by discounting evidence that conflicts with their underlying preferences without even realizing it.

A better approach is to develop tripwires in advance, identifying specific indicators about safety conditions in each of Triton's destinations that are monitored continuously by the director of fleet security. Here's an example:

Acapulco: Indicators of Improved Security Environment

- Cessation of reports of violence impacting civilians—including residents and standby tourists—in tourist zones, shore excursion areas, and primary commercial sites during the daytime
- Overall decrease in cartel-related violence
- Decrease in murder and violent crime rates
- Cessation of narco-motivated intimidation tactics in tourist zones and primary commercial areas
- Development of a sustainable security strategy, agreed upon by Mexican port authorities in collaboration with cruise line representatives

Acapulco: Indicators of Deteriorating Security Environment/ Markers for Port-of-Call Review

- Increased violence in tourist areas, shore excursion zones, and primary commercial routes, particularly during daytime hours
- Narco-violence in tourist zones, particularly the propensity to escalate into high-probability collateral damage
- Narco-motivated intimidation tactics in tourist zones and shore excursion routes
- Deteriorating relationships with local port security officials

As this example suggests, tripwires do not have to be overly detailed. Even basic indicators can help. Identifying what to look for ahead of time helps guard against cognitive bias and makes data gathering and analysis more efficient.

To maximize effectiveness, tripwires should be tied to protocols that specify what actions come next—whether it's conducting a security review of a Triton destination, taking additional security measures at a Marriott hotel, or rerouting more FedEx airplanes through Paris. Connecting tripwires to protocols reduces the time between warning and action. Military history is filled with examples where warnings were issued, but not in time to forestall disaster. General Douglas MacArthur testified that even if he had received three days' warning that North Korea would invade the South on June 25, 1950, it would have made no difference. He needed three weeks, not three days, to mobilize troops from Japan to the Korean peninsula. After Japanese forces attacked Pearl Harbor on December 7, 1941, American air units in the Philippines went on full alert and were ordered to take immediate defensive measures. The attack on Clark Field came nine hours later. It was not enough time to move all the B-17s out of harm's way. The attack on the Philippines was not a surprise, but it was devastating anyway, destroying twelve of the nineteen American B-17 bombers stationed there.[46] Without sufficient time to take action, warning in both the Korean War and World War II was useless.

Businesses that are good at managing political risk link tripwires to protocols so they can reduce the lag time between warning and action. At Marriott, Alan Orlob's in-house intelligence unit gathers information continuously. That information is fed into a five-tiered color-coded warning system that alerts all Marriott hotel managers about any changing threat conditions affecting them. Each tier includes an assigned list of mandatory tasks for managers to take. Hotels are regularly audited by a third party to test compliance. In the highest threat level, for example, called "threat condition red," steps include installing walk-through metal detectors and X-rays at every entrance, limiting the access points to the hotel, enhancing explosive detection, and, in Orlob's words, "procedures that are not so noticeable, like surveillance detection teams." This is no small operation. When Marriott acquired Starwood Hotels in the fall of 2016, it became the world's largest hotel company, with more than fifty-seven hundred properties, over a million rooms, and thirty brands worldwide.[47] On a weekly basis, Marriott is moving hotels up or down the threat level.

Earlier, we mentioned McDonald's Northwestern University model to collect information about possible sit-ins, protests, or other political risks to its restaurants. The model is coupled with crisis contingency plans that are ready to go if necessary. FedEx also understands the value of linking tripwires to protocols. The GOCC in Memphis can warn *and* act, rerouting planes when necessary. Marriott, McDonald's, and FedEx all have warning systems for timely warning and action.

3. How can we limit the damage when something bad happens?

The final layer of risk mitigation is damage control. The headline here is to take action before you need to—specifically, by developing relationships and contingency plans. FedEx and other resilient organizations have an exceptional ability to bend without breaking when bad things happen. The key to their resilience is flexibility, and the key to flexibility is having the people and plans pre-positioned and ready to go.

Building Relationships: Drink the Cup of Coffee!

There's a scene in the movie *Erin Brockovich* that Amy used in her UCLA public management course for many years. The movie chronicles the real-life story of how Brockovich brought a successful lawsuit against the Pacific Gas and Electric Company for contaminating drinking water in the small Southern California town of Hinkley. In the scene, the lawyer, named Ed Masry, goes with Erin, a down-on-her-luck high school dropout single mom scraping by as his assistant, to convince a family to start a class action lawsuit against the energy company. It's a make-or-break moment. If they cannot get the support of Donna and Pete Jensen, their cause is lost. After a long and tense discussion, Erin convinces the Jensens to sign the suit. The tension lifts and Donna offers some homemade bundt cake and coffee. But Ed is all business. "No thanks," he says curtly and heads for the door, eager to get back to work. Erin grabs him by the arm and whispers, "Ed, have a #$! cup of coffee." Erin knew what her boss didn't: Coffee was not a waste of time. It was a golden opportunity to deepen a personal connection.

Relationships are important in any endeavor. Building trust takes effort, time, and shared experiences. In the moment, drinking the cup of coffee feels inefficient. There are always too many meetings, too many priorities, too much to do, and too little time. Former secretary of state George Shultz has always said that he took the time to do what he called "gardening"—cultivating relationships with his counterparts—before he had to call and ask them to do something hard.

Companies that effectively manage political risks develop relationships with stakeholders early and often. Many work closely with community groups, NGOs, and local officials to win approval for projects and reduce the risk of being labeled a bad neighbor later. That's exactly what Alcoa did in Brazil before opening a bauxite mine there in 2009. Although the rural Brazilian region of Juruti contained the world's largest high-quality deposits of bauxite—the chief ore from which aluminum is produced—Alcoa executives were concerned about political risks there. They had watched competitors in Brazil struggle against fierce local opposition, political action, and physical security breaches that included railroad blockades, temporary mine closures, and even an armed takeover using bows, arrows, and clubs. They were determined to avoid the same fate by winning the support of stakeholders early on.

Alcoa drank the cup of coffee in a big way. Two years before the bauxite mine opened, the company launched a major public outreach and communications campaign to build relationships with residents, organized civil society groups, and government officials. Partnering with the Getúlio Vargas Foundation and the Brazilian Biodiversity Fund, Alcoa conducted a series of surveys and discussions to better understand local needs and views. The company held three public meetings to educate local residents and solicit their input. More than eight thousand people attended. Alcoa also held seventy meetings with community members. By 2008, an independent survey found that 89 percent of the local population supported the mine.[48]

But Alcoa didn't stop there. Executives believed that an effective community partnership in Juruti needed to be genuine and sustained. The company created a multi-stakeholder council to serve as an open channel between it, the government, and civil society. It developed sustainability metrics to track progress. And it established a $35 million development fund for sustainable initiatives proposed by the community. Initiatives included building a hospital, adding classrooms to local schools, creating a clean water system, and establishing a local job training program. These outreach efforts did not eliminate opposition to the mine, but they made a big difference.[49]

Walmart took drinking the cup of coffee even further.[50] Starting in the 1990s, Walmart came under attack from a number of activists and groups concerned about many issues, including the company's environmental record. By 2004, Walmart was ranked number one on the Fortune 500 list. But it was also facing a growing chorus of concern as it moved into urban markets in search of higher growth.[51] "When growth was easier, this idea of critics being ignored was O.K.," Walmart CEO Lee Scott said.[52] But with growth slowing, Walmart could not ignore it anymore. So Scott launched a strategy to respond to critics directly in the media while building better relationships with stakeholders.[53] He took a trip to the New Hampshire wilderness with Fred Krupp, president of the Environmental Defense Fund and one of Walmart's toughest critics. They talked about climate change, and Scott came back convinced that Walmart should do more.[54] The company promised to reduce greenhouse gas emissions in its stores by 20 percent in seven years and improve other environmental standards. With the help of environmental groups and scholars, the company started using an electronic product sustainability rating system for its products.[55] Scott also saw profit potential in going green: Walmart started selling energy-saving lightbulbs and cutting energy costs in its own operations.[56] And then coffee drinking got serious: Walmart created staff positions for Environmental Defense Fund representatives at its Bentonville, Arkansas, center.[57] Fred Krupp, who began as a fierce opponent, became one of Scott's staunchest supporters. He later reflected, "I almost think of Lee Scott as a Gorbachev leading Glasnost, because Lee was this figure that opened Walmart's walls up to the outside and changed how they did business."[58]

Relationship building is also a core part of Royal Caribbean International's risk mitigation efforts. The company takes a "destination stewardship approach" to its business, working with a range of local community groups, residents, government officials, and nonprofits to maintain the cultural, economic, environmental, and social integrity of places like Labadee, Haiti. Another way that Royal Caribbean International develops relationships with stakeholders is by arranging regular ship visits in port. "One of the very best things we can do for political risk is to take [local] people on the ship in port so they see our supply chain, they see our operations. There's no substitute for seeing it," said president and COO Adam Goldstein. "By trying as hard as we can to get people to see the ships, when something does happen they have a point of reference." Goldstein believes this human touchpoint is essential. "Maybe because in the world today technology is so dominant, it's so easy to communicate by text and email and video conference and telephone, I believe that people value personal visitation much more," he told us. "There's a real value in longevity...People come to believe that they can count on you, that if times are difficult, that there's a foundation upon which the dialogue rests that is at some level tried and trusted. It's very, very helpful to work your way through situations."

Here, too, timing matters. Relationships need to be developed *before* a crisis hits. For Royal Caribbean International, the advocacy of Haitian government officials, ethics experts, and NGOs helped the company weather the media storm following the 2010 earthquake. Adam Goldstein did not begin cold-calling people once negative news stories started breaking. He turned to old friends for help. As he put it, "You make

> "You make relationships when you want to, not when you need to—because when you need to, it's too late already."
> —Adam Goldstein, president and COO, Royal Caribbean Cruises, Ltd.

relationships when you want to, not when you need to—because when you need to, it's too late already."

Contingency Planning

Helmuth von Moltke, the nineteenth-century Prussian army commander, famously said that no battle plan survives contact with the enemy. Plans are often useless. It's the planning process that is valuable. Plans will almost never match the conditions of the future, but planning builds capacity to succeed anyway by developing what we call the three Rs: *roles*, *repertoires of action*, and *routines of coordination*. Roles clarify who does what. Repertoires provide broad options for what can be done. Routines of coordination determine how it can be done well.

Rule 1: Roles should be clear. By definition, contingency plans are used when normal processes are not enough and conditions are not ideal. In these circumstances, there is too much pressure, too many moving parts, and not enough time to be debating who should be doing what. The more that roles are delineated, the faster and better your organization can execute its contingency plan.

Rule 2: The more repertoires of action, the better. By repertoires of action, we do not mean an exhaustive list of rigid plans for every conceivable circumstance. Reality is too complex, and flexibility is too important. Rigid plans of action are likely to be ill-suited. Instead, repertoires of action develop fundamental skills for the totally unexpected and provide options that can be used in different combinations and ways.

Condi is a lifelong pianist and thinks about repertoires of action as a musician does. For her, a repertoire is a go-to repository of songs that can be easily recalled and deployed in different combinations for different circumstances. Her repertoire usually consists of about five pieces. Some, like the Schumann Piano Quintet, she plays all the time, while others, like the Brahms Piano Quintet, require much more practice before she's willing to play them outside of her living room. Her repertoire is the foundation on which she can build a performance. But it's just the starting point. Some concerts consist entirely of songs she has known and played for years. Most include a combination of old and new songs. With an occasional curveball...

In 2010, Condi played a concert with the Philadelphia Philharmonic. They performed a movement of a Mozart piano concerto that Condi had worked on for months. The other part of the program featured Condi playing with the Queen of Soul, Aretha Franklin. They rehearsed the day before and agreed on the repertoire. At intermission, just before they were to go onstage, Aretha's producer told Condi that Ms. Franklin wanted to sing something else—a song they had not rehearsed. Fortunately, the music wasn't difficult, and all those years of learning to sight-read pieces, all those years of practicing scales, and considerable concert experience led Condi to just say, "Fine." And the performance came off without a hitch.

Importantly, mastering and maintaining a repertoire takes practice. But sometimes it is mastering the fundamentals so that you can deal with a curveball—a sudden change in plans—that matters.

Repertoires of action play this role in many domains. Research on chess grandmasters finds that what distinguishes them from weaker chess players isn't native intelligence or more time spent playing chess. It's pattern recognition. Chess grandmasters have exceptional repertoires of action. When they see a new move, they compare it to the patterns stored in their heads to determine a path forward. The process is done in seconds, with remarkable accuracy, even when grandmasters are playing multiple games simultaneously.[59] Most of us grapple with something new by comparing it to something known, relying on experience as a guide through the unfamiliar. The more developed these repertoires are, the better we can handle new situations. The same is true for organizations. Good contingency planning develops broad options as well as fundamental skills that can be deployed to help the entire organization adapt to unforeseen circumstances.

Rule 3: Coordination routines are essential. Assigning roles is a start. Developing repertoires of action comes next. Coordination is where roles and repertoires come together. Coordination routines establish trust and patterns of interaction that smooth the functioning of groups under stress. The best way to develop coordination routines is practice.

In the defense world, coordination failures have deadly consequences. Perhaps the best-known example is Operation Eagle Claw, the failed operation to rescue fifty-three American hostages in Iran. Launched on April 24, 1980, the mission had to be aborted—but not before eight service members died when a helicopter collided with a transport plane in the desert.[60] The botched operation was one of the Carter presidency's darkest moments. Thirty-five years later, when asked what he would have done differently in office, President Carter immediately answered that he would have fixed Operation Eagle Claw.[61]

Two postmortems conducted at the time—one by the Senate and one by a special commission—concluded that coordination problems were the root cause of failure. The Army, Navy, Air Force, and Marines all insisted on having a piece of the rescue plan. Yet they never conducted any joint training. Instead, each service practiced its own part in isolation. When the rescue day arrived, many of the team members had never met before. Service commanders did not even have arrangements in place to be able to communicate with one another. Nobody in the Pentagon had paid enough attention to coordination.[62] The failure of Operation Eagle Claw led in 1987 to the creation of the U.S. Special Operations Command, a new integrated command led by a four-star general whose mission is to conduct special operations across the military services. Today, coordination across the services for special operations is vastly improved.

U.S. Special Operations Command offers a valuable lesson for business: Coordination should never be assumed, even when the stakes are high, the mission is clear, and the will to succeed is shared by all. Coordination does not just emerge organically. It has to be ingrained through practice and supported by leaders at the top. The natural state of all organizations, whether military units or corporate departments, is to work in silos or specialized functions. Silos are important. But they can also be counterproductive when unity of effort is required. Working across silos is an unnatural act. And managing political risk is an exercise in silo-crossing. Political risks do not just involve the finance department, the legal team, government relations, or the IT folks. Political risks cut across every part of a company, from strategy to operations to marketing. Planning for political risk contingencies means practicing coordination.

FedEx follows all three rules—assigning clear roles, developing repertoires of action, and establishing coordination routines. At FedEx, contingency planning is everyday life. "We believe in predictable surprises," notes former GOCC managing director Paul Tronsor.[63] At the Global Operations Control Center in Memphis, there's always a Plan B. But as Tronsor notes, executing any Plan B, even a routine one, "is a tremendous undertaking." Flying out of an alternate airport requires getting the right crews to the right places at the right times, with enough rest to remain in compliance. It requires making sure there's enough fuel where you need it, securing airport space and landing rights. Freight can be unloaded only if it is cleared by customs, and it can be put on trucks only if the trucks are positioned where the planes are landing.[64]

Establishing roles, repertoires, and coordination routines is essential. At FedEx, roles are clear. The flight dispatcher, known as the "Captain on the Ground," is responsible for assessing air routes and conditions. The freight movement center team focuses on constantly evaluating where freight is in transit. A service recovery specialist manages the development and implementation of the overall action plan for "movement solutions." A crew scheduling specialist is responsible for getting aircrews to the right places at the right times in compliance with applicable regulations. Contingency plans—or repertoires of action—are continually developed based on most likely scenarios. If the Paris airport hub goes down, for example, the default contingency plan is to reroute cargo to Frankfurt, Germany. If Frankfurt goes down, too—which happened in April 2010 when an Icelandic volcano erupted and spread a giant ash cloud over Western Europe—FedEx moves to a different contingency plan, making up a new one if necessary. And routines of coordination are established and reinforced at FedEx's GOCC. Success each day requires a complex, coordinated effort between flight dispatchers, freight movement center teams, crew scheduling, and global trade services to make sure international freight is in compliance with all laws and customs requirements.[65] Each day begins with a war room conference call among managers. Each major disruption ends with a team debrief of lessons learned.

That's not to say FedEx has a cookie-cutter approach to diverting aircraft. It doesn't, because it can't. When the Icelandic volcano erupted, conditions were changing so fast, European airports were closing, opening, and closing again within minutes. The usual Plan B, shifting to Frankfurt, was no good. So the GOCC developed a different Plan B that assumed Paris would remain closed and positioned flights and crews in Toulouse and Barcelona. But then Charles de Gaulle Airport in Paris reopened, so they shifted again, to what they called Plan A. FedEx had planned for that, too. "Since we had accounted for this possibility," Tronsor noted, "we were ready to go." FedEx restored service and then moved to clear the backlog, shipping 7.7 million pounds of cargo in two days.[66] Like Condi improvising during her concert with Aretha Franklin, FedEx succeeded by drawing on its existing repertoire and skills practiced every day.

KEY TAKEAWAYS: MITIGATING POLITICAL RISKS

- ☐ Prepare for the unexpected.
- ☐ Know what assets are most valuable *and* vulnerable.
- ☐ Reduce exposure by dispersing critical assets, flying the empty plane, and aligning with others in the industry.
- ☐ Set tripwires and develop protocols so that you have a system for timely warning and action.
- ☐ Remember to drink the cup of coffee! Limit the damage when something bad happens by building relationships with stakeholders before you need them.
- ☐ Develop contingency planning processes built on the three Rs: roles, repertoires of action, and routines of coordination.

9

Zulu Time: Responding to Crises

On July 16, 2009, Alan Orlob landed in Jakarta to conduct a security review of the Ritz-Carlton and JW Marriott hotels. The city's security situation seemed to be improving.[1] As Marriott International's vice president for global safety and security, Orlob knew that Indonesia had long struggled with Islamist terrorism. But in recent years, Jemaah Islamiyah (JI), the country's deadliest group, appeared to be weakening. Best known for the 2002 Bali nightclub bombings that killed more than two hundred, the terror group had not waged a significant attack in four years. New Indonesian security measures, enhanced counterterrorism efforts by American-trained Indonesian police, and the arrests or deaths of many top JI operatives led many analysts to believe that JI no longer had the capabilities to launch a major operation. A year earlier, the United States had lifted its travel warning on Indonesia.[2] More recent political news was also promising. Indonesia had just celebrated a peaceful democratic presidential election. Orlob went to bed that night in the Ritz-Carlton "feeling confident that the authorities were dealing successfully with the terrorism threat in the country."[3]

At 7:30 the next morning, Orlob was getting out of the shower when he heard an explosion. Out the window, he saw smoke billowing from the JW Marriott across the street. Having served more than twenty years in Army special forces, Orlob instinctively rushed toward the danger, not away from it. But before he could get outside, he felt another explosion—this one inside the Ritz.[4] It was a double suicide bombing, carried out by terrorists masquerading as guests. Investigators would later discover that the bombers had worked with an insider, the hotels' florist, to learn how to evade the hotels' stringent security measures.[5] The attack killed nine people and injured dozens.

Marriott activated its crisis response team to evacuate and account for all guests, support victims' families, assist investigators,

Romeo Gacad/Getty Images

John van Hasselt/Getty Images

tend to employees, and assess ongoing threats. The company's communications staff issued regular updates on Twitter, careful to avoid reporting developments until they could be verified. Within 150 minutes of the bombings, chairman and CEO Bill Marriott published a blog post expressing his condolences and providing details about what the company was doing to help victims and guests.[6]

The company's response was quick, decisive, and compassionate. There was just one problem. The terrorist attacks had garnered global news coverage, and much of it featured scathing and erroneous criticism of Marriott's security. "I was listening to the media reports. They were so inaccurate and it was really frustrating for me," Orlob told us. "I knew what had happened. I had been there from the beginning. And I was listening to this wild speculation from the media." Some senior executives did not want anyone from the company talking to the press. As a result, nobody was defending Marriott.

In truth, the Ritz-Carlton and JW Marriott were among the most secure hotels in the world. Marriott was widely recognized as an industry leader. The company considered security a significant competitive advantage in the business travel market, particularly in cities like Jakarta. Starting in the 1990s, as Marriott's international footprint grew, its investment in security did, too. By 2009, the company was operating thousands of properties in seventy countries.[7] Many destinations posed elevated risks of civil unrest, kidnapping, natural disasters, disease, and terrorism. Senior management recognized that security was important to the value of the Marriott brand. As Orlob put it, "They understood the damage that could ensue if terrorists decided to target Marriott because of its name and its reputation as an American company."[8] Robust security was a must-have for consumers and investors.[9]

At the time of the bombing, both the Ritz-Carlton and JW Marriott were operating under "condition red," the company's highest threat level.[10] Security at these two hotels was arguably the best in the city. At the JW Marriott, for example, vehicles were inspected at a roadway checkpoint away from hotel buildings separated by a blast wall and guarded by an armed police officer. In addition, the company had installed explosive vapor detection devices, brought in a bomb-sniffing dog, placed security cameras throughout the facility, and added specially trained security officers to conduct counter-surveillance. Anyone entering the hotel went through a metal detector monitored by security officers, and luggage was screened outside the building. These and other procedures were tested by an independent auditor on unannounced visits, so that implementation could be confirmed, failures reported, and employees penalized.[11] This was no lax security environment. When tragedy struck on July 17, 2009, it was not because Marriott was asleep at the wheel.

Frustrated that none of this context was in the news, Orlob made a gutsy decision: When a friend from CNN called for an interview, he said yes. That interview began changing the narrative. "I used the interview to tell our story, to talk about the type of security we did have in the hotel," Orlob recounted. "It gave us a chance to push our story out there rather than listening to all the negative media information that was coming out about our security procedures." Senior leadership at Marriott liked what they saw and asked him to do more. In the next few days, Orlob gave nearly two dozen interviews. His message: Marriott security was robust, but the company was committed to conducting a complete review of this attack, and if additional security measures were necessary, they would be implemented.[12]

Marriott's experience shows how to handle "Zulu time," when events erupt and response cannot wait until tomorrow. Everyone knows that crisis response should be coordinated across time zones and corporate functions. But good crisis response starts long before any crisis appears. Effective communication in the heat of the moment is important. It is never enough. Companies need to lay the foundation, learning from near misses, rewarding employees for doing difficult and courageous things, leading with core values, and taking steps to ensure that crisis response capabilities are honed without being hidebound. These "back room" practices enable "front room" successes when political risks get real.

In this chapter, we take you through the three questions companies should ask so that they can perform at their best when crisis conditions are worst.

Responding to Crises: Three Key Questions

1. Are we capitalizing on near misses?
2. Are we reacting effectively to crises?
3. Are we developing mechanisms for continuous learning?

1. Are we capitalizing on near misses?

The best way to deal with crises is not to have them. All organizations want to learn from failures. Not enough try to learn from near misses, events that could have ended poorly but didn't because luck saved the day. Individuals and organizations tend to take false comfort in near misses, seeing them as signs of success rather than warnings of potential failure. Even descriptors mislead. These events are often called "close calls" or "lucky breaks," not "near disasters that could get us the next time."

"A near miss can be evidence of two things," says Georgetown professor Cathy Tinsley. "It can be evidence of a system's resiliency, or it can be evidence of that system's vulnerability."[13] Too often, people conclude the system worked well when in reality it just got lucky. Why? Because we all like to think we are good at our jobs and because giving luck that much power is scary.[14] Tinsley and her colleagues have studied near misses in companies, government

> "When people observe a successful outcome, their natural tendency is to assume that the process that led to it was fundamentally sound, even when it demonstrably wasn't."
> —Catherine Tinsley, Robin Dillon, and Peter Madsen, *Harvard Business Review*, 2011

agencies, and lab experiments. They repeatedly find that people either disregard or misinterpret them: "When people observe a successful outcome, their natural tendency is to assume that the process that led to it was fundamentally sound, even when it demonstrably wasn't."[15]

Apple, for example, had an unusually troubled product launch of its iPhone 4 in 2010 because the company dismissed earlier consumer complaints as reassuring signs of loyalty rather than warning signs of technical deficiencies.[16] Customers had been complaining for years that signal strength declined when they touched the phone's external antenna, but they still lined up to buy iPhones. Instead of addressing these concerns, Apple ignored them. When the iPhone 4 came out, Apple was barraged with complaints that simply holding the device resulted in dropped calls. Steve Jobs and other executives blamed customers for holding the phone incorrectly and labeled the problem a "non-issue." As Tinsley and her colleagues write, "If Apple had recognized consumers' forbearance as an ongoing near miss and proactively fixed the phones' technical problems, it could have avoided the crisis."[17] Instead, *Consumer Reports* did not recommend the iPhone for the first time in product history.

The *Challenger* shuttle tragedy is a classic example of a disaster that could have been avoided if only managers had paid attention to near misses. On January 28, 1986, *Challenger* exploded shortly after liftoff when unusually cold weather caused O-ring seals in one of the solid rocket boosters to fail.[18] O-ring problems had been a common occurrence on previous shuttle flights, and although they had not failed before, they had come close. Just a year earlier, *Challenger* launched from Florida when the temperature had dropped to 51.8 degrees Fahrenheit, the lowest for a shuttle launch to date.[19] After the mission, engineers discovered that O-rings in both rocket boosters had experienced significant damage.[20] Engineers at O-ring manufacturer Morton Thiokol concluded that cold weather was the culprit and recommended against future shuttle launches if temperatures dipped below 53 degrees.[21] This was a major near miss, but NASA didn't see it. Instead, when a cold front sent temperatures in Florida plummeting to 36 degrees, NASA okayed the *Challenger* launch anyway. Thiokol engineers' worst fears came true: All seven astronauts, including Christa McAuliffe, the first teacher in space, were killed.

The Rogers Commission that investigated the *Challenger* disaster concluded that NASA accepted escalating risk because they "got away with it last time." They mistook near misses as signs of resilience, not vulnerability. Commissioner and physicist Richard Feynman likened the process to Russian roulette, noting that whenever the shuttle flew with O-ring erosion and nothing happened, "it…suggested, therefore, that the risk is no longer so high for the next flights."[22]

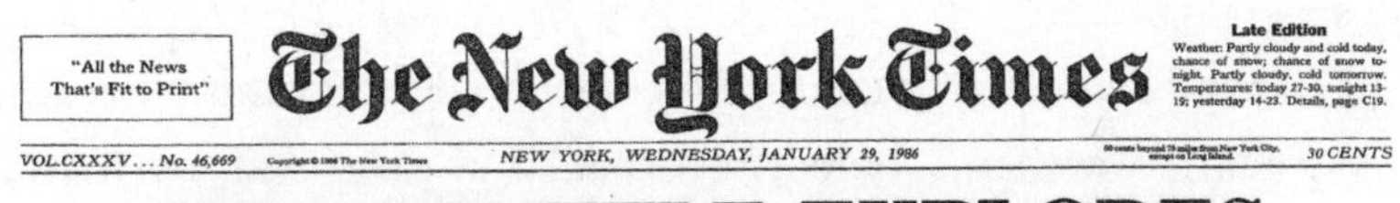

"All the News That's Fit to Print"

The New York Times

Late Edition

Weather: Partly cloudy and cold today, chance of snow; chance of snow tonight. Partly cloudy, cold tomorrow. Temperatures: today 27-30, tonight 13-19; yesterday 14-23. Details, page C19.

VOL.CXXXV . . . No. 46,669 — NEW YORK, WEDNESDAY, JANUARY 29, 1986 — 30 CENTS

THE SHUTTLE EXPLODES

6 IN CREW AND HIGH-SCHOOL TEACHER ARE KILLED 74 SECONDS AFTER LIFTOFF

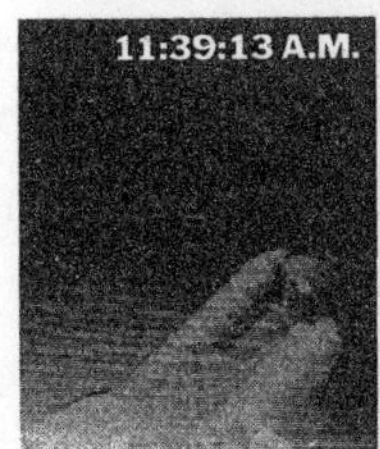

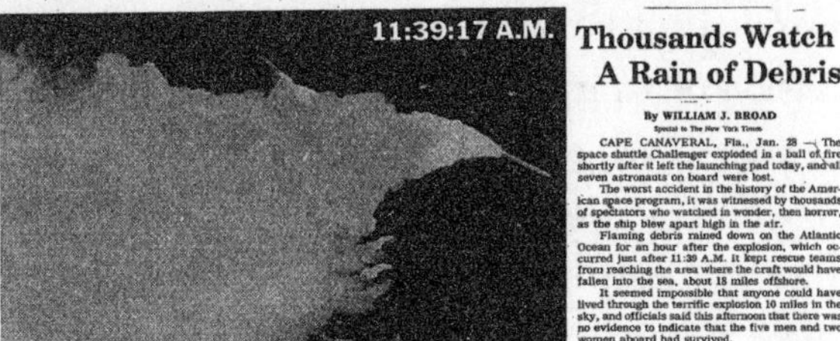

Thousands Watch A Rain of Debris

By WILLIAM J. BROAD

Special to The New York Times

CAPE CANAVERAL, Fla., Jan. 28 — The space shuttle Challenger exploded in a ball of fire shortly after it left the launching pad today, and all seven astronauts on board were lost.

The worst accident in the history of the American space program, it was witnessed by thousands of spectators who watched in wonder, then horror, as the ship blew apart high in the air.

Flaming debris rained down on the Atlantic Ocean for an hour after the explosion, which occurred just after 11:39 A.M. It kept rescue teams from reaching the area where the craft would have fallen into the sea, about 18 miles offshore.

It seemed impossible that anyone could have lived through the terrific explosion 10 miles in the sky, and officials said this afternoon that there was no evidence to indicate that the five men and two women aboard had survived.

New York Times

In these cases, Apple and NASA did not take near misses seriously enough. But in the case of aircraft carrier operations, the U.S. Navy does. In the summer of 2016, Amy spent some time aboard the USS *Carl Vinson* during flight training exercises at sea. There's a reason carriers are described as "the most dangerous 4.5 acres in the world."[23] The *Vinson* is just 1,090 feet long, with each runway or catapult only 350 feet in length.[24] (Runways at London's Heathrow Airport are ten times longer.)[25] Fighter jets are catapulted from the flight deck, accelerating from zero to 165 miles per hour in two seconds. Aircraft launch and land less than a minute apart, sometimes simultaneously. Rather than slowing down to land, pilots touch down at full throttle so they can take off again if the plane's tailhook fails to snag one of the arresting wires stretched across the flight deck. It is a chaotic work environment. The noise is deafening, with sailors communicating mostly by hand signals. Weather can be a huge factor. At night, visibility is poor and landing becomes exponentially more difficult. The movement of planes, people, fuel lines, parts, and pilots is constant, with a razor-thin margin of error. Safety hazards are everywhere: Any loose object—a wrench, a penny, a dropped binder clip—can be sucked into a jet engine, causing severe damage.

On the *Vinson*, every landing is considered a near miss. Because it is. Each is watched, graded, recorded, and debriefed, no matter what the conditions or time of day or night. A landing safety officer from each squadron both assists and assesses the pilots as they make all the corrections in the final thirty seconds before making the controlled crash. Landing on a carrier requires the confidence and precision of a surgeon and the humility of a clergyman. The pilot can, at best, achieve a grade of "okay" for successfully catching the three wire, a two-foot-by-two-foot space on the deck. The Navy knows that learning from near misses is the best way to prevent big failures.

Only a handful of nations in the world have aircraft carriers.[26]

Navinfo East

It is not because these ships are too difficult to build. It is because flight operations are that difficult to execute. Conducting flight operations is the ultimate exercise of learning from near misses.

The USS *Vinson* highlights three tips for any organization seeking to learn from near misses:

Tip 1: Plan for failure, not success.[27]

Organizations that learn from near misses are fundamentally pessimistic. They assume that failure is always just around the corner and invest in developing structures, processes, incentives, cultures, and technical tools to prevent it. They never assume that good outcomes today will continue tomorrow. In carrier aviation, landings are scrutinized no matter who sits in the cockpit, how many times they have flown, or what the circumstances are.

Marriott and FedEx also plan for failure. When Alan Orlob arrived in Jakarta, he had many reasons to be hopeful about Indonesia's security environment. But he was also wary, which was why the JW Marriott and Ritz-Carlton had such tight security measures in place even though there had not been a major JI terrorist attack in four years. FedEx relentlessly plans for contingencies because, as Fred Smith told us, "We brush up against" risks "so often." Soon after the company built a large hub in Guangzhou, China, for example, Smith took the board to meet with Chinese leader Jiang Zemin. But as tensions began rising in Sino-American relations, FedEx began building other regional hubs in Osaka, Anchorage, and Singapore. Smith was not about to wait for a crisis to start developing a Plan B. "While we're not sure how U.S.-China relations will play out," said Smith, "we've been trying to take steps to protect ourselves."

Organizations that adopt a "planning for failure" mentality are more likely to see near misses, take them seriously, and learn from them.

Tip 2: Look for weak signals.[28]

As Karl E. Weick and Kathleen M. Sutcliffe note, organizations that learn from near misses also look for weak signals that things may not be working as intended. They know that the earlier they identify a potential problem, the more time and options they have to prevent disaster. Performance indicators for people, processes, and parts are critical. Anything that does not perform as expected could be an early indicator of a serious problem. Of course, not every weak signal is. That's why it is important to look deeper, at possible systemic deficiencies, whenever weak signals are found. And then take strong action.

Remember General Electric's botched Honeywell deal? It was the first time that European regulators had ever rejected a major American merger. But just barely. Four years earlier, the European Commission made headlines for opposing the proposed merger of two American civilian aircraft giants, Boeing and McDonnell Douglas.[29] For months, it looked like that deal was doomed. The commission recommended blocking the merger, and competition experts from all fifteen EU member nations unanimously agreed. The merger went through only after Boeing agreed to several major eleventh-hour concessions. Boeing's 1997 deal was a signal that European regulators would no longer rubber-stamp American corporate mergers.[30]

Photograph released by the Coast Guard on April 22, 2010.
U.S. Coast Guard via European Pressphoto Agency.

In the *Deepwater Horizon* disaster, British Petroleum (BP) and its offshore drilling rig owner/operator, Transocean, responded poorly to a series of not-so-weak signals.[31] On April 20, 2010, a cement seal on the Macondo well in the Gulf of Mexico failed, creating an explosion that took the lives of eleven crew and caused one of the nation's worst environmental catastrophes.[32] Millions of barrels of oil flowed into the Gulf over the next eighty-seven days, contaminating ecosystems and damaging economies from Texas to Florida. Five years later, BP reached a $20.8 billion settlement with the U.S. government. It was the largest American pollution penalty ever paid.[33]

Investigations concluded that the *Deepwater Horizon* disaster stemmed from complex causes—and that failing to notice warning signs was a big one.[34] Internal BP documents showed that as early as 2009, BP engineers were expressing concerns about using certain casings for the well because they violated the company's safety and design guidelines. The casings were used anyway.[35] A month before the disaster, the oil rig was hit with a burst, or "kick," of explosive methane gas. According to the Coast Guard's joint investigation, kicks are considered "critical indicators" of potential safety hazards, but BP and Transocean employees dismissed the incident.[36]

Around the same time, the well's blowout preventer, which served as a last line of defense, was discovered leaking fluids at least three times.[37] Problems at the well were so common, *Deepwater Horizon* personnel referred to Macondo as the "well from hell."[38] In April, employees at Halliburton, BP's cementing contractor, warned that BP's well design violated Halliburton's best practices, and that a "severe" gas flow problem could result.[39] BP drilling engineer Brett Cocales responded in an internal email, "Who cares, it's done, end of story, will probably be fine..."[40]

Perhaps most important, BPs own investigation found that its site leaders and the Transocean rig crew discounted a negative-pressure test indicating that the cement barrier around the well casing might not be secure. These are critical tests, designed to assess the integrity of the well after it has been cemented. The first test showed pressure buildup in the drill pipe, a dangerous indication that gas had invaded the well. The finding, however, was "explained away" as an acceptable anomaly.[41] Although there were no industry standards to interpret or approve negative-pressure test results, BP's review concluded that *any* pressure in the drill pipe should have been considered unacceptable. "The negative-pressure test was an opportunity to recognize that the well did not have integrity and to take appropriate action to evaluate the well further," the report noted.[42] Other expert investigations came to the same conclusion. A National Academy of Engineering report called the negative-pressure test "an irrefutable sign" that the cement did not establish an effective seal.[43] James Dykes, cochair of the Coast Guard's Joint Investigation Team into the disaster, testified before Congress that "the crew's collective misinterpretation of the negative tests was a critical mistake that would escalate into the blowout, fire and eventual sinking of the Deepwater Horizon."[44] Missed signals compounded risks and contributed to disaster. By the time anyone on board *Deepwater Horizon* noticed that hydrocarbons were leaking from the well and into the rig, it was too late.

By contrast, Marriott is constantly searching for weak signals and reacting strongly to them. Marriott's Alan Orlob ensures that the thousands of hotels he oversees around the world are audited at unanticipated times to make sure they are following security procedures fully. If they aren't, individuals face disciplinary action. Partially meeting requirements is not an option. Threat condition blue, the company's lowest level of enhanced security, requires nearly forty different procedures.[45]

Weick and Sutcliffe discovered that one East Coast power company uses bees as weak signals. That's right. Bees. When the rate of bee stings for linemen in the field goes up, managers know that workers probably are not looking as carefully as they should before reaching for a power line. They don't assume operations "will probably be fine." Rising bee sting rates trigger greater attention to addressing safety risks within the company before something bad happens.[46]

Tip 3: Reward courageous acts.

Third and finally, organizations that learn from near misses develop cultures that reward courageous acts. Learning from near misses often requires someone to say, "Hold on a minute. Why are we moving full speed ahead when we may have a problem here?" The pressure to stay on schedule and on budget can be immense. Calling a time out to examine a weak signal is an act of courage. Recognizing those moments can make a difference.

The night before the *Challenger* launch, five engineers at Morton Thiokol recommended postponing the flight because they were concerned that predicted cold temperatures could cause a catastrophic O-ring failure.[47] NASA manager Lawrence Mulloy, the head of NASA's booster rocket program, infamously exclaimed, "For God's sake, Thiokol, when do you expect me to launch? Next April?"[48] Soon after, Thiokol managers overruled their own engineers, okaying the launch.[49] The Rogers Commission found that launch schedule pressures were very much on the minds of NASA managers. As a result, the courageous dissent of Thiokol engineers was not heeded or rewarded. "I fought like hell to stop that launch," said one of the engineers on the twentieth anniversary of the disaster. "I'm so torn up inside I can hardly talk about it even now."[50]

Compare the experience of Morton Thiokol engineers to a crew member working on the flight deck of the USS *Carl Vinson*. Twenty years before Amy landed on the carrier, professors Martin Landau and Donald Chisholm wrote about how a seaman serving on the *Vinson* lost a tool during flight operations. The seaman was concerned that the lost tool could be sucked into a jet engine and cause an engine failure. The Navy repeatedly warns carrier crews about the dangers of "foreign object debris." So when the seaman could not find his tool, he told the air boss. It was a big deal. About a dozen planes in the air had to be diverted to airfields on land. The flight deck had to be shut down. Hundreds of people had to stop what they were doing to "walk the deck," searching inch by inch until they found the missing tool. The next day, a formal ceremony was held. Instead of being punished, the seaman got an award. That's what we call rewarding courageous acts. It is one thing to tell the crew they should always report any foreign object debris. It's another to show that you mean it.[51]

Employees often have ideas about how to avoid failure or improve performance that they never tell the boss. A 2009 survey by the Cornell University Survey Research Institute found that 53 percent of respondents admitted they never spoke up about an idea or problem. When asked why, many said they thought it would be a waste of time or could hurt their careers.[52] After failure, postmortems reveal all sorts of information that could have been shared beforehand but wasn't. Rewarding courageous acts fosters a premortem culture—encouraging people in the organization to volunteer information about what could go wrong before it does go wrong.[53]

Learning from near misses is never easy. Organizations that do it well plan for failure, look for weak signals and respond strongly to them, and reward courageous acts that empower everyone to avert disaster.

2. Are we reacting effectively to crises?

No matter how hard an organization works to do everything right—understanding and communicating the risk appetite, integrating political risk analysis into the business, collecting good information, using analytic tools to reduce cognitive bias and groupthink, mitigating risks, and learning from near misses—big surprises can still occur. Your organization's response determines whether that crisis fades or festers. As Warren Buffett once said, "It takes twenty years to build a reputation and five minutes to ruin it. If you think about that, you'll do things differently."[54]

> "It takes twenty years to build a reputation and five minutes to ruin it. If you think about that, you'll do things differently."
> —Warren Buffett

Johnson & Johnson's handling of the Tylenol tampering deaths is still considered the gold standard of crisis response. When seven people were poisoned by laced Tylenol capsules in 1982, Tylenol was the best-selling nonprescription pain medication in the United States, with 35 percent market share.[55] It was also Johnson & Johnson's top-selling product.[56] Johnson & Johnson (J&J) public relations executives learned of the deaths from the press. It was

Yvonne Hemsey/Getty Images

the worst possible way for a crisis to unfold. News quickly spread. According to one news service, it was the biggest media event since President Kennedy's assassination.[57]

The company responded decisively. J&J pulled all Tylenol capsules from store shelves nationwide, offered to replace them with tablets free of charge, promised a reward for information leading to the arrest of anyone involved in the murders, issued warnings against using Tylenol, set up a toll-free hotline for consumers, and communicated directly with the public through news shows and paid advertising.[58] Within ten weeks, the company launched new tamper-resistant packaging for Tylenol products that became the industry standard.[59] The recall cost more than $100 million, with the total cost of the crisis estimated between $500 million and $1 billion.[60] Many thought Johnson & Johnson would never recover. Yet within two months, its stock had returned to its fifty-two-week high,[61] and within a year Tylenol had resumed its place as the leading pain relief medication.[62]

Although the Tylenol crisis occurred more than thirty years ago, Johnson & Johnson's approach can be distilled into five steps for any company confronting a crisis.

Step 1: Assess the situation.

The first step in crisis management is to get a better handle on what is happening. Early moments of a crisis are swirling with uncertainty. What is the problem? How serious is it? Is the crisis over or just beginning? How do you know? Don't jump to conclusions. Assess the situation.

Assessing the situation takes discipline and time. Yet modern communications technologies are straining discipline and compressing time. Twitter, YouTube, Facebook, and "citizen-journalist" Internet reporting are ever-present and fast-moving. Crisis management isn't what it used to be.

We see these pressures every time we teach our cyber crisis simulation. The simulation involves a hypothetical technology company called Frizzle, which offers Internet-related services and products, including search, email, cloud computing, mobile payments, and drone delivery services. Founded by an East German immigrant, Frizzle is headquartered in California but operates globally, with 75 percent of revenues generated outside the United States. Like many Silicon Valley companies, Frizzle believes deeply in protecting the privacy of its users. Its mission statement declares, "Doing What's Right lies at the core of who we are and how we operate. At Frizzle, Doing What's Right means having the courage to protect our users, their information, and their trust in us."

Frizzle

The crisis starts when executives learn that Frizzle's email system has been breached in an attack targeting the accounts of Chechen activists. Frizzle's security team believes the attack originated from Eastern Europe. The U.S. Department of Defense has publicly acknowledged that the Russian government appears to be behind an escalating number of attacks ostensibly perpetrated by individuals and other proxy groups against American companies and government agencies. Still, at this early stage, the Frizzle security team is unable to determine the person or organizations behind the attack, although they believe they have identified the computer used. Company data may still reside on it. Executives must decide how to respond, including whether and how to work with the U.S. government; whether to "hack back" against the perpetrators; how to communicate the breach to customers, partners, and the public; and what, if any, longer-term steps should be taken to improve Frizzle's cyber security and political risk management.

In addition to Stanford MBAs, we have run this simulation for national reporters and senior congressional staff.[63] Each time, most of our Frizzle "executives"—who come from all over the world and all different industries and backgrounds—want to get in front of the story as fast as they possibly can. This instinct is natural. Yet moving too fast runs some hidden risks. The biggest one is that the engineering team does not yet know what it is dealing with. Is the worst over or yet to come? Typically, a few hours into an attack, it is impossible to know. As one real-world chief information security officer of a major tech company told us, "The first twenty-four to forty-eight hours of a major breach are usually crazy. We have to let the engineers do their thing to stop the bleeding. It's all very foggy. It takes discipline to stay calm." Staying calm is especially important in cyber crises because if adversaries are tipped off too soon, they can change their methods and inflict even more damage before the company can bolster its defenses. The company also has to contend with breach reporting and remediation requirements that vary by state and country and could turn company offices into a crime scene, making it harder to stop the attack. Going public as fast as possible may seem like a good idea but may make life worse for the customers and the company. While responding quickly is important, executives today need to resist the urge to respond so fast that they provide inaccurate information, worsen the damage, or make promises about fixes that they cannot deliver.

> "The first twenty-four to forty-eight hours of a major breach are usually crazy. We have to let the engineers do their thing to stop the bleeding. It's all very foggy. It takes discipline to stay calm."
> —Tech company chief information security officer

Target could have used this advice when it was hit with a cyber attack during the 2013 Christmas shopping season. The breach was a watershed event, one of the largest thefts of consumer information. An estimated forty million payment cards and personal records of seventy million Target shoppers were stolen.[64] The breach and resulting negative publicity came at a terrible time for the retail giant, and Target's response made it worse. Eager to get in front of the story, Target sent frequent updates. But they contained conflicting information, giving the impression that executives did not understand what they were facing. Customers flooded Target with complaints and questions, jamming phone lines and causing the company's credit card website to crash.[65] Efforts to provide information backfired and efforts to reassure customers ended up annoying them. The stock price tumbled, and within six months, CEO Gregg Steinhafel resigned.

Communications experts often highlight the importance of issuing statements immediately: Studies find that 20 percent of online news stories about a subject appear within just eight hours of its occurrence.[66] Research also finds that the longer executives wait to take action, the less moral they seem, even if they ultimately make a decision judged to be moral.[67] But Target shows that speedier is not always better. As we discuss below, the best way to navigate this terrain is for executives to communicate values immediately, explaining what they stand for and what steps they intend to take.

The upshot is this: Do not say what you know. You could end

up being wrong. Instead, say what values you believe in and what actions you will take to get to the bottom of the crisis while you figure out what is going on.

Step 2: Activate the team.

In 1982, Johnson & Johnson did not have a crisis response team, so CEO James Burke formed one as soon as the news broke.[68] J&J's experience is exemplary, but twenty-first-century crises demand more. Today, no company should be designating a crisis response team or formulating a plan *after* a crisis breaks. Companies should already have a system in place for reporting crises, a plan for gathering and sharing relevant information, and well-defined roles that are updated and practiced. Not everything can be anticipated, but having these basic capabilities in place provides a head start.

Marriott's Alan Orlob likens corporate crisis response to military training. As he puts it, "The military spends a lot of time training soldiers so that when confronted by the enemy, they don't need to think. They react to the training they received."[69] Marriott regularly conducts tabletop exercises simulating various scenarios to hone processes, define roles, and learn new lessons. When the Jakarta JW Marriott was attacked by terrorists in 2003, it took just thirty minutes to assemble Marriott International's crisis team on a conference call in the middle of the night. The roles and tasks were already clear.

Step 3: Lead with values.

Reputation expert Daniel Diermeier finds that when crises erupt, managers too often get sidetracked figuring out who is to blame.[70] That is not what customers and other stakeholders want to hear. They want to hear what your company stands for and why. They want to know what you will do to earn back their trust. They want to know that you care, that you are committed, and that you are contrite.

J&J CEO James Burke knew what his company stood for. Johnson & Johnson's credo, crafted in 1943 by founding family member Robert Wood Johnson, states, "We believe our first responsibility is to the doctors, nurses, and patients, to mothers and fathers and all others who use our products and services." Burke took it seriously. To him, the credo meant that J&J had to safeguard the well-being of its customers even though the Tylenol deaths did not result from any corporate wrongdoing. The most important priority was protecting public health, not shareholder value. "The credo is all about the consumer," Burke later said. When the deaths occurred, "the credo made it very clear at that point exactly what we were all about. It gave me the ammunition I needed to persuade shareholders and others to spend the $100 million on the recall. The credo helped sell it."[71] It was Burke who pushed for a nationwide recall against the wishes and advice of the FBI and the Food and Drug Administration, who thought a recall might embolden the perpetrator and stoke public anxiety.[72]

Burke's second goal was saving the Tylenol brand. This would only be possible, he believed, by meeting the crisis head-on, undertaking enormous costs to pull the product, addressing public fears fast and fully, and then relaunching a better tamper-resistant Tylenol product as fast as possible. At the time, Burke's approach defied conventional marketing wisdom, which counseled keeping a low profile and circling the wagons until the crisis passed. "Before 1982, nobody ever recalled anything," said Albert Tortorella, a managing director at Burson-Marsteller, the public relations firm that advised Johnson & Johnson. "Companies often fiddle while Rome burns."[73]

Johnson & Johnson was a victim of a crime. Most companies facing political crises are not. For them, the lesson from J&J is the power of accepting responsibility. Assuming full responsibility for a crisis, even one not of your making, and demonstrating that your organization truly cares about rebuilding trust can go a long way. In the medical field, for example, research finds that honest disclosure of mistakes reduces malpractice lawsuits dramatically.[74] Conversely, dodging responsibility for a crisis or issuing halfhearted expressions of concern is likely to backfire and spark greater furor.[75]

That's what United Airlines CEO Oscar Munoz learned in April 2017 when he issued a lackluster apology for having to, in his words, "re-accommodate these customers" after video surfaced showing police forcibly removing a sixty-nine-year-old passenger from an overbooked United flight to make room for United employees. The passenger, Dr. David Dao, was seated on the last flight of the day. "I won't go, I'm a physician, have to work tomorrow, eight o'clock...," Dao explained. Police then proceeded to drag him off the plane in front of horrified passengers. Dao sustained a concussion, a broken nose, and broken teeth. "Oh my God! Look at what you did to him!" screamed one passenger in the video.

Munoz's uncaring apology fueled outrage online and in the press, prompting calls for new legislation to change airline overbooking practices and protect consumers. Hours later, Munoz exacerbated the crisis by issuing a letter to United employees (which leaked immediately) blaming Dao for being "disruptive and belligerent."[76] Munoz eventually reversed course, saying, "No one should ever be mistreated this way," and promising a review of United policies, but the public relations damage was severe.[77] It was a textbook case of how *not* to handle a crisis. "The back-against-the-wall, through-gritted-teeth apology isn't generally a winning strategy," noted Jeremy Robinson-Leon, a public relations partner at Group Gordon.[78]

The moral of the story is that genuine contrition matters. Corporate crises are ultimately about trust. The best way to restore trust is to own the problem, know your company's core values, and manage to them. That is particularly true today, when polls show that trust in business executives is not much higher than it is in used-car salesmen.[79] As J&J CEO James Burke reflected before his death in 2012, "Trust has been an operative word in my life. [It] embodies almost everything you can strive for that will help you to succeed. You tell me any human relationship that works without trust, whether it is a marriage or a friendship or a social interaction; in the long run, the same thing is true about business."[80]

Step 4: Tell your story.

As we discuss above, companies need to be careful about letting their desire to say something fast cause them to say something wrong that could erode stakeholder trust. But taking time to gather facts does not mean that companies should stay silent. They need to tell their story rather than hiding from the press and difficult conversations. As FedEx's Fred Smith told us, "We live in an unprecedented real-time diffuse communications environment and you're generally not in control of the narrative that somebody wants to advance and you have to be equally adept in that milieu to be able to deal with it."

> "We live in an unprecedented real-time diffuse communications environment and you're generally not in control of the narrative that somebody wants to advance and you have to be equally adept in that milieu to be able to deal with it."
>
> —Fred Smith, founder, chairman, and CEO, FedEx

Smith is no stranger to these real-time communications challenges. On Thursday, January 26, 2017, a FedEx delivery driver tried to stop some protesters from burning American flags outside a shopping mall in Iowa. A video circulated online showing the driver, Matt Uhrin, using a fire extinguisher to put out the fire, pushing back the protesters, and taking one of the flags away. It went viral. Then erroneous reports surfaced that FedEx had decided to discipline or fire Uhrin and an uproar ensued. Online petitions gathered thousands of signatures. "Let's make sure Matt Uhrin keeps his job at FedEx," noted one petition movement. "He was standing up for our American flag and should be commended, not punished."[81]

FedEx's crisis team unit jumped into action. As Smith told us, the company made a decision to support the driver and communicated it quickly. On Friday, FedEx communications adviser Jim Masilak sent an initial statement to the Daily Caller News Foundation saying that the company had "reviewed the facts of the incident and interviewed our courier to better understand what took place. As with all personnel issues, we are handling the matter internally."[82] By 7:30 on Saturday morning, FedEx issued a press release and sent it out on Twitter, stating, "We have reviewed the matter in Iowa City involving driver Matt Uhrin. He remains a FedEx employee & we have no plans to change his status." The crisis quickly subsided.

FedEx is in many ways a best-practice crisis response company because it has to respond to crises nearly all the time, from driver interactions caught on video to lost packages. "We're primed to respond in this way perhaps more so than other companies because we operate in real time with all kinds of major equipment (such as airplanes)," Smith reflected. "We also try to actively respond to complaints on social media. Given our state-of-the-art tracking system, we're usually able within a few seconds to tell customers where their packages are."

How can companies in other industries—where the business model does not demand real-time response to customer concerns—handle sudden crises effectively? How can they react quickly without falling into the Target trap? The answer is by carefully distinguishing between facts and values. Facts take time to unfold. Values can be communicated immediately.

When the 2009 Jakarta terrorist attacks struck two Marriott-operated properties, some senior executives wanted the company to stay as far away from the press as possible. That's a common and natural response. Alan Orlob, though, sensed that there could be benefits to surfing the media wave and talking directly about how seriously Marriott took security when the eyes of the world were on them. As he told us, "There's a huge advantage to being able to get your word out when there's an event like that." Orlob was careful to avoid speculating or commenting about what could have gone wrong; instead, he focused on communicating his determination to find out and fix it. He told Marriott's story.

When Royal Caribbean International got hit with a wave of bad publicity after the 2010 earthquake in Haiti, Adam Goldstein was also quick to communicate what mattered to him and why. His message: Cruise ships were not docking in Labadee to party, they were docking there to help—bringing relief supplies as well as badly needed revenues from tourists to help the stricken nation recover. Goldstein delivered the message himself, through traditional media and his blog. He put a human face on the corporation's response and explained how Royal Caribbean International was helping Haiti. Reporters cut and pasted from the blog as though they were quoting him directly. It was the first time Goldstein used his blog to communicate during a crisis. Now it is standard practice for him. Goldstein was ahead of his time. A 2014 study found that two-thirds of Fortune 500 CEOs still had no social media presence.[83]

Third parties, such as NGOs, foreign government officials, and academic experts, can also play an important role in telling your story by lending credibility in times of crisis. This kind of support helped Royal Caribbean International. Because communications in Haiti were in disarray after the earthquake, the cruise line could not get an immediate statement from the Haitian government. But a Haitian official named Leslie Voltaire was visiting New York at the time, so Goldstein asked if he would issue a brief statement explaining that the government wanted Royal Caribbean International ships to keep coming. Voltaire did. "That was very helpful," Goldstein told us. "It was not just about us anymore."

Orlob found the same thing. After a Marriott property in Islamabad was struck by terrorists, a terrorism expert in Singapore named Dr. Rohan Gunaratna wrote an article posted on the well-respected SITE Intelligence Group blog about the increasing threat to hotels and the security measures that Marriott was taking. Professor Gunaratna called the Marriott in Islamabad "the world's most protected hotel."[84] Immediately after the attack, many American companies and officials said they no longer wanted to stay in the Islamabad Marriott. Orlob could use Dr. Gunaratna's article to show them what type of security Marriott actually had to confront the rising terrorist threat there. "It wasn't just me telling the story. It was an outside expert telling the story," Orlob told us. It made a difference.

Step 5: Do not fan the flames.

Finally, organizations need to be aware that they are always speaking to multiple audiences. Each can fan the flames, creating new risks and worsening the crisis. Media reports. Statements by local and state leaders. Grassroots boycotts. Congressional hearings and legislative proposals. Federal investigations and regulations. Actions by international governments and customers. Each of these actions and audiences can affect the others. As Daniel Diermeier notes, "Once the company is portrayed as a villain, many public officials will vie for the role of hero."[85]

That's exactly what happened to British Petroleum after the *Deepwater Horizon* oil spill. As oil slicks washed ashore and live underwater video showed the broken well spewing oil continuously into the Gulf, BP CEO Tony Hayward declared that the explosion was not BP's fault, that the environmental impact was likely to be "very, very modest,"[86] and that everything was under control.[87] The attempt at reassurance backfired horribly, casting the quiet geologist as a callous corporate villain who was more concerned about blaming others than accepting responsibility or showing compassion. So Hayward went to Louisiana to apologize in person and put a human face on BP's response. But his comments there got him in more trouble. "There's no one who wants this thing over more than I do. I'd like my life back," he said to a crowd of reporters, on camera.[88] Public anger boiled over. "These are the most idiotic statements I've ever heard," declared irate Louisiana governor Bobby Jindal. "If I was on that board, I would wonder about trusting a multibillion-dollar company to somebody who's making those kind of statements."[89] Hayward ending up having to apologize for his apology tour.

BP's expensive national advertising campaign also struck the wrong chord, suggesting the company had the spill under control when it didn't. "We will get this done, we will make this right," Hayward declared in one television spot. Crisis management consultant Glenn Selig likened it to a doctor in an emergency room full of dying people telling family members that everything will be fine.[90]

Tony Hayward became the most vilified man in America. Daily headlines covered his gaffes. Everyone piled on. Presidential spokesman Robert Gibbs took aim at him from the White House press room. Congressional leaders of both parties pummeled BP and its chief executive. Hayward's appearance at a June 17 House hearing was described as "a public execution."[91] The next day, Hayward was removed from day-to-day control over the company's oil spill response. In July, he announced his resignation. At a gathering of board members, he said handling the *Deepwater Horizon* crisis was like "stepping out from the pavement and being hit by a bus."[92]

The Spy Plane Crisis and Condi's Multiple Audience Challenge

The risks posed by multiple audiences affect governments, not just companies. Soon after Condi began serving as national security adviser, a Chinese fighter jet collided with an American surveillance plane in international airspace, leading to the death of the Chinese pilot and an emergency landing of the American plane in China. The American crew were detained on Hainan Island while the two governments negotiated the terms of their release. For President Bush, the goals were clear: The crew had to be treated well and released; there would be no compromising of American values by apologizing for conducting surveillance in international airspace; and the relationship with China needed to be maintained. Neither side wanted to escalate the situation. But negotiations were complicated by the multiple audience problem. "Every time you speak," Condi reflected, "all parties are listening. You can't say, 'Okay, China, you only listen to this part. Congress, you only listen to that part.' You have to think about all of your audiences in each statement." At one point, every day a spokesperson would go out in front of the press. The White House would want to say something new, but each time a new statement would escalate the rhetoric from different audiences, which made the crisis all the more difficult to resolve. So the crisis team met twice a day every day, carefully working the communications strategy to show that the two governments were working on the problem without triggering an escalation spiral. After seven days of intense negotiations, the United States and China agreed to a deal: The crew were released, and the Chinese received a letter from U.S. ambassador to China Joseph Prueher expressing regret for the pilot's loss of life without issuing an apology for the incident.

Multiple audiences also became a challenge for United Airlines, causing its crisis to escalate. Within forty-eight hours, the passenger dragging incident moved from social media to mainstream media; triggered calls for congressional hearings and a federal investigation; outrage in China, one of United's most important foreign markets (where more than one hundred million Chinese viewed the video); and a $255 million loss in shareholder value. We capture the forty-eight-hour escalation in the chart below.

United's Unfriendly Skies: Escalating Political Risks

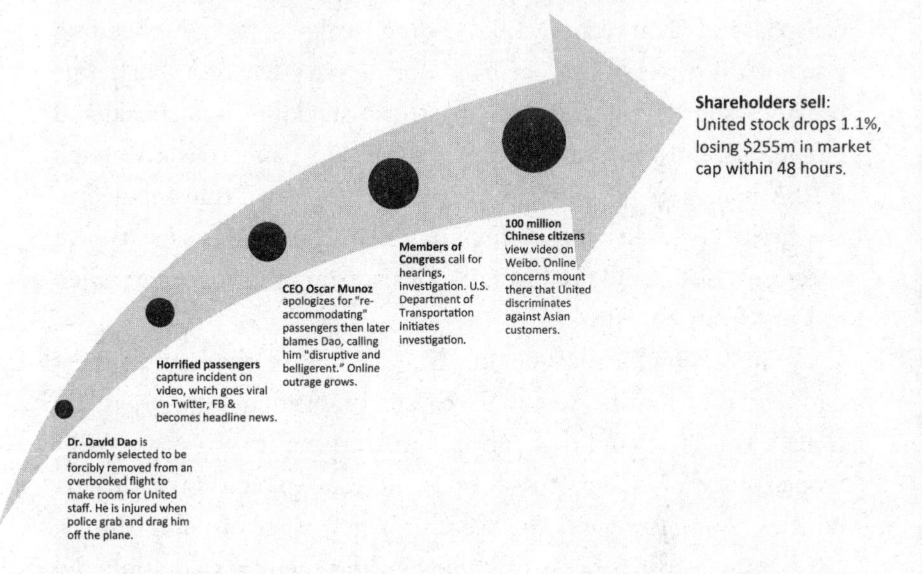

Venture capitalist Marc Andreessen described the predicaments of BP and United Airlines well. He told us, "Things happen in the world, right? Some of those things then become big deals in the press. And then there's a feedback loop. Something that becomes a big deal in the press, that's going to cause governments to come after you. Or vice versa. Governments coming after you can cause things to happen in the press...That's a dynamic that results in your company becoming a political punching bag in a way that's kind of hard to recover from."

3. Are we developing mechanisms for continuous learning?

Responding well to a crisis in the moment is part of the battle. Developing mechanisms to remember the right lessons from that crisis is another.

Here, too, NASA provides a tragic tale of a learning failure. Seventeen years after the *Challenger* tragedy, the space shuttle *Columbia* exploded, killing all seven astronauts on board. This time the fatal cause was foam shedding from the shuttle's external fuel tank, which damaged a thermal shield on the wing during liftoff and caused it to fail on reentry. Like O-ring weaknesses, foam shedding was not a surprise. It had occurred during sixty-five of seventy-nine previous shuttle launches.[93] At first, the shedding was considered dangerous. But the more it happened, the less dangerous it seemed. NASA managers fell into the exact same cognitive trap that led to the first shuttle disaster, seeing sixty-five near misses as sixty-five successes. NASA did not just fail to learn from near misses. It failed to learn from tragedy.

Our Stanford colleague Jim March, one of the world's most eminent sociologists, spent his career examining how organizations learn. He found that continuous learning involves two skills: "the exploration of new possibilities and the exploitation of old certainties."[94] *Exploration* is the search for new ways of doing things. *Exploitation* is the process of implementing them. Exploration and exploitation often compete and conflict. "The essence of exploration is experimentation with new alternatives,"[95] March wrote. "The essence of exploitation is the refinement and extension of existing competences, technologies, and paradigms." One process is creative, disruptive, and uncertain. The other is efficient, order-inducing, and predictable. Companies that excel at continuous learning keep exploration and exploitation in productive tension.[96] This is hard to do.

Even Johnson & Johnson has struggled to balance exploration

and exploitation. Back in 1982, CEO James Burke developed new ways to manage crises that flew in the face of conventional wisdom. He excelled at exploration. Exploitation has been more challenging. In 2012, a Wharton Business School article asked, "Has the Company Lost Its Way?"[97] The article found that J&J wasn't sustaining its own best practices. In the 2000s, under the leadership of CEO William Weldon, the company suffered a string of major product recalls, including household name brands like Benadryl and Children's Tylenol as well as products ranging from contact lenses to Rolaids to artificial hips. J&J also faced heightened regulatory scrutiny, critical congressional hearings, and several state lawsuits over improper marketing of its antipsychotic medication Risperdal.[98] In 2011, the Food and Drug Administration put three facilities under consent decree.[99] Johnson & Johnson issued at least eleven major product recalls, nearly twice as many as health care product giant Pfizer or Procter & Gamble, the largest consumer products company in the world.[100] Quality control problems cost an estimated $1 billion in lost sales.[101]

Many believe that one reason for J&J's decline was the company's drift from its core values as the number of its subsidiaries mushroomed, global business grew, and profit pressures increased. "I think the credo used to be quite real there," says Erik Gordon, a professor at the University of Michigan's Ross School of Business. "There was a time when people really believed in it and took great pride in it. But those days are long gone."[102] *Fortune* described the period as a "cascading reputational and quality-control crisis" that had "engulfed" the company's consumer business.[103]

In February 2012, when CEO Weldon stepped down and Alex Gorsky took the helm, Gorsky's first presentation to the board outlining his long-term vision centered on the company credo.[104] Among his priorities: creating a unified company out of 250 different global subsidiaries, each operating relatively autonomously. Values were at the core. Today, across Johnson & Johnson there are "credo challenges" where business decisions are evaluated according to the credo. There are also biannual credo surveys that ask employees to assess how well the business is upholding the credo.[105] J&J still has its share of crises, and it is still struggling to respond effectively to them, but the company is taking major steps to relearn the lessons of 1982.[106]

The best learning organizations we know may surprise you: top-notch football teams. We admit it, we both love football. Condi's father was a collegiate athletic administrator who taught her the intricacies of the sport, among other ways, by insisting she play in his backyard holiday game called "The Rice Bowl." Amy's grandfather was a judge who spent his free time recruiting young men from nearby western Pennsylvania steel towns to play for his alma mater, the University of Michigan.

But it also happens to be true. Years ago, Martin Landau and Donald Chisholm seized on football as the ultimate learning organization. "American football may be a game of inches, but above all else, it is a game where success depends on the consistent and progressive reduction of error," they wrote.[107] In football, error is everywhere and success and failure are obvious. In every game, only one team wins. Losing coaches do not keep their jobs for long. The most successful coaches study wins as well as losses, subjecting "every aspect of their plans and executions to careful analysis." Good coaches balance exploration and exploitation and engage in both processes continuously. Activities like watching game tape, devising plays to exploit opponents' weaknesses and capitalize on your strengths, and adjusting the lineup for better matchups are exercises in exploration—they are innovations to gain advantage. Activities like practicing hurry-up offense and conducting drills to hone the capabilities of specialized positions, including backup players, so they are ready to substitute in at a moment's notice are exercises in exploitation. Notably, Landau and Chisholm wrote that "many (if not most) of the coaching profession see their task as teaching."[108] Football teams really are learning organizations. Whether it's the National Football League or the NCAA, the best teams may not have the best talent; what they often do have are the best learning processes.

Consider one of our favorite examples, the turnaround track record of former Stanford coach Jim Harbaugh, who took Stanford from a tough 1–11 season to become a BCS bowl qualifier and top-ranked team in just four seasons. Harbaugh did the same thing in the NFL. When he joined the San Francisco 49ers in 2011, the team had not had a winning season in eight years. In his first season as head coach, the 49ers, with very little turnover in the roster, won 13 games, the division title, and made it to the NFC Championship Game.[109] Then in 2014 Harbaugh moved to the University of Michigan. Before he arrived, the Wolverines went 5–7.[110] During Harbaugh's first season, he took essentially the same players and finished with 10 wins, 3 losses, and a number 12 national ranking. Three teams, three turnarounds. What made the difference? Harbaugh's intensity, his exceptional ability to motivate a team, and his relentless focus on learning and competition. Everything to him is competitive. Improvement is a mind-set. "You are getting better or you are getting worse. You never stay the same," he likes to say.[111] He's not afraid to try something new or repeat what works. He takes exploration and exploitation seriously.

Harbaugh is a good reminder that continuous learning takes a heavy dose of leadership to work. Jim March is right that learning requires processes that enable both exploration and exploitation. But real life is not so sterile. Organizations in the real world are filled with people who respond to leaders and values that inspire. Creating mechanisms for continuous learning must involve both the head and the heart—a cold-nosed assessment of what to keep doing, what to stop doing, what to start doing, and an inspirational approach to get everyone to join the journey.

KEY TAKEAWAYS: RESPONDING TO CRISES

☐ The best way to deal with crises is not to have them. Capitalize on near misses by planning for failure, looking for weak signals, and rewarding courageous acts.

☐ Follow the five golden rules for crisis response:
(1) Assess the situation.
(2) Activate the team.
(3) Lead with values.
(4) Tell your story.
(5) Do not fan the flames.

☐ Develop mechanisms for continuous learning that balance the creative search for new ideas (exploration) and the systematic implementation of proven best practices (exploitation).

10

Strengthening Your Political Risk Muscles

When we started teaching our political risk course several years ago, some future trends seemed clear. North Korea's Kim Jong-un would pose a growing and grave nuclear danger. China's rise would probably challenge American influence in the Asia-Pacific. The brittle state system of the Middle East—cobbled together on the back of a napkin as the Ottoman Empire ended—would continue to generate instability and human suffering. Yet many developments were not so evident back then. We might have known that Russia would be a problem, but not that it would annex Crimea or wage information warfare campaigns via Facebook and Twitter. We expected the European Union would face stresses, but we did not expect Brexit. And many events were simply unimaginable. Who would have thought that Donald Trump would be elected president of the United States? That Brazil's Luiz Inacio Lula da Silva would go from popular presidential candidate to prison? Or that North Korean leader Kim Jong-un would cross the demilitarized zone to shake hands with South Korean president Moon Jae-in, marking the first time that a North Korean leader had set foot in the South since 1953?

Politics has always been an uncertain business. Technological innovations; government institutions; individual leaders; the ambitions, emotions, and aspirations of peoples—these are large forces.

Understand	Analyze
1. What is my organization's political risk appetite?	**1. How can we get good information about the political risks we face?**
Develop processes (e.g., annual risk setting workshops) to make risk appetite explicit and updated.	Collect information that is specific to your needs, includes perception and emotions of key stakeholders, and answers the right questions.
2. Is there a shared understanding of our risk appetite? If not, how can we foster one?	**2. How can we ensure rigorous analysis?**
Create a common language for discussing risk and a consistent process for identifying, evangelizing, and owning risk.	Harness tools like scenario planning, red teams, and thinking backwards. The goal is not to predict the future but to make better decisions by "re-perceiving."
3. How can we reduce blind spots?	**3. How can we integrate political risk analysis into business decisions?**
Develop processes that foster imagination, a better understanding of others' perspectives, and truth-telling to guard against groupthink.	Bake in political risk thinking instead of bolting it on at the end of a business decision. Political risk analysts need to be close to business units, understand their needs, and deliver useful inputs.

Sometimes they move gradually and incrementally. At other times, they move suddenly and seismically. No one can see precisely how human history will unfold.

But managing political risk does not have to be pure guesswork. You do not have to know exactly where political risk will come from if you are well prepared—if you are looking in all directions, considering political risks at the highest levels, and developing planning and thinking across your organization. Just as world-class athletes enhance their performance through strength and conditioning training, companies can improve their performance by

Mitigate	Respond
1. How can we reduce exposure to the risks we have identified?	**1. Are we capitalizing on near misses?**
Identify where asset value and vulnerability converge; build the nuclear triad (disperse critical assets); fly the empty plane (build flexible surge capacity); align with others in the industry.	Plan for failure, not success; look for weak signals; reward courageous acts.
2. Do we have a good system in place for timely warning and action?	**2. Are we reacting effectively to crises?**
Develop proactive, timely situational awareness for risks "knocking on the door" and tripwires that trigger protocols and actions.	Follow five key steps: Stop the bleeding, activate the team, communicate what matters to you and why, tell your story, and beware of multiple audiences.
3. How can we limit the damage when something bad happens?	**3. Are we developing mechanisms for continuous learning?**
Drink the cup of coffee: Build relationships with key stakeholders before you need them.	Use counterfactuals; train, train, train; continuously reinforce company values as a touchstone for action.

building their all-around political risk muscles. We hope you will think of our framework as a workout plan or training guide to get your organization into better shape. Understanding, analyzing, mitigating, and responding to risks are the key elements. Our guiding questions provide more detailed exercises to hone your political risk capabilities. We pull together the main ones in the table above.

The most effective organizations have three big things in common: They take political risk seriously, they approach it systematically, and they lead from the top.

Some companies have no choice: They are born into industries that are buffeted by political action. Royal Dutch Shell invented modern-day scenario planning in the 1960s because executives knew they faced a volatile Middle East and a rising organization called OPEC, and they needed better tools to anticipate the future price of oil. FedEx has been managing political risk ever since Fred Smith delivered his first package. Any event that could interfere with a customer experience, whether it's a labor strike in Europe, food riots in Venezuela, or a tornado in Oklahoma, is his business. As Smith likes to say, the most important thing FedEx delivers is trust. He has been setting the company's culture and approach to risk for nearly half a century.

For other industries like movie studios and toy companies, the imperative to manage political risk is less obvious. Sony Pictures started caring a lot more about political risk after it was forced off the grid by a North Korean cyber attack. The Lego Group embraced political risk management only after a brush with bankruptcy.

Others see the writing on the wall too late. SeaWorld executives knew they were in an industry that carried significant political risks from animal rights groups and shows that put humans in tanks with dangerous killer whales. Yet the company did not take political risk seriously enough, manage it systematically, or drive action from the top. Instead, executives bet that the future would resemble the past—that Shamu would always be the company's most valuable asset. Risks were not managed so much as they were wished away.

Bad surprises will always happen. But organizations that take a serious, systematic, and senior-driven approach to political risk management are likely to be surprised less often and recover better. Companies that don't get these basics right are more likely to get blindsided—as were British Petroleum CEO Tony Hayward and United Airlines CEO Oscar Munoz.

British Petroleum chief executive Tony Hayward testifies before the oversight and investigations panel of the Energy and Commerce Committee, June 17, 2010.
Alex Brandon/Associated Press.

As these embattled corporate leaders learned, if something bad happens, it won't just be "the risk people" who have to answer for it.

Acknowledgments

This book began in a Stanford classroom. Nearly two hundred students have now taken our political risk seminar. Around a third have come from countries outside the United States—from places as wide-ranging as Brazil, China, India, Spain, and the Democratic Republic of the Congo. Their ideas and perspectives have sharpened our thinking, and their enthusiasm is what led us to put our thoughts on paper. This book is dedicated to them.

From the development of our course to the drafting of this manuscript, our institutional home bases—the Stanford Graduate School of Business (GSB), the Hoover Institution, and Stanford's Freeman Spogli Institute for International Studies (FSI)—have been generous in support and helpful at every step. We would like to thank the leadership of each organization for sustaining this project and our work: GSB dean Jonathan Levin, Hoover director Tom Gilligan, and FSI director Michael McFaul.

We would also like to express our gratitude to the people who took time out of their busy schedules to assist us and in doing so enabled us to write a better book. Special thanks are due to the business practitioners who agreed to sit for interviews, including Marc Andreessen, Bibi Bleekemolen, Cam Burks, Pat Donovan, Adam Goldstein, Tom Hill, Vinod Khosla, Karen Laureano-Rikardsen, Alan Orlob, Fred Smith, Joe Sullivan, Peter Thiel, and Peter Whelpton. Others spoke to us on background. We hope they know how grateful we are. We are also greatly appreciative of the comments we received from Craig Mallery, Keith Hennessey, and

Wayne Kabak, who carefully reviewed every word of the manuscript and provided invaluable feedback.

Over several years, we have been aided by an all-star team of research and course assistants led by Taylor Johnson McLamb and Charles Nicas. This book quite simply could not have been written without them. Katherine Boyle, Alexa Corse, Caroline Keller-Lynn, Iris Malone, Andrew Milich, Julia Payson, and Michael Robinson provided outstanding research and fact-checking. Since our political risk seminar began, we have been fortunate to have a number of other assistants, many of whom contributed to the development of case studies in this book. They included Sarah Benjamin, Nandi Chhabra, Matthew Decker, Torey McMurdo, Astasia Myers, Jenna Nicholas, Jessica Renier, Sarah Shirazyan, and Derick Stace-Naughton.

Many colleagues have discussed ideas, read parts of the book, or answered research queries from one or both of us. To Bill Barnett, Coit Blacker, Nick Burns, Bobby Chesney, Martha Crenshaw, Tino Cuellar, Kristen Eichensehr, Karl Eikenberry, Rod Ewing, Jim Fearon, Niall Ferguson, Joe Felter, Tom Fingar, Frank Fukuyama, Andrea Gilli, Toomas Ilves, Sean Kanuck, David Kennedy, Steve Krasner, Sarah Kreps, Herb Lin, Jane Holl Lute, Eric Min, Michael Morell, Chick Perrow, Bill Perry, Jason Reinhardt, Scott Sagan, Matt Spence, Eli Sugarman, John Taylor, Mike Tomz, Harold Trinkunas, John Villasenor, Matt Waxman, Jessica Weeks, and Keren Yahri-Milo, thank you.

We are both grateful to Sean Desmond, our gifted editor, and all of the fine people of Twelve Books.

Amy would like to thank her incredible Hoover team who make everything possible: Caroline Beswick, Nga-my Pham Nguyen, and Russell Wald. She is also deeply grateful to the faculty, fellows, students, and staff at the Center for International Security and Cooperation, for creating such a vibrant intellectual home. Literary agent Christy Fletcher has provided years of great advice. Thank you, Lisa Hammann and Courtney Kingston, for cofounding Room 130. Thanks to the Zegart and Mallery clans—and especially Craig, Alex, Jack, and Kate, for indulging in scary international security dinner conversations every night.

Finally, Amy would like to thank Condi for welcoming her into that comparative politics seminar back in 1991, inspiring her to become a political scientist, and being there, always, ever since. Condi's immense talent is equaled only by her generosity of spirit. Working with her—first as a student and now as a colleague—has been the honor and joy of a lifetime.

Condi would like to thank her dedicated staff. She would not have been able to complete this book while juggling her other commitments without their untiring support. Enduring thanks goes to her chief of staff Shannon York (and her predecessor Georgia Godfrey), her office manager Jules Thompson (and her predecessor Caroline Beswick), and her longtime assistant Marilyn Stanley. For Condi, working on this book, and the seminar that predates it, has been a rare and rewarding experience. Amy was a graduate student of hers many moons ago. Amy has always been a first-rate scholar, and she has since become a world-class author, professor, expert, and leader, both within her field and at our university. Teaching alongside her and collaborating on this project has been one of the true pleasures of Condi's professional life. Deepest thanks to her for that, and for her tireless efforts in bringing this book to fruition.

Notes

CHAPTER 1: THE *BLACKFISH* EFFECT

1. William Alden, "Public Offering Values SeaWorld at $2.5 Billion," *New York Times*, April 18, 2013, https://dealbook.nytimes.com/2013/04/18/seaworld-prices-i-p-o-at-top-of-range/?_r=0.

2. Samantha Bonar, "How *Blackfish* Director Gabriela Cowperthwaite Became SeaWorld's Worst Nightmare," *LA Weekly*, February 6, 2014, www.laweekly.com/arts/how-blackfish-director-gabriela-cowperthwaite-became-sea-worlds-worst-nightmare-4417148.

3. Rupert Neate, "Sea World Fights to Restore Its Image as Shares Sink in the Wake of Blackfish," *Guardian*, November 6, 2015, www.theguardian.com/environment/2015/nov/06/seaworld-blackfish-pr-profits-share-prices.

4. Tim Zimmermann, "First Person: How Far Will the Blackfish Effect Go?," *National Geographic*, January 13, 2014, http://news.nationalgeographic.com/news/2014/01/140113-blackfish-seaworld-killer-whale-orcas/. In October, CNN aired the movie alongside an organized Twitter campaign and cross-promotions on several of its popular shows, including *Crossfire* and *Anderson Cooper 360*. When *Blackfish* aired, CNN included #Blackfish on the screen to integrate Twitter and live-blogged conversations about the movie on CNN.com. Weeks later, Netflix released the film, and backlash against SeaWorld grew even more. Simon Rogers, "The #Blackfish Phenomenon: A Whale of a Tale Takes Over Twitter," Twitter, November 6, 2013, https://blog.twitter.com/2013/the-blackfish-phenomenon-a-whale-of-a-tale-takes-over-twitter.

5. Ibid.; Aly Weisman, "Big Music Acts Cancel SeaWorld Performance After 'Blackfish' Doc Shows Mistreatment of Whales," *Business Insider*, December 10, 2013, www.businessinsider.com/willie-nelson-barenaked-ladies-heart-cancel-seaworld-performance-after-blackfish-documentary-2013-12.

6. Christopher Palmeri and Mary Schlangenstein, "Virgin America Drops SeaWorld in Next Blow to Orca Parks," Bloomberg, October 14, 2014, www.bloomberg.com/news/articles/2014-10-14/virgin-america-drops-seaworld-in-next-blow-to-orca-parks; Stephen Messenger, "Hyundai Motor Cuts Ties with SeaWorld," *The Dodo*, November 14, 2014, www.thedodo.com/hyundai-cuts-ties-seaworld-819812155.html.

7. Roberto A. Ferdman, "What the Documentary 'Blackfish' Has Done to Sea World," *Washington Post*, December 12, 2014, www.washingtonpost.com/blogs/wonkblog/wp/2014/12/12/chart-what-the-documentary-blackfish-has-done-to-seaworld/.

8. Aly Weisman, "Why the Director of 'Blackfish' Hasn't Made a Penny Off the Film," *Business Insider*, March 19, 2014, www.businessinsider.com/blackfish-director-gabriela-cowperthwaite-made-no-money-from-film-2014-3; Rupert Neate, "SeaWorld Still Battling Blackfish Fallout as Profits Fall by $10m for the Year," *Guardian*, November 5, 2015, www.theguardian.com/us-news/2015/nov/05/seaworld-blackfish-fallout-profits-fall-by-10m.

9. Zimmermann, "How Far Will the Blackfish Effect Go?"

10. Ibid.

11. Many articles and books talk about emerging markets. Many others offer prognostications about the future of geopolitics. Legal experts examine corruption and the risk of contract breaches. Supply chain experts talk about global vulnerabilities and how to create more resilient organizations that can withstand sudden disruptions from natural disasters. But rarely do these disparate threads come together to offer a coherent tapestry of how political actions affect business or what business leaders can do to better handle political uncertainty. Research and teaching about "strategy beyond markets" in business schools has increased, but it is still tiny and underdeveloped. One recent study reviewed three years of the *Strategic Management Journal*, arguably the most prestigious business strategy academic journal, and found that fewer than 10 percent of its papers examined political risk topics. Between 2012 and 2014, fewer than 3 percent of the nearly two thousand presentations at the Strategic Management Conference, the premier academic strategy conference in the country, focused on political risk. John De Figueiredo, Michael Lenox, Felix Oberholzer-Gee, and Richard Vanden Bergh, *Strategy Beyond Markets* (Bingley, UK: Emerald, 2016), xvi.

12. In July 2015, "political risk" returned 251 hits, which included several materials we published for our course. "Business risk" returned 2,806 hits, and "global business" returned 4,518 hits.

13. Samantha Azzarello and Blu Putnam, "BRIC Country Update: Slowing Growth in the Face of Internal and External Challenges," *Market Insights*, CME Group, July 25, 2012, www.cmegroup.com/education/files/ed133-market-insights-bric-2012-8-1.pdf.

14. "Dating Game: When Will China Overtake America?," *Economist*, December 16, 2010, www.economist.com/node/17733177. In 2010, the *Economist* predicted the size of China's economy (calculating for purchasing power parity) would surpass that of the United States in 2019. In 2014, the IMF announced that using the PPP method, China had surpassed the United States as the world's largest economy, nearly five years ahead of predictions. See International Monetary Fund, World Economic Outlook Database, April 2015, www.imf.org/external/pubs/ft/weo/2015/01/weodata/index.aspx. If you had bet in 1950 what

countries would be advanced economies today, the smart money would have been on resource-rich nations in Africa, not the Asian tigers of Singapore, Hong Kong, Taiwan, and South Korea. Michael Spence, *The Next Convergence: The Future of Economic Growth in a Multispeed World* (New York: Farrar, Straus & Giroux, 2011); World Bank, Commission on Growth and Development, *The Growth Report Strategies for Sustained Growth and Inclusive Development*, 2008, https://openknowledge.worldbank.org/bitstream/handle/10986/6507/449860PUB0Box3101OFFICIAL0USE0ONLY1.pdf?sequence=1.

15. Renée Johnson and Geoffrey S. Becker, "U.S.-Russia Meat and Poultry Trade Issues," Congressional Research Service, April 2, 2010, http://nationalaglawcenter.org/wp-content/uploads/assets/crs/RS22948.pdf.

16. Globalization has also transformed higher education. Each year, about 40 percent of our Stanford MBA students have come from outside the United States, from countries including Brazil, China, Egypt, India, Israel, Lebanon, Mexico, Nigeria, Poland, Rwanda, Spain, and Ukraine.

CHAPTER 2: MOVE OVER, HUGO CHÁVEZ

1. Rory Carroll, "Chávez Bans Sale of Coke Zero in Venezuela," *Guardian*, June 11, 2009, www.theguardian.com/world/2009/jun/11/venezuela-coke-zero-hugo-chavez.

2. "Factbox: Venezuela's Nationalizations Under Chavez," Reuters, October 7, 2012, www.reuters.com/article/2012/10/08/us-venezuela-election-nationalizations-idUSBRE89701X20121008.

3. Witold J. Henisz and Bennet A. Zelner, "The Hidden Risks in Emerging Markets," *Harvard Business Review*, April 2010, reprinted in Harvard Business Review, *Thriving in Emerging Markets* (Boston: Harvard Business Review Publishing, 2011), 204.

4. Nader's book *Unsafe at Any Speed* attacked the safety record of American automobile manufacturers, who at the time were largely unregulated. Nader claimed that in 1964 alone, more than forty-seven thousand people were killed in auto accidents, and he accused U.S. car companies of designing vehicles with an emphasis on style rather than consumer safety. When he presented his findings at a Senate hearing in 1966, a firestorm erupted when it was revealed that General Motors had hired private investigators to find derogatory information to discredit him as a witness. In September 1966, President Lyndon Johnson signed the National Traffic and Motor Vehicle Safety Act, which established federal safety standards for U.S.-made cars, including seat belts for all passengers. Patricia Cronin Marcello, *Ralph Nader: A Biography* (Westport, CT: Greenwood Press, 2004), 17–27.

5. "Passenger Forcibly Removed from United Flight, Prompting Outcry," *All Things Considered*, National Public Radio, April 10, 2017, www.npr.org/sections/thetwo-way/2017/04/10/523275494/passenger-forcibly-removed-from-united-flight-prompting-outcry; Daniel Victor and Matt Stevens, "United Passenger Dragged from Overbooked Flight," *New York Times*, April 10, 2017,

www.nytimes.com/2017/04/10/business/united-flight-passenger-dragged.html; Roger Cheng, "United Airlines Gets Black Eye over Passenger Ejection Video," CNET, April 10, 2017, www.cnet.com/news/united-airlines-passenger-ejected-in-intense-facebook-video/; press release from Eleanor Holmes Norton, April 10, 2017, http://norton.house.gov/media-center/press-releases/norton-wants-hearing-on-abusive-removal-of-united-airlines-passenger.

6. Victor Reklaitis, "United's Stock Falls 1.1%, Wipes Out $255 Million off the Airline's Market Cap," MarketWatch, April 12, 2017, www.marketwatch.com/story/uniteds-stock-is-set-to-fall-5-and-wipe-1-billion-off-the-airlines-market-cap-2017-04-11.

7. James Griffiths and Serenitie Wang, "Man Filmed Being Dragged Off United Flight Causes Outrage in China," CNN, April 11, 2017, www.cnn.com/2017/04/11/asia/united-passenger-dragged-off-china-reaction/.

8. Quoted in Mohamad Bazzi, "The Two Greatest Threats to U.S.-Iran Détente," Reuters, January 22, 2016, http://blogs.reuters.com/great-debate/2016/01/22/the-two-greatest-threats-to-a-united-states-iran-detente/.

9. Cara Lyttle, "FDI in Iran Soars with Sanctions Relief," *Financial Times*, June 20, 2016, www.ft.com/cms/s/3/549d0dac-36d6-11e6-9a05-82a9b15a8ee7.html#axzz4DsLV4f3e.

10. "California's Economy Is Bigger Than All but Five Nations, World Bank Data Says," *San Jose Mercury News*, July 5, 2016, www.mercurynews.com/2016/07/05/californias-economy-is-bigger-than-all-but-five-nations-world-bank-data-says/.

11. "Governor Abbott Rejects Obama Administration's Request to Lift Iran Sanctions," Office of the Texas Governor, May 16, 2016, http://gov.texas.gov/news/press-release/22315.

12. Andrew Soergel, "Economy Still Reeling from West Coast Slowdown," *U.S. News & World Report*, February 23, 2016, www.usnews.com/news/articles/2016-02-23/a-year-later-west-coast-labor-disputes-cost-still-unresolved; Laura Stevens and Paul Ziobro, "Ports Gridlock Reshapes the Supply Chain," *Wall Street Journal*, March 5, 2015, www.wsj.com/articles/ports-gridlock-reshapes-the-supply-chain-1425567704.

13. Ibid.; Robert J. Bowman, "A Vow After West Coast Port Disruption: Never Again," *SupplyChainBrain*, June 1, 2015, www.supplychainbrain.com/content/general-scm/global-supply-chain-mgmt/single-article-page/article/a-vow-after-west-coast-port-disruption-never-again/.

14. Quoted in Devon Maylie, "Alcoa Invests Near Planned Mines," *Wall Street Journal*, March 24, 2008, www.wsj.com/articles/SB120631154713558085.

15. Quoted in ibid.

16. Lu Wei, "Dream of the Web," speech at Diaoyutai State Guesthouse, February 9, 2015, http://cmp.hku.hk/2015/02/17/lu-wei-on-the-dream-of-the-web/.

17. "Jane Stanford: The Woman Behind Stanford University," Stanford University, http://archive.is/80g7.

18. Mike Lennon, "Hackers Hit 100 Banks in 'Unprecedented' $1 Billion Cyber Heist: Kaspersky Lab," *SecurityWeek*, February 15, 2015, www.securityweek.com/hackers-hit-100-banks-unprecedented-1-billion-cyber-attack-kaspersky-lab.

19. Statement from the press secretary, the White House, February 15, 2018.

20. The effort to integrate Europe began in the aftermath of World War II, with the creation of the NATO military alliance (1949), the European Coal and Steel Community (1951), and the European Economic Community (1957). Membership in European institutions expanded over the decades and culminated in the creation of the European Union in 1991.

21. Democracies fight wars against non-democracies. The key finding is that democracies almost never wage wars on other democracies. There is a rich literature in political science about what explains the democratic peace and the unique advantages of democratic regimes in international affairs more broadly. See, for example, Michael W. Doyle, "Kant, Liberal Legacies, and Foreign Affairs," *Philosophy and Public Affairs* 12, no. 3 (Summer 1983): 205–35; Bruce Russett, *Grasping the Democratic Peace* (Princeton, NJ: Princeton University Press, 1993); John M. Owen, "How Liberalism Produces Democratic Peace," *International Security* 19, no. 2 (Fall 1994): 87–125; James D. Fearon, "Domestic Political Audiences and the Escalation of International Disputes," *American Political Science Review* 88, no. 3 (September 1994): 577–92.

22. "Security Council Subsidiary Bodies: An Overview," United Nations, www.un.org/sc/committees/index.shtml; "UN Sanctions," Security Council Report, November 25, 2013, www.securitycouncilreport.org/atf/cf/%7B65BFCF9B-6D27-4E9C-8CD3-CF6E4FF96FF9%7D/special_research_report_sanctions_2013.pdf, p. 3.

23. Yossi Sheffi, *The Resilient Enteprise: Overcoming Vulnerability for Competitive Advantage* (Cambridge, MA: MIT Press, 2005), 165–66, citing Christopher B. Pickett, "Strategies for Maximizing Supply Chain Resilience: Learning from the Past to Prepare for the Future" (Master of Engineering in Logistics thesis, MIT, June 2003), http://hdl.handle.net/1721.1/28579.

24. Adrian Edwards, "Global Forced Displacement Hits Record High," UNHCR, June 20, 2016, www.unhcr.org/en-us/news/latest/2016/6/5763b65a4/global-forced-displacement-hits-record-high.html.

25. William Spindler, "Ukraine Internal Displacement Nears 1 Million as Fighting Escalates in Donetsk Region," ed. Leo Dobbs, UNHCR, February 6, 2015, www.unhcr.org/54d4a2889.html.

26. Amnesty International, "Syria's Refugee Crisis in Numbers," updated December 20, 2016, www.amnesty.org/en/latest/news/2016/02/syrias-refugee-crisis-in-numbers/.

27. The Rohingya are a Muslim minority group in Burma who have been denied citizenship and for decades have faced discrimination and persecution by the Burmese government. The United Nations classifies them as one of the most persecuted refugee groups in the world. Cf. Austin Ramzy, "Rohingya Refugees

Fleeing Myanmar Await Entrance to Squalid Camps," *New York Times*, October 18, 2017, https://www.nytimes.com/2017/10/18/world/asia/rohingya-refugees-myanmar.html; Lucy Westcott, "Who Are the Rohingya and Why Are They Fleeing Myanmar?," *Newsweek*, May 11, 2015, www.newsweek.com/who-are-rohingya-and-why-are-they-fleeing-myanmar-330728.

28. Paul Collier, *Wars, Guns, and Votes: Democracy in Dangerous Places* (New York: HarperCollins, 2009).

29. Andrew Flowers, "How Thailand's Coup Could Affect Its Economy," FiveThirtyEight, May 23, 2014, http://fivethirtyeight.com/datalab/how-thailands-coup-could-affect-its-economy/.

30. Marek Strzelecki, "Poland Shale Boom Falters as State Targets Higher Taxes," Bloomberg, May 21, 2013, www.bloomberg.com/news/2013-05-20/poland-shale-boom-falters-as-state-targets-higher-taxes-energy.html.

31. Ibid.

32. "Poland Says Will Not Tax Shale Gas Output Until 2020," Reuters, May 22, 2013, www.reuters.com/article/2013/05/22/poland-shale-idUSL6N0E320Q20130522; "Poland Says Law on Shale Gas to Be Ready by Year End," Reuters, November 26, 2013, www.reuters.com/article/2013/11/26/poland-shale-law-idUSL5N0JB1A120131126.

33. World Bank, *Doing Business 2015: Going Beyond Efficiency*, 12th ed., www.doingbusiness.org/~/media/WBG/DoingBusiness/Documents/Annual-Reports/English/DB15-Full-Report.pdf, p. 87.

34. Ibid., p. 88.

35. Cited in Witold J. Henisz and Bennet A. Zelner, "The Hidden Risks in Emerging Markets," *Harvard Business Review*, April 2010, reprinted in Harvard Business Review, *Thriving in Emerging Markets* (Boston: Harvard Business Review Publishing, 2011), https://hbr.org/2010/04/the-hidden-risks-in-emerging-markets.

36. Quoted in "When a Country Defaults, Who Comes Knocking?," NPR, October 9, 2011, www.npr.org/2011/10/09/141195893/when-a-country-defaults-who-comes-knocking.

37. "To Default, or Not to Default?," *Economist*, June 20, 2011, www.economist.com/blogs/dailychart/2011/06/sovereign-defaults-and-gdp.

38. "Usual Suspects," *Economist*, July 31, 2014, www.economist.com/blogs/graphicdetail/2014/07/daily-chart-23.

39. Michael Tomz and Mark L. J. Wright, "Empirical Research on Sovereign Debt and Default," *Annual Review of Economics* 5 (August 2013): 263, www.annualreviews.org/doi/abs/10.1146/annurev-economics-061109-080443; Michael Tomz and Mark L. J. Wright, "Do Countries Default in 'Bad Times'?," *Journal of the European Economic Association* 5, nos. 2–3 (April–May 2007): 352–60, https://web.stanford.edu/~tomz/pubs/TW2007.pdf.

40. Ian Bremmer and Preston Keat, *The Fat Tail: The Power of Political Knowledge in an Uncertain World* (New York: Oxford University Press, 2010), 75–76.

41. "Ian Bremmer on Sovereign Defaults," Reuters, March 23, 2009, http://blogs.reuters.com/felix-salmon/2009/03/23/ian-bremmer-on-sovereign-defaults/.

42. "Correa Defaults on Ecuador Bonds, Seeks Restructuring," Bloomberg via *Market Pipeline*, December 12, 2008, http://marketpipeline.blogspot.com/2008/12/correa-defaults-on-ecuador-bonds-seeks.html.

43. Virginia Harrison and Chris Liakos, "Greece Defaults on $1.7 Billion IMF Payment," CNNMoney, June 30, 2015, http://money.cnn.com/2015/06/30/news/economy/greece-imf-default/.

44. Sarah Chayes, *Thieves of State: Why Corruption Threatens Global Security* (New York: Norton, 2015).

45. Patrick Radden Keefe, "Corruption and Revolt," *New Yorker*, January 19, 2015, www.newyorker.com/magazine/2015/01/19/corruption-revolt. See also Cleangovbiz.org, OECD, "The Rationale for Fighting Corruption," 2014, www.oecd.org/cleangovbiz/49693613.pdf.

46. World Bank, "Helping Countries Combat Corruption: The Role of the World Bank," September 1997, www1.worldbank.org/publicsector/anticorrupt/corruptn/cor02.htm, p. 8.

47. Quoted in *World Policy Journal* blog, February 12, 2016, www.worldpolicy.org/blog/2016/02/12/talking-policy-sarah-chayes-corruption.

48. World Bank, "Helping Countries Combat Corruption."

49. Transparency International, "Corruption Perceptions Index 2014," 2014, www.transparency.org/whatwedo/publication/cpi2014.

50. Alvin Shuster, "In Some Countries, Bribes Remain Tax Deductible," *New York Times*, March 20, 1997, www.nytimes.com/1977/03/20/archives/in-some-countries-bribes-remain-tax-deductible-postlockheed-picture.html?_r=0.

51. Martin T. Biegelman and Daniel R. Biegelman, *Foreign Corrupt Practices Act Compliance Guidebook* (Hoboken, NJ: John Wiley & Sons, 2010), 2.

52. Richard L. Cassin, "The 2016 FCPA Enforcement Index," The FCPA Blog, January 2017, http://www.fcpablog.com/blog/2017/1/3/the-2016-fcpa-enforcement-index.html.

53. Richard L. Cassin, "Teva Announces $59 million FCPA Settlement," The FCPA Blog, December 22, 2016, http://www.fcpablog.com/blog/2016/12/22/teva-announces-519-million-fcpa-settlement.html.

54. One key difference is that the FCPA allows "facilitating payments" that speed the process of business decisions but do not alter the outcome. The U.K. Bribery Act bans facilitating payments.

55. "Fifa Corruption Inquiries: Officials Arrested in Zurich," BBC, May 27, 2015, www.bbc.com/news/world-europe-32895048.

56. Stephen Heifetz and Evan Sherwood, "Those Other Economic Sanctions: Section 311 Special Measures," *Banking Law Journal*, September 2014, www.steptoe.com/assets/htmldocuments/Banking%20Law%20Journal%20-%20September%202014.pdf.

57. Anna Yukhananov and Warren Strobel, "After Success on Iran, U.S. Treasury's Sanctions Team Faces New Challenges," Reuters, April 14, 2014, www.reuters.com/article/2014/04/15/us-usa-sanctions-insight-idUSBREA3D1O820140415; Steven R. Weisman, "Success in Macao Bank Case Demonstrates Reach of U.S. Financial Sanctions," *New York Times*, June 27, 2007, http://mobile.nytimes.com/2007/06/27/business/worldbusiness/27iht-bank.1.6354294.html?referrer=.

58. "Brief History," OPEC, n.d., www.opec.org/opec_web/en/about_us/24.htm.

59. Greg Myre, "The 1973 Arab Oil Embargo: The Old Rules No Longer Apply," NPR, October 16, 2013, www.npr.org/sections/parallels/2013/10/15/234771573/the-1973-arab-oil-embargo-the-old-rules-no-longer-apply.

60. Michael L. Ross, "How the 1973 Oil Embargo Saved the Planet," *Foreign Affairs*, October 15, 2013, www.foreignaffairs.com/articles/north-america/2013-10-15/how-1973-oil-embargo-saved-planet.

61. Danielle Venton, "Rare-Earth Mining Rises Again in United States," *Wired*, May 11, 2012, www.wired.com/2012/05/rare-earth-mining-rises-again/.

62. "Manipulation of China's Rare Earth Minerals Supply Could Backfire," Voice of America, October 25, 2011, www.voanews.com/content/chinas-rare-earth-minerals-supply-manipulation-could-backfire-132605798/168140.html.

63. "Update 2—China Loses Appeal of WTO Ruling on Rare Earth Exports," Reuters, August 7, 2014, www.reuters.com/article/2014/08/07/china-wto-rareearths-idUSL6N0QD5T820140807.

64. "Manipulation of China's Rare Earth Minerals Supply Could Backfire," Voice of America; Richard Martin, "Molycorp's $1 Billion Rare-Earth Gamble," *Fortune*, November 18, 2011, http://fortune.com/2011/11/18/molycorps-1-billion-rare-earth-gamble/.

65. The White House, "Remarks by the President on Fair Trade," March 13, 2012, www.whitehouse.gov/the-press-office/2012/03/13/remarks-president-fair-trade; "Update 2—China Loses Appeal of WTO Ruling on Rare Earth Exports," Reuters.

66. "Manipulation of China's Rare Earth Minerals Supply Could Backfire," Voice of America.

67. Quoted in Emily Steel, "Nestlé Takes a Beating on Social-Media Sites," *Wall Street Journal*, March 29, 2010, www.wsj.com/articles/SB10001424052702304434404575149883850508158.

68. Greenpeace UK, "Have a Break?," Vimeo, March 17, 2010, https://vimeo.com/10236827.

69. Quoted in Chris Rose, "Campaign Case Study: How Greenpeace Changed Corporate Behaviour over Rainforest Destruction," Three Worlds, July 26, 2013, http://threeworlds.campaignstrategy.org/?p=265. See also Elliott Fox, "Nestlé Hit by Facebook 'Anti-social' Media Surge," *Guardian*, March 19, 2010, www.guardian.co.uk/sustainable-business/nestle-facebook; Paul Armstrong, "Greenpeace,

Nestlé in Battle over Kit Kat Viral," CNN, March 20, 2010, www.cnn.com/2010/WORLD/asiapcf/03/19/indonesia.rainforests.orangutan.nestle/.

70. Julie Creswell and Rachel Abrams, "Shopping Becomes a Political Act in the Trump Era," *New York Times*, February 10, 2017, www.nytimes.com/2017/02/10/business/nordstrom-trump.html.

71. "Case Study: Always #LikeAGirl," Campaign, October 12, 2015, www.campaignlive.co.uk/article/case-study-always-likeagirl/1366870; "Case Study: Always #LikeAGirl," D&AD, www.dandad.org/en/d-ad-always-like-a-girl-campaign-case-study-insights/; Hannah Goldberg, "This Ad Completely Redefines the Phrase, 'Like a Girl,'" *Time*, June 26, 2014.

72. Scott Stewart, "The Persistent Threat to Soft Targets," Stratfor, July 26, 2012, www.stratfor.com/weekly/persistent-threat-soft-targets.

73. "List of Terrorist Attacks That Have Struck Europe in 2016," *Indian Express*, July 25, 2016, http://indianexpress.com/article/world/world-news/list-of-terrorist-attacks-that-have-struck-europe-in-2016/; Lana Clements, "EU Death Knell: Eurozone Growth HALVES as French Economy Grinds to a Halt," *Express*, July 29, 2016, www.express.co.uk/finance/city/694739/European-economic-growth-HALVES-as-France-grinds-to-a-halt.

74. Quoted in "Brexit Heightens Uncertainty in Global Economy, Says G20," *Guardian*, July 24, 2016, www.theguardian.com/world/2016/jul/24/brexit-heightens-risks-to-global-economy-says-g20.

75. Julia La Roche, "The Amazing and Heartbreaking Story of the CEO Who Lived and Rebuilt His Firm After 9/11: Howard Lutnick," *Business Insider*, September 11, 2011, www.businessinsider.com/cantor-fitzgerald-9-11-story-howard-lutnick-2011-9.

76. John Chambers, "What Does the Internet of Everything Mean for Security?," World Economic Forum, January 21, 2015, www.weforum.org/agenda/2015/01/companies-fighting-cyber-crime/.

77. "All Fortune 500 Companies Have Been Hacked, 97% Know It, the Other 3% Don't," Homeland Security News Wire, January 8, 2014, www.homelandsecuritynewswire.com/srcybersecurity20140108-all-fortune-500-companies-have-been-hacked-97-know-it-the-other-3-don-t.

78. Jonathan Weber, "Google Notifies Users of 4,000 State-Sponsored Cyber Attacks per Month" Reuters, July 12, 2016, www.reuters.com/article/us-google-cyberattack-idUSKCN0ZR2IU.

79. Elaine Edwards, "Cyber Security Experts Warned of a Hacked World," *Irish Times*, February 15, 2017, www.irishtimes.com/business/technology/cyber-security-experts-warned-of-a-hacked-world-1.2976432. See also ISACA, "State of Cybersecurity: Implications for 2016," www.isaca.org/cyber/Documents/state-of-cybersecurity_res_eng_0316.pdf.

80. Peter Elkind, "Inside the Hack of the Century," Part 2, *Fortune*, June 25, 2015, http://fortune.com/sony-hack-part-two/.

81. "Net Losses: Estimating the Global Cost of Cybercrime," Center for Strategic and International Studies, June 2014, www.mcafee.com/us/resources/reports/rp-economic-impact-cybercrime2.pdf, p. 2.

82. "GDP (Official Exchange Rate)," *The World Factbook*, Central Intelligence Agency, www.cia.gov/library/publications/the-world-factbook/fields/2195.html#xx.

83. Robert Dethlefs, "How Cyber Attacks Became More Profitable Than the Drug Trade," *Fortune*, May 1, 2015, http://fortune.com/2015/05/01/how-cyber-attacks-became-more-profitable-than-the-drug-trade/.

84. Adam Janofsky, "Equifax Breach Could Cost Billions," *Wall Street Journal*, September 15, 2017, https://www.wsj.com/articles/equifax-breach-could-cost-billions-1505474692.

85. Ibid.

86. Between September 2014 and June 2015, the U.S. Department of Defense faced thirty million known attempted cyber intrusions. Only 0.1 percent of them compromised a cyber system. Department of Defense, Cybersecurity Culture and Compliance Initiative (DC3I), September 2015, www.defense.gov/Portals/1/Documents/pubs/OSD011517-15-RES-Final.pdf, p. 1. During that same period, the Office of Personnel Management fended off ten million known cyber attacks per month. James Eng and Wendy Jones, "OPM Chief Says Government Agency Thwarts Ten Million Hack Attempts a Month," Reuters via NBC News, June 16, 2015, www.nbcnews.com/tech/security/opm-chief-says-government-agency-thwarts-10-million-hack-attempts-n376476.

87. Bruce Schneier, "Who Are the Shadow Brokers?," *Atlantic*, May 23, 2017, www.theatlantic.com/technology/archive/2017/05/shadow-brokers/527778/.

88. National Intelligence Council, "Assessing Russian Activities and Intentions in Recent US Elections," Office of the Director of National Intelligence, ICA 2017-01D, January 6, 2017, www.dni.gov/files/documents/ICA_2017_01.pdf.

89. Mike Isaac and Scott Shane, "Facebook's Russia-Linked Ads Came in Many Disguises," *New York Times*, October 2, 2017.

90. Colin Stretch, Testimony Before the United States Senate Select Committee on Intelligence, Hearing on Social Media Influence in the 2016 U.S. Elections, November 1, 2017.

91. James R. Clapper, "Worldwide Threat Assessment of the U.S. Intelligence Community," Office of the Director of National Intelligence, February 26, 2015, www.dni.gov/files/documents/Unclassified_2015_ATA_SFR_-_SASC_FINAL.pdf, p. 1. The Navy has become so worried about vulnerabilities in GPS systems that it has started teaching cadets how to navigate with stars and sextants again, just in case. NSA director/U.S. Cyber Command commander Admiral Michael Rogers in 2016 warned that the next wave of hacking will alter data, not just steal, destroy, or release it. Imagine a world where military leaders cannot trust their missile defense systems, where a company's product designs have been

sabotaged but nobody realizes it, where an individual's medical records may suddenly include the wrong blood type, where your bank account seems just a little off each month but you can't be sure anything is wrong.

92. Quoted in *2014 Global Survey on Reputation Risk*, Deloitte, October 2014, www2.deloitte.com/content/dam/Deloitte/global/Documents/Governance-Risk-Compliance/gx_grc_Reputation@Risk%20survey%20report_FINAL.pdf, p. 8.

93. Cyber experts note that "air gapped" systems that are not directly connected to the Internet are not safe from attack.

94. Aimee Picchi, "Target Breach May Have Started with Email Phishing," CBS MoneyWatch, February 13, 2014, www.cbsnews.com/news/target-breach-may-have-started-with-email-phishing/; Brian Krebs, "Email Attack on Vendor Set Up Breach at Target," KrebsOnSecurity, February 12, 2014, http://krebsonsecurity.com/tag/fazio-mechanical-services/.

95. Peter Elkind, "Inside the Hack of the Century," Part 1, *Fortune*, June 25, 2015, http://fortune.com/sony-hack-part-1/.

96. Paul Farhi, "Bill O'Reilly's Fox News Career Comes to a Swift End Amid Growing Sexual Harassment Claims," *Washington Post*, April 19, 2017, www.washingtonpost.com/lifestyle/style/bill-oreilly-is-officially-out-at-fox-news/2017/04/19/74ebdc94-2476-11e7-a1b3-faff0034e2de_story.html?utm_term=.b56789107826. Emily Steel and Michael S. Schmidt, "Bill O'Reilly Settled New Harassment Claim, Then Fox Renewed His Contract," *New York Times*, October 21, 2017, www.nytimes.com/2017/10/21/business/media/bill-oreilly-sexual-harassment.html?_r=0.

97. Mike Isaac, "Uber Founder Travis Kalanick Resigns as C.E.O.," *New York Times*, June 21, 2017, www.nytimes.com/2017/06/21/technology/uber-ceo-travis-kalanick.html. See also Mike Isaac, "Uber Fires 20 Amid Investigation into Workplace Culture," *New York Times*, June 6, 2017, www.nytimes.com/2017/06/06/technology/uber-fired.html; Mike Isaac, "Inside Uber's Aggressive, Unrestrained Workplace Culture," *New York Times*, February 22, 2017, www.nytimes.com/2017/02/22/technology/uber-workplace-culture.html.

CHAPTER 3: HOW WE GOT HERE

1. Cecilia Yap and Clarissa Batino, "Cargo Containers Jam Manila Docks in Rush-Hour Truck Ban," Bloomberg, May 12, 2014, www.bloomberg.com/news/articles/2014-05-11/cargo-containers-jam-manila-docks-amid-truck-ban.

2. "Mayor Erap Lifts Truck Ban in Manila," GMA News Online, September 13, 2014, www.gmanetwork.com/news/story/379022/news/metro/mayor-erap-lifts-truck-ban-in-manila.

3. Yap and Batino, "Cargo Containers."

4. Bea Cupin, "Isko Moreno: Port Congestion Preceded Manila Truck Ban," Rappler, September 8, 2014, www.rappler.com/business/industries/208-infrastructure/68572-isko-moreno-truck-ban-port-congestion.

5. Louella Desiderio, "Toyota Auto Parts Shipments Down 10%," *Philippine Star*, January 22, 2015, www.philstar.com/business/2015/01/22/1415302/toyota-auto-parts-shipments-down-10; Chelsea Cruz, "Port Congestion Dampens Toyota Philippines' Parts Exports," *InterAksyon*, January 21, 2015, http://interaksyon.com/business/103504/port-congestion-dampens-toyota-philippines-parts-exports.

6. "Sales Volume Overseas," 75 Years of Toyota, Toyota-Global.com, 2012, www.toyota-global.com/company/history_of_toyota/75years/data/automotive_business/sales/sales_volume/overseas/index.html.

7. John Gunnell, *Standard Catalog of Chevrolet, 1912–2003* (Iola, WI: Krause Publications, 2011); Andy Thompson, *Cars of the Soviet Union: The Definitive History* (Sparkford, Somerset, UK: Haynes Publishing, 2008); Matt Gasnier, "France 1950: Renault 4CV and Citroen Traction Avant Shine," *Best Selling Cars Blog*, http://bestsellingcarsblog.com/1951/01/france-1950-renault-4cv-and-citroen-traction-avant-shine/.

8. "Sales Volume Overseas," Toyota-Global.com.

9. Dan Mihalascu, "Russia's Best-Selling Car No Longer a Lada for the First Time Since the 1970s," CarScoops, January 2, 2015, www.carscoops.com/2015/01/russias-best-selling-car-no-longer-lada.html.

10. Fairphone exemplifies just how much supply chains have globalized. Between 1995 and 2007, the number of transnational companies more than doubled, from 38,000 to 79,000, and foreign subsidiaries nearly tripled, from 265,000 to 790,000. "World Investment Report 1996: Investment, Trade and International Policy Agreements," United Nations, August 1996; "World Investment Report 2008: Transnational Corporations, and the Infrastructure Challenge," United Nations, July 2008.

11. Yogesh Malik, Alex Niemeyer, and Brian Ruwadi, "Building the Supply Chain of the Future," *McKinsey on Supply Chain: Select Publications*, January 2011, https://commdev.org/userfiles/779922_McKinsey_on_Supply_Chain_Select_Publications_20111.pdf.

12. Demetri Sevastopulo, "Vietnam Riots Land Another Blow on the Global Supply Chain," *Financial Times*, May 20, 2014, www.ft.com/intl/cms/s/0/abc9ba84-e01c-11e3-9534-00144feabdc0.html#axzz44yd9dVmh.

13. Clement Tan, "Li & Fung Sees Limited Impact from Vietnam Factory Unrest," Bloomberg, May 15, 2014, www.bloomberg.com/news/articles/2014-05-15/li-fung-sees-limited-impact-from-vietnam-factory-unrest.

14. Ravi Anupindi, *Boeing: The Fight for Fasteners*, Case 1-428-787, Tauber Institute for Global Operations, University of Michigan, November 17, 2009; Ravi Anupindi, "Case Study: Boeing's Dreamliner," *Financial Times*, October 10, 2011, www.ft.com/cms/s/0/a7d38332-ef70-11e0-941e-00144feab49a.html#axzz3c78p4A2S.

15. Dave Demerjian, "Small Fasteners Cause Big Problems for Boeing," *Wired*, November 10, 2008, www.wired.com/2008/11/the-little-fast/.

16. Quoted in "Boeing CEO Blames Industry for 787 Bolt Shortage," Reuters, September 11, 2007, www.reuters.com/article/2007/09/11/us-boeing-alcoa-idUSN1141086620070911.

17. Yoshi Sheffi, *The Resilient Enterprise: Overcoming Vulnerability for Competitive Advantage* (Cambridge, MA: MIT Press, 2005), 88–90.

18. Martin Landau and Donald Chisholm, "The Arrogance of Optimism: Notes on Failure-Avoidance Management," *Journal of Contingencies and Crisis Management* 3, no. 2 (June 1995): 67–80, at 71.

19. Accenture research found that significant supply chain disruptions reduced the share price of impacted companies by an average of 7 percent. Cited in World Economic Forum, *Building Resilience in Supply Chains*, An initiative of the Risk Response Network in collaboration with Accenture, January 2013, www3.weforum.org/docs/WEF_RRN_MO_BuildingResilienceSupplyChains_Report_2013.pdf, p. 7.

20. ManMohan S. Sodhi and Christopher S. Tang, *Managing Supply Chain Risk* (New York: Springer Publishing, 2012), 70, citing Hicks 2002.

21. Sheffi, *The Resilient Enterprise*, 13.

22. Christopher S. Tang and Joshua D. Zimmerman, "Managing New Product Development and Supply Chain Risks: The Boeing 787 Case," *Supply Chain Forum* 10, no. 2 (2009): 74–86.

23. E2open and Exostar, *Boeing 787: Global Supply Chain Management*, Case Study, 2013, http://zygxy.jwzhn.com/foreign/Files/File/Boeing_case_study.pdf.

24. "787 Model Summary: Orders," Boeing, February 2017, http://active.boeing.com/commercial/orders/displaystandardreport.cfm?cboCurrentModel=787&optReportType=AllModels&cboAllModel=787&ViewReportF=View+Report.

25. IBM, "The Smarter Supply Chain of the Future Report," 2009, www-935.ibm.com/services/us/gbs/bus/html/gbs-csco-study.html, p. 13.

26. Russ Banham, "Political Risk and the Supply Chain," *Risk Management*, June 1, 2014, www.rmmagazine.com/2014/06/01/political-risk-and-the-supply-chain/.

27. World Economic Forum, *Building Resilience in Supply Chains*.

28. Mary Driscoll, "Risk Management: Extreme Weather Increasingly Disrupts Global Supply Chains," APQC, June 28, 2013, www.apqc.org/knowledge-base/documents/risk-management-extreme-weather-increasingly-disrupts-global-supply-chains.

29. Zachary Davies Boren, "There Are Officially More Mobile Devices Than People in the World," *Independent*, October 7, 2014, www.independent.co.uk/life-style/gadgets-and-tech/news/there-are-officially-more-mobile-devices-than-people-in-the-world-9780518.html.

30. Roger Cheng, "By 2020, More People Will Own a Phone Than Have Electricity," CNET, February 3, 2016, www.cnet.com/news/by-2020-more-people-will-own-a-phone-than-have-electricity/.

31. Other emerging technologies—from artificial intelligence to crypto currencies—are poised to make profound impacts as well. See Amy Zegart, "The Tools of Espionage Are Going Mainstream," *The Atlantic*, November 27, 2017, https://www.theatlantic.com/international archive/2017/11/deception-russia-election

-meddling-technology-nationa-security/546644, and Reid Hoffman, "Why the Blockchain Matters," *WIRED Magazine*, May 15, 2015, https://www.wired.co.uk/article/bitcoin-reid-hoffman.

32. "Time Magazine's 'Person of the Year' Is...You," NBC News, December 17, 2006, www.nbcnews.com/id/16242528/ns/us_news-life/t/time-magazines-person-year-you/#.VwvD2xMrKRs.

33. Mancur Olson, *The Logic of Collective Action* (Cambridge, MA: Harvard University Press, 1971); Sidney Tarrow, *Power in Movement: Social Movements, Collective Action and Politics* (New York: Cambridge University Press, 1994).

34. In the 2012 American presidential election, only 53.6 percent of eligible voters ended up casting ballots. See Drew DeSilver, "U.S. Voter Turnout Trails Most Developed Countries," Pew Research Center, August 2, 2016, www.pewresearch.org/fact-tank/2015/05/06/u-s-voter-turnout-trails-most-developed-countries/. A *USA Today*/Suffolk University Poll examining the 2012 election found that among unlikely voters, 41 percent said they were not bothered about not voting because they felt their vote did not make a difference anyway. See Susan Page, "What the Unlikely Voters Think," *USA Today*, August 15, 2012, http://usatoday30.usatoday.com/news/politics/story/2012-08-15/non-voters-obama-romney/57055184/1.

35. Marc Fisher, "In Tunisia, Act of One Fruit Vendor Sparks Wave of Revolution Through Arab World," *Washington Post*, March 26, 2011, www.washingtonpost.com/world/in-tunisia-act-of-one-fruit-vendor-sparks-wave-of-revolution-through-arab-world/2011/03/16/AFjfsueB_story.html.

36. Ibid.

37. Worker Rights Consortium, "Update on Bangladesh Apparel Factory Disaster," press release, www.workersrights.org/press/WRC%20Update%20on%20Bangladesh%20Apparel%20Factory%20Disaster.pdf; Sarah Stillman, "Death Traps: The Bangladesh Garment-Factory Disaster," *New Yorker*, May 1, 2013, www.newyorker.com/online/blogs/newsdesk/2013/05/death-traps-the-bangladesh-garment-factory-disaster.html.

38. Taslima Akhter, "A Final Embrace," *Time*, May 8, 2013, http://time.com/3387526/a-final-embrace-the-most-haunting-photograph-from-bangladesh/.

39. Michael Guerrerio, "The Number: Ten Cents," *New Yorker*, May 16, 2013, www.newyorker.com/news/news-desk/the-number-ten-cents; Patrick Lo, "H&M Responds Slowly to Bangladesh Factory Collapse Killing 1,100," CorpWatch, May 19, 2013, www.corpwatch.org/article.php?id=15840; Steven Greenhouse, "Global Retailers Join Safety Plan for Bangladesh," *New York Times*, May 13, 2013, www.nytimes.com/2013/05/14/world/asia/bangladeshs-cabinet-approves-changes-to-labor-laws.html.

40. Sara Ayech, "LEGO: Everything Is NOT Awesome," *Making Waves* (Greenpeace blog), July 8, 2014, www.greenpeace.org/international/en/news/Blogs/makingwaves/lego-awesome-video/blog/49850/.

41. Simon Mainwaring, "How Lego Rebuilt Itself as a Purposeful and Sustainable Brand," *Forbes*, August 11, 2016, www.forbes.com/sites/

simonmainwaring/2016/08/11/how-lego-rebuilt-itself-as-a-purposeful-and-sustainable-brand/#4004d3256f3c.

42. Dominique Mosbergen, "Lego Saying 'No' to Plastic, Invests Millions into Search for 'Sustainable Material,'" *Huffington Post*, June 24, 2015, www.huffington-post.com/2015/06/24/lego-plastic-sustainable-materials_n_7651190.html; Mainwaring, "How Lego Rebuilt Itself as a Purposeful and Sustainable Brand"; Lorenza Brascia, "Lego Puts Big Bucks Behind Push to Go Green," CNN, June 25, 2015, http://money.cnn.com/2015/06/23/news/companies/lego-sustainable-material/.

43. Quoted in *2014 Global Survey on Reputation Risk*, Deloitte, October 2014, www2.deloitte.com/content/dam/Deloitte/global/Documents/Governance-Risk-Compliance/gx_grc_Reputation@Risk%20survey%20report_FINAL.pdf, p. 5.

44. *Global Risks 2015*, World Economic Forum Report, http://reports.weforum.org/global-risks-2015/, pp. 28–30.

CHAPTER 4: MIND GAMES AND GROUPTHINK

1. Michael Elliott, "The Anatomy of the GE-Honeywell Disaster," *Time*, July 8, 2001.

2. The EU has expanded since 2001 from fifteen member states to twenty-eight (including the United Kingdom, which voted in 2016 to leave the union, a process that remains under way). At the time of the proposed GE-Honeywell merger, the European Union consisted of Austria, Belgium, Denmark, Finland, France, Germany, Greece, Italy, Ireland, Luxembourg, the Netherlands, Portugal, Spain, Sweden, and the United Kingdom. The thirteen member states that have joined since then are Bulgaria, Croatia, the Czech Republic, Cyprus, Estonia, Hungary, Latvia, Lithuania, Malta, Poland, Romania, Slovakia, and Slovenia. See "About the EU," European Union, March 20, 2017, http://europa.eu/about-eu/countries/member-countries/.

3. Raymond J. Ahearn, "U.S.-European Union Trade Relations: Issues and Policy Challenges," CRS Issue Brief for Congress, May 1, 2006, www.au.af.mil/au/awc/awcgate/crs/ib10087.pdf; Elliott, "Anatomy of the GE-Honeywell Disaster."

4. Quoted in "Spiking the World's Biggest Merger," *Economist*, July 3, 2001.

5. Andrew Ross Sorkin, "Failure to Acquire Honeywell Is Sour Finish for G.E. Chief," *New York Times*, July 3, 2001, www.nytimes.com/2001/07/03/business/failure-to-acquire-honeywell-is-sour-finish-for-ge-chief.html.

6. Elliott, "Anatomy of the GE-Honeywell Disaster"; Michael D. Watkins and Max H. Bazerman, "Predictable Surprises: The Disasters You Should Have Seen Coming," *Harvard Business Review*, April 2003, 5; Matt Murray, Philip Shishkin, Bob Davis, and Anita Raghavan, "As Honeywell Deal Goes Awry for GE, Fallout May be Global," *Wall Street Journal*, June 15, 2001, www.wsj.com/articles/SB992563873127359695.

7. Quoted in "Merger Muddle," *Economist*, June 21, 2001, www.economist.com/node/666703.

8. See, for example, *2013 World Investment and Political Risk*, Multilateral Investment Guarantee Agency, World Bank Group, 2014, www.miga.org/documents/WIPR13.pdf.

9. International Telecommunication Union, United Nations, *Global Cybersecurity Index 2017*, www.itu.int/dms_pub/itu-d/opb/str/D-STR-GCI.01-2017-PDF-E.pdf.

10. *2014 Global Survey on Reputation Risk*, Deloitte, October 2014, www2.deloitte.com/content/dam/Deloitte/global/Documents/Governance-Risk-Compliance/gx_grc_Reputation@Risk%20survey%20report_FINAL.pdf.

11. Thomas Davenport, "Why No One Wants to Be a Chief Information Officer Any More," *Fortune*, March 10, 2016, http://fortune.com/2016/03/10/why-no-one-wants-to-be-a-chief-information-officer-any-more/.

12. "Stanford Salutes Professor William J. Perry," YouTube, February 12, 2016, https://www.youtube.com/watch?v=p7HSCDHZRYA, at 3:38.

13. Fred Smith and Brian Dumaine, "How I Delivered the Goods," CNN, October 1, 2002, http://money.cnn.com/magazines/fsb/fsb_archive/2002/10/01/330568/.

14. Ibid.

15. "Universal Signs Deal for Beijing Theme Park," Associated Press via *Hollywood Reporter*, September 15, 2015, www.hollywoodreporter.com/news/universal-beijing-theme-park-deal-823339.

16. Remarks by Kirtee Kapoor, DavisPolk, Stanford University Directors' College, June 21, 2016.

17. The most authoritative account is the President's Foreign Intelligence Advisory Board investigation, which was declassified in 2015. See "The 1982 War Scare Declassified and For Real," National Security Archive, the George Washington University, October 24, 2015, http://nsarchive.gwu.edu/nukevault/ebb533-The-Able-Archer-War-Scare-Declassified-PFIAB-Report-Released/.

18. Approximately thirty thousand Americans die in car accidents annually, compared to one fatality about every two years from shark attacks in the United States.

19. Aaron Brown, "You're More Likely to Die in a Black Friday Sale Than a Shark Attack," *Daily Express*, November 12, 2015, www.express.co.uk/life-style/science-technology/618951/Black-Friday-Death-Injury-Shark-Attack.

20. World Health Organization Influenza Fact Sheet, November 2016, www.who.int/mediacentre/factsheets/fs211/en/; "Ebola: Mapping the Outbreak," BBC News, January 14, 2016, www.bbc.com/news/world-africa-28755033; Aurelio Locsin, "Is Air Travel Safer Than Car Travel?," *USA Today*, http://traveltips.usatoday.com/air-travel-safer-car-travel-1581.html.

21. Amos Tversky and Daniel Kahneman, "Judgment Under Uncertainty: Heuristics and Biases," *Science*, New Series, vol. 185, no. 4157 (September 27, 1974): 1124–31.

22. Amos Tversky and Daniel Kahneman, "Extensional Versus Intuitive Reasoning: The Conjunction Fallacy in Probability Judgment," *Psychological Review* 90, no. 4 (October 1983): 293–315.

23. Daniel Kahneman, *Thinking, Fast and Slow* (New York: Farrar, Straus & Giroux, 2011), 158.

24. Steven Strogatz, "It's My Birthday Too, Yeah," *New York Times*, October 1, 2012, http://opinionator.blogs.nytimes.com/2012/10/01/its-my-birthday-too-yeah/.

25. R. A. Olsen, "Desirability Bias Among Professional Investment Managers: Some Evidence from Experts," *Journal of Behavioral Decision Making* 10 (1997): 65–72. As Kahneman wrote in 2011, "In terms of its consequences, the optimistic bias may well be the most significant of the cognitive biases." See Kahneman, *Thinking, Fast and Slow*, 255.

26. Albesh B. Patel, *Investing Unplugged: Secrets from the Inside* (New York: Springer, 2005).

27. N. D. Weinstein, "Optimistic Biases About Personal Risks," *Science* 246 (December 8, 1989): 1232–33.

28. Joseph P. Simmons and Cade Massey, "Is Optimism Real?," *Journal of Experimental Psychology* 141, no. 4 (2012): 630–34.

29. D. Granberg and E. Brent, "When Prophecy Bends: The Preference–Expectation Link in U.S. Presidential Elections, 1952–1980," *Journal of Personality and Social Psychology* 45 (1983): 477–81; Zlatan Krizan, Jeffrey C. Miller, and Omesh Johar, "Wishful Thinking in the 2008 U.S. Presidential Election," *Psychological Science* 2, no. 1 (2010): 140–46, https://public.psych.iastate.edu/zkrizan/pdf/Krizan_etal_2009.pdf.

30. S. P. Hayes Jr., "The Predictive Ability of Voters," *Journal of Social Psychology* 7 (1936): 183–91.

31. Simmons and Massey, "Is Optimism Real?"

32. Nate Cohn, "Why the Surprise over 'Brexit'? Don't Blame the Polls," *New York Times*, June 24, 2016, www.nytimes.com/2016/06/25/upshot/why-the-surprise-over-brexit-dont-blame-the-polls.html?_r=0.

33. Dave Mosher and Skye Gould, "How Likely Are Foreign Terrorists to Kill Americans? The Odds May Surprise You," *Business Insider*, January 31, 2017, www.businessinsider.com/death-risk-statistics-terrorism-disease-accidents-2017-1.

34. Yossi Sheffi, *The Resilient Enterprise: Overcoming Vulnerability for Competitive Advantage* (Cambridge, MA: MIT Press, 2007), 26.

35. Michael Tomz and Mark L. J. Wright, "Do Countries Default in 'Bad Times,'" *Journal of the European Economic Association* 5 (April–May 2007): 352–60, https://web.stanford.edu/~tomz/pubs/TW2007.pdf.

36. Data from Global Terrorism Database, www.start.umd.edu/gtd/. All observations are coded based on news and media reports. Therefore the numbers reported are a lower bound on the total number of terrorist attacks.

37. Sherman Kent, "A Crucial Estimate Relived," *Studies in Intelligence* 36, no. 5 (Spring 1964): 111–19.

38. Ibid.

39. Warren Buffett, Annual Letter to Shareholders, Berkshire Hathaway, February 27, 2009, www.berkshirehathaway.com/letters/letters.html.

40. The nuclear countries are: United States, Russia, the United Kingdom, France, China, India, Pakistan, and North Korea. In addition, Israel is widely believed to possess nuclear weapons.

41. When the Soviet Union collapsed, three former Soviet republics—Ukraine, Belarus, and Kazakhstan—had nuclear weapons on their soil and ultimately, with the assistance of the forward-looking Nunn-Lugar Cooperative Threat Reduction Program, gave them up.

42. Sonali Singh and Christopher R. Way, "The Correlates of Nuclear Proliferation," *Journal of Conflict Resolution* 48, no. 6 (December 2004): 859–85.

43. Nassim Taleb, *The Black Swan: The Impact of the Highly Improbable* (New York: Random House, 2010), xxii.

44. Ian Bremmer and Preston Keat, *The Fat Tail: The Power of Knowledge in an Uncertain World* (Oxford: Oxford University Press, 2010), 21.

45. Ibid., 179–80.

46. Diane Vaughan, *The Challenger Launch Decision: Risky Technology, Culture, and Deviance at NASA* (Chicago: University of Chicago Press, 1996); Richard Betts, "Surprise Despite Warning," *Political Science Quarterly* 94, no. 4 (Winter 1980–81): 551–72.

47. Roberta Wolhstetter, "Cuba and Pearl Harbor," *Foreign Affairs*, July 1965, 699; Richard Betts, *Surprise Attack: Lessons for Defense Planning* (Washington, DC: Brookings Institution Press, 1982), 41, 97–99. See also Frederic L. Borch, "Comparing Pearl Harbor and 9/11: Intelligence Failure? American Unpreparedness? Military Responsibility?," *Journal of Military History* 67 no. 3 (July 2003): 845–60, https://muse.jhu.edu/article/44242/pdf.

48. Vaughan, *The Challenger Launch Decision*.

49. *Report of Columbia Accident Investigation Board*, Volume 1, NASA, August 26, 2003, www.nasa.gov/columbia/home/CAIB_Vol1.html.

50. For industry differences, see A. L. Pablo, "Managerial Risk Interpretations: Does Industry Make a Difference?," *Journal of Managerial Psychology* 14, no. 2 (1999): 92–107.

51. Hans M. Kristensen and Robert S. Norris, "Status of World Nuclear Forces," Federation of American Scientists, https://fas.org/issues/nuclear-weapons/status-world-nuclear-forces/; "Nuclear Notebook: Nuclear Arsenals of the World," *Bulletin of the Atomic Scientists*, http://thebulletin.org/nuclear-notebook-multimedia.

52. Condoleezza Rice, *No Higher Honor: A Memoir of My Years in Washington* (New York: Crown, 2011), pp. 122–30.

53. Ibid.

54. Ibid.

CHAPTER 5: MOVING BEYOND INTUITION

1. Royal Caribbean International is one of several cruise lines owned and operated by its parent company, Royal Caribbean Cruises, Ltd.

2. "Haiti Earthquake Fast Facts," CNN, December 28, 2016, www.cnn.com/2013/12/12/world/haiti-earthquake-fast-facts/.

3. Myat Su Yin and John Walsh, "A Review of the Appropriateness of Royal Caribbean's Actions in Visiting Haiti after the 2010 Earthquake," *Journal of Travel and Tourism Research*, Spring/Fall 2010, 1; Leslie Gaines-Ross, "Reputation Warfare," *Harvard Business Review*, December 2010.

4. Chuck Bennett, "Ship of Ghouls," *New York Post*, January 19, 2010, http://nypost.com/2010/01/19/ship-of-ghouls/.

5. During the Haiti earthquake Goldstein was president and CEO of Royal Caribbean International. In 2014, he became president and chief operating officer of the parent company.

6. Royal Caribbean Cruises, Ltd. Annual Report 2015, www.rclcorporate.com/content/uploads/RCL-2015-Annual-Rreport-WEB.pdf.

7. "Royal Caribbean Provides Tourists, Relief to Haiti," NPR, January 19, 2010, www.npr.org/templates/story/story.php?storyId=122716579; Scott Mayerowitz, "Cruise-Ship Tourists Visit Haiti," ABC News, January 19, 2010, http://abcnews.go.com/Travel/cruise-ship-tourists-visit-haiti-royal-caribbean-liners/story?id=9595955.

8. Jeneen Interlandi, "Cruises to Haiti Stir Controversy," *Newsweek*, January 27, 2010, www.newsweek.com/cruises-haiti-stir-controversy-70855.

9. Interlandi, "Cruises to Haiti Stir Controversy."

10. Leslie Gaines-Ross, "Reputation Warfare," *Harvard Business Review*, December 2010, p. 7, https://hbr.org/2010/12/reputation-warfare.

11. On November 20, 2016, after several rounds of voting during a fourteen-month process, businessman Jovenel Moïse was elected president. He took office in February 2017.

12. "Haiti Earthquake Facts and Figures," Disasters Emergency Committee, www.dec.org.uk/articles/haiti-earthquake-facts-and-figures.

13. Mary Mederios Kent, "Earthquake Magnifies Haiti's Economic and Health Challenges," Population Reference Bureau, October 2010, www.prb.org/Publications/Articles/2010/haiti.aspx.

14. Kim Wall and Caterina Clerici, "Haiti Sees Tourism Promises Fade Amidst Electoral Tensions," *Time*, January 26, 2016, http://time.com/4192693/haiti-tourism/, quote at 1:08.

15. Kate Rice, "Haiti Expects Carnival Port to Spur Further Tourism Development," *Travel Weekly*, August 11, 2014, www.travelweekly.com/Cruise-Travel/Haiti-expects-Carnival-port-to-spur-further-tourism-development; interview with Peter Whelpton.

16. "Labadee, Haiti," Royal Caribbean International, www.royalcaribbean.com/findacruise/ports/group/home.do?portCode=LAB.

17. Rice, "Haiti Expects Carnival Port to Spur Further Tourism Development."

18. Interlandi, "Cruises to Haiti Stir Controversy."

19. "Royal Caribbean Provides Tourists, Relief to Haiti," NPR.

20. Royal Caribbean, press release, January 15, 2010, www.royalcaribbean.com/ourCompany/pressCenter/pressReleases/info.do.

21. Blog posts, June 11, 2010, and June 23, 2010, www.royalcaribbeanblog.com/category/category/haiti.

22. Sea World Entertainment, Inc., is the parent company that owns or licenses several brands, including SeaWorld, Shamu, and Busch Gardens, and operates about a dozen theme parks in the United States, including SeaWorld theme parks in Orlando, San Antonio, and San Diego.

23. Justin Chang, "Review: *Blackfish*," *Variety*, January 26, 2013, http://variety.com/2013/film/reviews/blackfish-1117949104/.

24. Secretary of Labor v. SeaWorld of Florida, LLC, OSHRC Docket No. 10-1705, Decision and Order, Administrative Law Judge Ken S. Welsch, June 11, 2012, www.oshrc.gov/decisions/pdf_2012/10-1705.pdf. Lynne Schaber, a Senior Trainer 1 at SeaWorld, stated that employees were told that "if you found yourself in the pool with Tilikum, you might not survive" (pp. 22–23).

25. Secretary of Labor v. SeaWorld, p. 9; "Autopsy: SeaWorld Trainer Died from Drowning, Traumatic Injuries," CNN, April 1, 2010, www.cnn.com/2010/US/03/31/florida.seaworld.autopsy/; Orange County Sheriff's Office Investigative Report, Case Number 2010-016715, Detective Samara Melich, EID 2685, April 28, 2010.

26. Tara John, "California Bans Captive Breeding of Killer Whales at Sea-World," *Time*, October 9, 2015, http://time.com/4067762/california-bans-captive-breeding-killer-whales-orcas-seaworld/. SeaWorld contested the legal authority of the Coastal Commission to issue the domestic breeding ban.

27. "SeaWorld Launches National Television Advertising Campaign," press release, SeaWorld, 2015, https://seaworldparks.com/en/corporate/media/company-news/2015/seaworld-launches-national-television-advertising-campaign.

28. Becky Peterson, "'Are Your Tanks Filled with Orca Tears?': SeaWorld Twitter Campaign Backfires as Marine Park Hashtag #AskSeaWorld Is Hijacked by Animal Rights Campaigners," *Daily Mail*, March 31, 2015, www.dailymail.co.uk/travel/travel_news/article-3019299/Are-tanks-filled-orca-tears-SeaWorld-Twitter-campaign-backfires-water-park-hashtag-AskSeaWorld-hijacked-animal-rights-campaigners.html.

29. Ibid.

30. Joel Manby, "SeaWorld CEO: We're Ending Our Orca Breeding Program. Here's Why," *Los Angeles Times*, March 17, 2016, www.latimes.com/opinion/op-ed/la-oe-0317-manby-sea-world-orca-breeding-20160317-story.html.

31. "The Only Place Where Real and Amazing Live," TV commercial, Sea-World, www.ispot.tv/ad/A68O/seaworld-the-only-place-where-real-and-amazing-live.

32. Sandra Pedicini, "First Orcas, Now Orlando: SeaWorld's Challenges Just Don't Let Up," *Orlando Sentinel*, August 21, 2016, www.orlandosentinel.com/business/tourism/os-seaworld-new-problems-20160818-story.html.

33. Ibid.

34. Ibid.

35. This step served to reduce violence, but it by no means eliminated the possibility of violence. In 2004, an uprising against former president Jean-Bertrand Aristide spread, resulting in the shooting death of a security guard outside the front gate of Royal Caribbean's Labadee property. The incident prompted Royal Caribbean to cancel port visits there for three months. Marc Lacey, "An 'Uphill Battle' to Polish Haiti's Image," *New York Times*, February 15, 2007, www.nytimes.com/2007/02/15/world/americas/15iht-haiti.4609127.html?_r=0.

36. Secretary of Labor v. SeaWorld of Florida, LLC, pp. 24–29.

37. Ibid.

38. Quoted in ibid., pp. 36–37.

39. PETA's SeaWorld campaign website, called SeaWorldofhurt.com, attracted about two dozen visitors per day before *Blackfish*. In 2015, the site had 1.3 million daily visitors all year long. Hugo Martin, "PETA Rakes in More Donations as It Denounces SeaWorld," *Los Angeles Times*, February 16, 2016, www.latimes.com/business/la-fi-peta-donations-20160216-story.html.

40. Caty Borom Chattoo, "Anatomy of the Blackfish Effect," *Huffington Post*, March 25, 2016, www.huffingtonpost.com/caty-borum-chattoo/anatomy-of-the-blackfish-_b_9511932.html.

41. SeaWorld Entertainment 2013 Annual Report. The six SeaWorld theme parks and companion parks were: SeaWorld Orlando, SeaWorld San Antonio, SeaWorld San Diego, Aquatica Orlando, Aquatica San Diego, and Discovery Cove (which is next to SeaWorld Orlando). The remaining five theme parks operated by SeaWorld Entertainment were: Busch Gardens Tampa, Busch Gardens Williamsburg, Sesame Place, Water Country USA, and Adventure Island (which is next to Busch Gardens Tampa).

42. Secretary v. SeaWorld, Judge Welsch Decision and Order, p. 3.

43. 2013 Annual Report, SeaWorld Entertainment, pp. 1–6; Kenneth Brower, "SeaWorld vs. the Whale That Killed Its Trainer," *National Geographic*, August 4, 2013.

44. Secretary vs. SeaWorld, Judge Welsch Decision and Order, pp. 19-21; Kenneth Brower, "SeaWorld vs. the Whale That Killed Its Trainer," *National Geographic*, August 4, 2013; David Kirby, "Near Death at SeaWorld: Worldwide Exclusive Video," *Huffington Post*, July 24, 2012, www.huffingtonpost.com/david-kirby/near-death-at-seaworld-wo_b_1697243.html.

45. Michael Cieply, "SeaWorld's Unusual Retort to a Critical Documentary," *New York Times*, July 18, 2013, www.nytimes.com/2013/07/19/business/media/seaworlds-unusual-retort-to-a-critical-documentary.html.

46. Chabeli Herrera, "Royal Caribbean Reestablishes Stop in Haiti, Deems It Safe," *Miami Herald*, January 26, 2016, www.miamiherald.com/news/business/tourism-cruises/article56710248.html.

CHAPTER 6: THE ART OF BOAT SPOTTING

1. We are grateful to Mary Driscoll from APQC for sharing this case study with us. APQC is a leading nonprofit organization that partners with more than five hundred global member organizations across industries to improve business productivity. Case study from APQC, "Best Practices Report, Enterprise Risk Management: Seven Imperatives for Process Excellence," 2014. See also Jens Hansegard, "Building Risk Management at Lego," *Wall Street Journal*, August 5, 2013, http://blogs.wsj.com/riskandcompliance/2013/08/05/building-risk-management-at-lego/; Mark L. Frigo and Hans Læssøe, "Strategic Risk Management at the Lego Group," *Strategic Finance*, February 2012.

2. Case study from APQC, "Best Practices Report."

3. Ibid. See also Hansegard, "Building Risk Management at Lego"; Frigo and Læssøe, "Strategic Risk Management at the Lego Group."

4. Case study from APQC, "Best Practices Report." See also Hansegard, "Building Risk Management at Lego"; Frigo and Læssøe, "Strategic Risk Management at the Lego Group."

5. Frigo and Læssøe, "Strategic Risk Management at the Lego Group," p. 31.

6. "Lego Is Building Itself Up to Pass Mattell as the World's Largest Toymaker," The Motley Fool, March 4, 2016, www.fool.com/investing/general/2016/03/04/lego-is-building-itself-up-to-pass-mattel-as-the-w.aspx.

7. Hansegard, "Building Risk Management at Lego."

8. Some astronauts flew more than once.

9. Tariq Malik, "NASA's Space Shuttle by the Numbers: 30 Years of a Spaceflight Icon," Space.com, July 21, 2011, www.space.com/12376-nasa-space-shuttle-program-facts-statistics.html.

10. In 2014, U.S. carriers flew an average 22,211 flights per day, or 675,000 per month. Bureau of Transportation Statistics, United States Department of Transportation, www.rita.dot.gov/bts/acts/customized/table?adfy=2014&adfm=1&adty=2015&adtm=1&aos=6&artd=1&arti&arts&asts=1&astns&astt&ascc&ascp=1.

11. Quoted in Alan Levin, "There'd Be 272 Crashes a Day If Jets Failed Like Shuttles," Bloomberg, October 31, 2014, www.bloomberg.com/news/articles/2014-10-31/there-d-be-272-crashes-a-day-if-jets-failed-like-shuttles.

12. See, for example, "Disney Named World's Most Powerful Brand," Walt Disney Company, February 18, 2016, https://thewaltdisneycompany.com/disney-named-worlds-most-powerful-brand/; "Disney Tops List of the World's Most Reputable Companies for 2016," Walt Disney Company, March 23, 2016, https://thewaltdisneycompany.com/disney-tops-list-of-the-worlds-most-reputable-companies-for-2016/; "The Harris Poll Releases Annual Reputation Rankings for the 100 Most Visible Companies in the U.S.," press release, Harris Poll, February 18, 2016, www.theharrispoll.com/business/Reputation-Rankings-Most-Visible-Companies.html.

13. Andrey P. Anohkin, Simon Golosheykin, and Andrew C. Heath, "Heritability of Risk Taking in Adolescence: A Longitudinal Twin Study," *Twin Research and Human Genetics* 12, no. 4 (August 2009): 366-71, http://www.ncbi.nlm.nih.gov/pmc/articles/PMC3077362/.

14. David Cesarini, Magnus Johannesson, Paul Lichtenstein, and Örjan Sandewall, "Genetic Variation in Financial Decision Making," *Journal of Finance* 65, no. 5 (October 2010): 1725–54; Xavier Caldu and Jean-Claude Dreher, "Hormonal and Genetic Influences on Processing Reward and Social Information," *Annals of New York Academy of Sciences* 1118 (2007):43–73, http://www.ncbi.nlm.nih.gov/pubmed/17804523.

15. Claudia R. Sahm, "How Much Does Risk Tolerance Change?," Working Paper, Finance and Economics Discussion Series, Federal Reserve Board, June 26, 2008, www.federalreserve.gov/PubS/feds/2007/200766/revision/200766pap.pdf.

16. *2014 Global Survey on Reputation Risk*, Deloitte, October 2014, www2.deloitte.com/content/dam/Deloitte/global/Documents/Governance-Risk-Compliance/gx_grc_Reputation@Risk%20survey%20report_FINAL.pdf, p. 5.

17. Tom Aabo, John Fraser, and Betty J. Simkins, "The Rise and Evolution of the Chief Risk Officer: Enterprise Risk Management at Hydro One," *Journal of Applied Corporate Finance* 17, no. 3 (June 2005).

18. Case study from APQC, "Best Practices Report."

19. "About Us," CEMEX, www.cemex.com/AboutUs/WorldwideLocations.aspx.

20. *2014 Global Survey on Reputation Risk*, Deloitte, p. 15.

21. Case study from APQC, "Best Practices Report." See also Hansegard, "Building Risk Management at Lego"; Frigo and Læssøe, "Strategic Risk Management at the Lego Group."

22. APQC, "Best Practices Report." See also Hansegard, "Building Risk Management at Lego"; Frigo and Læssøe, "Strategic Risk Management at the Lego Group."

23. APQC, "Best Practices Report," p. 40.

24. Quoted in *2014 Global Survey on Reputation Risk*, Deloitte, p. 7.

25. Quoted in ibid., pp. 1–6.

26. Ibid., p. 9.

27. Video, "A Message from Tom Hill, President and CEO of BAAM," Blackstone, www.blackstone.com/the-firm/asset-management/hedge-fund-solutions-(baam).

28. Hansegard, "Building Risk Management at Lego."

29. National Intelligence Council, "Global Trends 2030: Alternative Worlds," Office of the Director of National Intelligence, December 2012, www.dni.gov/index.php/about/organization/global-trends-2030.

30. "Cybersecurity Futures 2020," Center for Long-Term Cybersecurity, University of California at Berkeley, https://cltc.berkeley.edu/scenarios/.

31. Hansegard, "Building Risk Management at Lego"; Kristina Narvaez, "Value Creation Through Enterprise Risk Management," PowerPoint presentation, ERM Strategies, July 2013, www.erm-strategies.com/blog/wp-content/uploads/2013/07/Value-Creation-Through-Enterprise-Risk-Management.pdf. In 2008, the Lego Group created four scenarios based on megatrends defined by the World Economic Forum. These included "More of the Same," "Brave New World," "Cut-Throat Competition," and "Murphy's Surprise." For each, it identified key issues that might happen as a result of these trends and action steps for managing those issues. For more, see Frigo and Læssøe, "Strategic Risk Management at the Lego Group," p. 33.

32. Paul Bracken and Martin Shubik, "War Gaming in the Information Age: Theory and Purpose," *Naval War College Review* 54, no. 2. (Spring 2001).

33. Paul Bracken, *The Second Nuclear Age: Strategy, Danger, and the New Power Politics* (New York: Macmillan, 2012), 85.

34. Ibid., 87.

35. Geoff Wilson and Will Saetren, "Quite Possibly the Dumbest Military Concept Ever: A 'Limited' Nuclear War," *National Interest*, May 27, 2016, http://nationalinterest.org/blog/the-buzz/quite-possibly-the-dumbest-military-concept-ever-limited-16394.

36. Tucker Bailey, James Kaplan, and Allen Weinberg, "Playing War Games to Prepare for a Cyberattack," McKinsey, July 2012, www.mckinsey.com/business-functions/business-technology/our-insights/playing-war-games-to-prepare-for-a-cyberattack.

37. For a business war game primer, see Benjamin Gilad, *Business War Games* (Pompton Plains, NJ: Career Press, 2009).

38. Christine Negroni, "Dutch Safety Board: Ukraine Should Have Closed Its Airspace Before MH-17 Was Shot Down," *Air & Space Magazine*, October 13, 2015, www.airspacemag.com/daily-planet/dutch-safety-board-ukraine-should-have-closed-its-airspace-before-mh-17-was-shot-down-180956921/?no-ist.

39. Alastair Jamieson, "Why Was Malaysia Airlines MH17 Flying over Ukraine? Time, Money," NBC News, July 18, 2014, www.nbcnews.com/storyline/ukraine-plane-crash/why-was-malaysia-airlines-mh17-flying-over-ukraine-time-money-n159161.

CHAPTER 7: ANALYZING RISKS LIKE A PHYSICIST

1. Kiku Telecommunications is a fictitious company.

2. "Myanmar's Ethnic War Grinds On," Stratfor, October 8, 2015, www.stratfor.com/analysis/myanmars-ethnic-war-grinds; "Why Is There Communal Violence in Myanmar," BBC, July 3, 2014, www.bbc.com/news/world-asia-18395788; "Reforming Telecommunication in Burma," report, Human Rights Watch, May 2013, www.hrw.org/report/2013/05/19/reforming-telecommunications-burma/human-rights-and-responsible-investment-mobile.

3. Ian Bremmer and Preston Keat, *The Fat Tail: The Power of Political Knowledge in an Uncertain World* (Oxford: Oxford University Press, 2010), 179–80.

4. PricewaterhouseCoopers and Eurasia Group, "How Managing Political Risk Improves Global Business Performance," March 2006, summary of findings available at https://globenewswire.com/news-release/2006/03/30/341195/96448/en/Study-on-Political-Risk-Management-by-PricewaterhouseCoopers-and-Eurasia-Group-Reveals-Multinational-Companies-Need-a-Rigorous-Political-Risk-Management-Framework.html.

5. Drew Erdmann, Ezra Greenberg, and Ryan Harper, "Geostrategic Risks on the Rise," McKinsey & Company, May 2016, www.mckinsey.com/business-functions/strategy-and-corporate-finance/our-insights/geostrategic-risks-on-the-rise.

6. This enthusiasm was widespread. A 2013 McKinsey study noted that the country was a "highly unusual but promising prospect for businesses and investors," with sixty million people, a large labor pool, vast swaths of developable land, significant natural resources, a strategic location (neighboring half a billion people in the world's fastest growing region), and an emerging economy. Heang Chhor et al., "Myanmar's Moment: Unique Opportunities, Major Challenges," McKinsey Global Institute, June 2013, www.mckinsey.com/global-themes/asia-pacific/myanmars-moment.

7. Nomination of General Michael V. Hayden, USAF, to be Director of the Central Intelligence Agency, Hearing Before the Select Committee on Intelligence, United States Senate, 109th Congress, Second Session, May 18, 2006, www.intelligence.senate.gov/hearings/nomination-general-michael-v-hayden-usaf-be-director-central-intelligence-agency-may-18#.

8. Nicholas Charron, Victor Lapuente, and Lewis Dijkstra, "Regional Governance Matters: A Study on Regional Variation in Quality of Government Within the EU," Working Paper, European Commission, 2012, http://ec.europa.eu/regional_policy/sources/docgener/work/2012_02_governance.pdf. See also Enterprise Surveys/World Bank Group corruption surveys, which in some cases subdivide by regions or states within individual countries. In Romania, for example, surveys find that the percent of firms expected to give gifts to secure government contracts ranges from zero percent in the Northeast, Northwest, South, and West regions to 29.3 percent in the Central region. www.enterprisesurveys.org/data/exploretopics/corruption.

9. Juan Forero and Taos Turner, "Challenger Mauricio Macri Wins Argentine Presidential Runoff," *Wall Street Journal*, November 22, 2015, www.wsj.com/articles/argentines-cast-votes-for-president-1448209335.

10. Daniel Bases, Richard Lough, and Sarah Marsh, "Argentina, Lead Creditors Settle 14-Year Debt Battle for $4.65 Billion," Reuters, March 1, 2016, www.reuters.com/article/us-argentina-debt-idUSKCN0W2249.

11. Peter Schechter, "Argentina's Mauricio Macri Needs Concrete Wins," *Forbes*, August 15, 2016, www.forbes.com/sites/realspin/2016/08/15/argentinas-mauricio-macri-needs-concrete-wins/#2990dd452c11.

12. Ibid.

13. Bruce Watson, "Cruise Line Visit to Haiti Highlights Ugly Side of Paradise," AOL.com, January 22, 2010, www.aol.com/article/2010/01/22/cruise-line-visit-to-haiti-highlights-ugly-side-of-paradise/19328050/?gen=1.

14. The Dubai Ports World discussion is drawn mostly from Condoleezza Rice, William Barnett, and Cecilia Hyunjung Mo, "The Dubai Ports Controversy," Stanford Graduate School of Business, Case GS-73, 2009, www.gsb.stanford.edu/faculty-research/case-studies/dubai-ports-controversy; see also "Key Questions About the Dubai Port Deal," CNN, March 6, 2006, www.cnn.com/2006/POLITICS/03/06/dubai.ports.qa/.

15. Ibid.

16. Ibid.

17. Quoted in Julio J. Rotemberg, "The Dubai Ports World Debacle and Its Aftermath," Harvard Business School Case 9-707-014, August 29, 2007, p. 4.

18. Quoted in Jim V, eHei [*sic*: VandeHei], and Jonathan Weisman, "Republicans Split with Bush on Ports: White House Vows to Brief Lawmakers on Deal with Firm Run by Arab State," *Washington Post*, February 23, 2006, www.washingtonpost.com/archive/politics/2006/02/23/republicans-split-with-bush-on-ports-span-classbankhead-white-house-vows-to-brief-lawmakers-on-deal-with-firm-run-by-arab-statespan/346ad4cb-6723-467b-b8d8-e362667d0acd/?utm_term=.c2e46387e6c1.

19. Rodney C. Ewing and Jeroen Ritsema, "Underestimating Nuclear Accident Risks: Why Are Rare Events So Common?," *Bulletin of Atomic Scientists*, May 3, 2011, http://thebulletin.org/fukushima-what-dont-we-know/underestimating-nuclear-accident-risks-why-are-rare-events-so-common; "A Brief History of Nuclear Accidents Worldwide," Union of Concerned Scientists, www.ucsusa.org/nuclear-power/nuclear-power-accidents/history-nuclear-accidents#.V_FWvJMrJBx.

20. Quoted in Miles Traer, "Fukushima Five Years Later: Stanford Nuclear Expert Offers Three Lessons from the Disaster," Stanford News Service, March 4, 2016, http://news.stanford.edu/press-releases/2016/03/04/pr-fukushima-lessons-ewing-030416/.

21. The IAEA's 2010 report finds that Japan operated 54 nuclear reactors. The United States had 104 reactors and France had 58. See "International Status and Prospects of Nuclear Power," www.iaea.org/sites/default/files/np10.pdf.

22. Ewing, "Underestimating Nuclear Accident Risks."

23. Minoura published his findings in respected scientific journals. Officials at the Tokyo Electric Power Company, which owns the Fukushima Daiichi nuclear plant, were aware of his findings but dismissed them. Ewing, "Underestimating Nuclear Accident Risks." See also "Scientist Warned of Tsunami Disaster in Japan," PRI, January 17, 2012, www.pri.org/stories/2012-01-17/scientist-warned-tsunami-disaster-japan; "Nuclear Aftershocks," *Frontline*, PBS, January 17, 2012, at 15:48–19:19, www.pbs.org/wgbh/frontline/film/nuclear-aftershocks/.

24. Alice Park, "A Cardiac Conundrum," *Harvard Magazine*, March–April 2013, http://harvardmagazine.com/2013/03/a-cardiac-conundrum; Amy Beth

Zegart, "What March Madness Tells Us About Forecasting," *Insights by Stanford Business*, Stanford Graduate School of Business, March 18, 2013, www.gsb.stanford.edu/insights/what-march-madness-tells-us-about-forecasting.

25. David S. Jones, *Broken Hearts: The Tangled History of Cardiac Care* (Baltimore: Johns Hopkins University Press, 2012).

26. Richard P. Feynman, "Cargo Cult Science," commencement address, California Institute of Technology, June 14, 1974, http://calteches.library.caltech.edu/51/2/CargoCult.htm.

27. Richards J. Heuer, *Psychology of Intelligence Analysis* (Center for the Study of Intelligence, CIA, 1999).

28. Norman Maier, "Reasoning in Humans I," *Journal of Comparative Psychology* 10 (1930): 115–43, 10.1037/h0073232.

29. Atul Gawande, *The Checklist Manifesto: How to Get Things Right* (New York: Henry Holt, 2009), 108.

30. Ibid., 150.

31. Irving L. Janis, *Victims of Groupthink: A Psychological Study of Foreign Policy Decisions and Fiascoes* (Boston: Houghton Mifflin, 1972).

32. Angela Wilkinson and Roland Kupers, "Living in the Futures," *Harvard Business Review*, May 2013, https://hbr.org/2013/05/living-in-the-futures.

33. Pierre Wack, "Scenarios: Uncharted Waters Ahead," *Harvard Business Review*, September 1985, https://hbr.org/1985/09/scenarios-uncharted-waters-ahead.

34. Peter Schwartz, *The Art of the Long View* (New York: Doubleday, 1991), 7–9; Wack, "Scenarios: Uncharted Waters Ahead."

35. Wilkinson and Kupers, "Living in the Futures." They note that scenario planning at Shell has not always been well supported or received.

36. Barbara Bilodeau and Darrell K. Rigby, "A Growing Focus on Preparedness," *Harvard Business Review*, July–August 2007, https://hbr.org/2007/07/a-growing-focus-on-preparedness; Darrell Rigby and Barbara Bilodeau, "Management Tools and Trends 2015," Bain & Company, June 10, 2015, www.bain.com/Images/BAIN_BRIEF_Management_Tools_2015.pdf.

37. Bilodeau and Rigby, "Management Tools and Trends."

38. Pierre Wack, "Scenarios: Shooting the Rapids," *Harvard Business Review*, November 1985, https://hbr.org/1985/11/scenarios-shooting-the-rapids; Schwartz, *The Art of the Long View*; Peter Schwartz, *Learnings from the Long View* (San Francisco: Global Business Network, 2011); Wack, "Scenarios: Uncharted Waters Ahead."

39. Schwartz, *The Art of the Long View*, xiii.

40. Ibid., p. 9; Pierre Wack, "Scenarios: The Gentle Art of Re-perceiving," Shell International Petroleum Company, 1985.

41. Intel's use of red teams from Rossi Sheffi, *The Resilient Enterprise: Overcoming Vulnerability for Competitive Advantage* (Cambridge, MA: MIT Press, 2005), 53–55. Goldman Sachs's use of red teams from Micah Zenko,

Red Team: How to Succeed by Thinking Like the Enemy (New York: Basic Books, 2015), 178.

42. Red team cyber "penetration testing" is required for many large companies. As Micah Zenko writes, the Commodity Futures Trading Commission, the Health Insurance Portability and Accountability Act, and the Payment Card Industry Data Security Standard all require that companies use penetration testing to identify vulnerabilities and verify safeguards. Zenko, *Red Team*, 177–78.

43. For more on red team best practices and pitfalls, see Zenko, *Red Team*.

44. Jayson E. Street, "Breaking in Bad," DEF CON 23 presentation, published December 11, 2015, www.youtube.com/watch?v=2vdvINDmlX8.

45. Ibid.; Zenko, *Red Team*, 202–6.

46. Street, "Breaking in Bad." One national U.S. bank hired Street to test cyber security at ten West Coast branches. Posing as a technician needing to examine "power fluctuations," Street was granted access throughout the first branch. He plugged in a small device called a Pwn Plug that looks like a power adapter but is actually a computer armed with hacking tools for remote access. After the fourth branch, Street says, the bank told him, "Stop now please. We give up." Robert McMillan, "The Little White Box That Can Hack Your Network," *Wired*, March 2, 2012, www.wired.com/2012/03/pwnie/.

47. Zenko, *Red Team*, 5.

48. Heuer, *Psychology of Intelligence Analysis*, 71. See also Todd Conklin, *Pre-Accident Investigations: An Introduction to Organizational Safety* (Boca Raton, FL: CRC Press, 2012); Deborah J. Mitchell, J. Edward Russo, and Nancy Pennington, "Back to the Future: Temporal Perspective in the Explanation of Events," *Journal of Behavioral Decision Making* 2 (1989): 25–38.

49. A 1989 study by researchers at Wharton, Cornell, and the University of Colorado found that thinking backwards—what they call "prospective hindsight"—increased by 30 percent the ability to correctly identify reasons for future outcomes. Mitchell, Russo, and Pennington, "Back to the Future."

50. Pope John Paul II ended the use of official devil's advocates in the Catholic Church in 1983 to make the process faster and less adversarial. He produced more beatifications and canonizations in two decades than his 263 predecessors did over the previous two millennia. Zenko, *Red Team*, ix–xii; Rachel Martin and Ben Zimmer, "Who Is the 'Devil's' Advocate," NPR, March 3, 2013, www.npr.org/2013/03/03/173350724/who-is-the-devils-advocate.

51. Richard K. Betts, *Surprise Attack: Lessons for Defense Planning* (Washington, DC: Brookings Institution, 1982); Alexander L. George and Eric K. Stern, "Harnessing Conflict in Foreign Policy Making: From Devil's to Multiple Advocacy," *Presidential Studies Quarterly* 32, no. 3 (September 2002): 484–508.

52. Jens Hansegard, "Building Risk Management at Lego," *Wall Street Journal*, August 5, 2013.

53. We are grateful to Mary Driscoll from APQC for sharing this case study with us. APQC is a leading nonprofit organization that partners with more

than five hundred global member organizations across all industries to improve business productivity. Case study from APQC, "Best Practices Report, Enterprise Risk Management: Seven Imperatives for Process Excellence," 2014. See also Hansegard, "Building Risk Management at Lego"; Mark L. Frigo and Hans Læssøe, "Strategic Risk Management at the Lego Group," *Strategic Finance*, February 2012.

54. Ibid.

55. Quoted in Hansegard, "Building Risk Management at Lego."

56. Ibid.

57. Full disclosure: Phil Knight, the founder of Nike, came up with the idea for the company while he was attending business school at Stanford, and the business school today is named after him.

58. Mike Ozanian, "The Forbes Fab 40: The World's Most Valuable Sports Brands 2015," *Forbes*, October 22, 2015, www.forbes.com/sites/mikeozanian/2015/10/22/the-forbes-fab-40-the-most-valuable-brands-in-sports-2015/#51ea0fc22e2a.

59. Quoted in Shelly Banjo, "Inside Nike's Struggle to Balance Cost and Worker Safety in Bangladesh," *Wall Street Journal*, April 21, 2014, https://www.wsj.com/articles/inside-nikes-struggle-to-balance-cost-and-worker-safety-in-bangladesh-1398133855.

60. Quoted in ibid.

61. Ibid.

62. Quoted in ibid.

63. Ibid.

CHAPTER 8: THE NUCLEAR TRIAD, THE EMPTY PLANE, AND OTHER WAYS TO MITIGATE RISKS

1. Andrew Cave, "The $30,000-a-Night Jet That Flies Empty," *Forbes*, August 29, 2016; "About FedEx," FedEx website, http://about.van.fedex.com/our-story/company-structure/express-fact-sheet.

2. Ibid. FedEx also delivers 7.3 million packages daily to the United States and Canada by ground and offers a host of business logistics services.

3. Henry Samuel, "France Braced for Wave of Strikes over Labour Reform as Hollande Insists: 'I Won't Give In,'" *Telegraph*, May 17, 2016, www.telegraph.co.uk/news/2016/05/17/french-braces-for-wave-of-strikes-over-labour-reform-as-hollande/.

4. Quoted in Cave, "The $30,000-a-Night Jet That Flies Empty." See also Karl E. Weick and Kathleen M. Sutcliffe, *Managing the Unexpected: Resilient Performance in an Age of Uncertainty* (San Francisco: Jossey-Bass, 2007).

5. Bonny Harrison and Jeff Martinez, "Fueling E-commerce: FedEx Super Hub's Physical Structure Powers Virtual Business," FedEx Blog, August 1, 2016, http://about.van.fedex.com/blog/fueling-e-commerce-fedex-super-hubs-physical-structure-powers-virtual-business-2/.

6. Jeffrey F. Rayport, "The Miracle of Memphis," *MIT Technology Review*, December 20, 2010, www.technologyreview.com/s/422081/the-miracle-of-memphis/; Harrison and Martinez, "Fueling E-commerce."

7. Cave, "The $30,000-a-Night Jet That Flies Empty"; "About FedEx."

8. Harrison and Martinez, "Fueling E-commerce"; Cave, "The $30,000-a-Night Jet That Flies Empty"; "About FedEx"; Rayport, "The Miracle of Memphis."

9. "In Control, Around the Clock," FedEx website, https://smallbusiness.fedex.com/global-operations-center.html.

10. Ibid.

11. Jason Douglas, "Every Plane Has a Name," FedEx Blog, September 30, 2015, http://about.van.fedex.com/blog/every-plane-bears-a-name/; "FedEx Executive Leadership," FedEx website, http://about.van.fedex.com/our-story/leadership/.

12. FedEx, "In Control, Around the Clock."

13. Paul Tronsor, "Business Unusual: Flight Planning and the Iceland Volcano Eruption," FedEx Blog, May 4, 2010, http://about.van.fedex.com/blog/business-unusual-flight-planning-and-the-iceland-volcano-eruption/.

14. "In Control, Around the Clock," FedEx Updates, October 2015.

15. Ibid.

16. Brian Dumaine, "FedEx CEO Fred Smith on . . . Everything," *Fortune*, May 11, 2012, http://fortune.com/2012/05/11/fedex-ceo-fred-smith-on-everything/.

17. Quoted in ibid.

18. Quoted in "Frederick W. Smith," Academy of Achievement, interview, www.achievement.org/achiever/frederick-w-smith/#interview.

19. APQC, "Risk Management: Extreme Weather Increasingly Disrupts Global Supply Chains," K04425, 2013, p. 2; Andrea J. Stroud, "Supply Chain Disruption: What Your Organization Should Know About Managing Risk in the Supply Chain," APQC K04424, 2013. APQC is a member-based nonprofit and one of the leading proponents of benchmarking and best-practice business research. "Managing the Risk of Supply Chain Disruption," May 2013 APQC Summary Report, www.apqc.org/knowledge-base/download/289037/K04362_Survey%20Summary%20Report-Finance%20and%20Supply%20Chain%20Risk.pdf.

20. IRM Security, *Finally the Board Is Paying Attention to Cyber. Now What?* 2016, http://info.irmsecurity.com/riskybusinessreport, p.8.

21. 2014 SeaWorld Annual Report, http://s1.q4cdn.com/392447382/files/doc_financials/Annual%20Reports/2014-SEAS-Annual-Report.pdf; Arthur Levine, "SeaWorld in 2017: New Coasters, Rides, and Shows to Turn the Tide," *USA Today*, September 26, 2016, www.usatoday.com/story/travel/experience/america/theme-parks/2016/09/26/seaworld-new-coasters-rides-shows-2017/91129692/.

22. This point is debated. FBI cyber division chief Joseph Demarest and cyber security expert Kevin Mandia found that the Sony hack was the work of a sophisticated cyber adversary using malware that was undetectable by standard antivirus software.

23. Peter Elkind, "Inside the Hack of the Century," Part 2, *Fortune*, June 25, 2015, http://fortune.com/sony-hack-part-two/; Sophie Curtis, "Sony Saved Thousands of Passwords in a Folder Named 'Password,'" *Telegraph*, December 5, 2014, www.telegraph.co.uk/technology/sony/11274727/Sony-saved-thousands-of-passwords-in-a-folder-named-Password.html.

24. Peter Elkind, "Inside the Hack of the Century," Part 1, *Fortune*, June 25, 2015, http://fortune.com/sony-hack-part-1/.

25. Ibid.

26. Nenad Pacek and Daniel Thorniley, *Emerging Markets: Lessons for Business Success and the Outlook for Different Markets*, 2nd ed. (London: *The Economist* in association with Profile Books, 2007), 44–45.

27. "Permian Basin," Occidental Petroleum Company, www.oxy.com/OurBusinesses/OilandGas/UnitedStates/Permian/Pages/default.aspx.

28. We are grateful to Paul Bracken for drawing the parallels between U.S. nuclear strategy and businesses. See Bracken, *The Second Nuclear Age: Strategy, Danger, and the New Power Politics* (New York: Macmillan, 2012).

29. Meryl Gordon, "Howard Lutnick's Second Life," *New York Magazine*, December 10, 2001, http://nymag.com/nymetro/news/sept11/features/5486/index1.html.

30. Julia La Roche, "The Amazing and Heartbreaking Story of the CEO Who Lived and Rebuilt His Firm After 9/11: Howard Lutnick," *Business Insider*, September 11, 2011, www.businessinsider.com/cantor-fitzgerald-9-11-story-howard-lutnick-2011-9.

31. Ivy Schmerken, "Cantor's eSpeed System Rebounds, Replacing Voice Brokerage," *Wall Street & Technology*, October 10, 2001, www.wallstreetandtech.com/careers/cantors-espeed-system-rebounds-replacing-voice-brokerage/d/d-id/1254841?.

32. Ibid.

33. Richard Blake, "Cantor Fitzgerald: Miracle on Wall Street," *Institutional Investor*, September 3, 2009, www.institutionalinvestor.com/article/2287395/banking-and-capital-markets-banking/cantor-fitzgerald-miracle-on-wall-street.html#.WBJ_5JMrJBw; Susanne Craig, "The Survivor Who Saw the Future for Cantor Fitzgerald," *New York Times*, September 3, 2011, http://dealbook.nytimes.com/2011/09/03/the-survivor-who-saw-the-future-for-cantor-fitzgerald/?_r=0.

34. Schmerken, "Cantor's eSpeed System Rebounds."

35. "Boeing 787 Dreamliner: A Timeline of Problems," *Telegraph*, July 28, 2013, www.telegraph.co.uk/travel/comment/Boeing-787-Dreamliner-a-timeline-of-problems/; Nicola Clark, "Boeing Announces Delay in Deliveries of 787 Dreamliner," *New York Times*, October 10, 2007, www.nytimes.com/2007/10/10/business/worldbusiness/10iht-boeing.4.7837959.html.

36. Gary S. Lynch, *Single Point of Failure: The 10 Essential Laws of Supply Chain Risk Management* (Hoboken, NJ: John Wiley & Sons, 2009), 188.

37. Yossi Sheffi, *The Resilient Enterprise: Overcoming Vulnerability for Competitive Advantage* (Cambridge, MA: MIT Press, 2005), 184, citing Chris J. McDonald,

"The Evolution of Intel's Copy Exact! Technology Transfer Method," *Intel Technology Journal*, 1998.

38. Stephen Prince, *Classical Film Violence: Designing and Regulating Brutality in Hollywood Cinema, 1930–1968* (New Brunswick, NJ: Rutgers University Press, 2003).

39. Roxanna Guildrod-Blake, "It's Time to Break Down Silos: Former NIRI President Points to FedEx as Model of IR, PR Integration," *Bulldog Reporter*, July 29, 2010, www.bulldogreporter.com/its-time-break-down-silos-former-niri-president-points-fedex-model-ir-pr-integratio/.

40. Pacek and Thorniley, *Emerging Markets*, 40.

41. "MH17 Ukraine Plane Crash: What We Know," BBC, September 28, 2016, www.bbc.com/news/world-europe-28357880.

42. Ibid.; Alastair Jamieson, "Why Was Malaysia Airlines MH17 Flying over Ukraine? Time, Money," NBC News, July 18, 2014, www.nbcnews.com/storyline/ukraine-plane-crash/why-was-malaysia-airlines-mh17-flying-over-ukraine-time-money-n159161.

43. "Mexico Travel Warning," U.S. Department of State, October 10, 2014, http://travel.state.gov/content/passports/english/alertswarnings/mexico-travel-warning.html; "U.S. Relations with Mexico," U.S. Department of State, September 10 2014, www.state.gov/r/pa/ei/bgn/35749.htm.

44. "Crime in the United States: Uniform Crime Reports," Federal Bureau of Investigation, 2013, www.fbi.gov/about-us/cjis/ucr/crime-in-the-u.s/2013/crime-in-the-u.s.-2013/violent-crime/murder-topic-page/murdermain_final.

45. Kate Abbey-Lambertz, "These Are the Major U.S. Cities with the Highest Murder Rates, According to the FBI," *Huffington Post*, November 12, 2014, www.huffingtonpost.com/2014/11/12/highest-murder-rate-us-cities-2013_n_6145404.html; Anthony Harrup, "Mexican Homicide Rate Fell 12.5% in 2013, Statistics Agency Says," *Wall Street Journal*, July 24, 2014, http://online.wsj.com/articles/mexican-homicide-rate-fell-12-5-in-2013-statistics-agency-says-1406155624.

46. Betts, *Surprise Attack: Lessons for Defense Planning* (Washington, DC: Brookings Institution, 1982), 91; William Bartsch, *December 8, 1941: MacArthur's Pearl Harbor* (College Station: Texas A&M University Press, 2012), 409.

47. "Marriott Closes $13-Billion Purchase of Starwood to Become World's Largest Hotel Chain," *Los Angeles Times*, September 23, 2016, www.latimes.com/business/la-fi-marriott-starwood-20160923-snap-story.html.

48. Abdala and Archell, "Alcoa's Juruti Mining Project Seeking to Set Sustainability Benchmark."

49. Ibid.; Maylie, "Alcoa Invests Near Planned Mines."

50. Walmart case abstracted from Daniel Diermeier, *Reputation Rules: Strategies for Building Your Company's Most Valuable Asset* (New York: McGraw-Hill, 2011), 112–16; Renee Montagne, "Wal-Mart CEO Stepping Down After 9 Years," NPR, January 30, 2009, www.npr.org/templates/story/story.php?storyId=100049709.

51. Diermeier, *Reputation Rules*, 112–16.

52. Quoted in ibid., 114.

53. Ibid., 112–16.

54. Montagne, "Wal-Mart CEO Stepping Down After 9 Years."

55. Diermeier, *Reputation Rules*, 112–16.

56. Montagne, "Wal-Mart CEO Stepping Down After 9 Years."

57. Diermeier, *Reputation Rules*, 112–16.

58. Quote from Montagne, "Wal-Mart CEO Stepping Down After 9 Years."

59. Herbert A. Simon, *The Sciences of the Artificial* (Cambridge, MA: MIT Press, 1996); Herbert A. Simon, *Reason in Human Affairs* (Stanford, CA: Stanford University Press, 1983); William G. Chase and Herbert A. Simon, "Perception in Chess," *Cognitive Psychology* 4, no. 1 (January 1973): 55–81; Roger Frantz, *Two Minds: Intuition and Analysis in the History of Economic Thought* (New York: Springer, 2005), 118.

60. Zegart, *Flawed by Design* (Stanford, CA: Stanford University Press, 1999), 229–30; Mark Bowden, "The Desert One Debacle," *Atlantic*, May 2006, www.theatlantic.com/magazine/archive/2006/05/the-desert-one-debacle/304803/.

61. Eugene Scott, "Carter: 'I Wish I'd Sent One More Helicopter' for U.S. Hostages in Iran," CNN, August 20, 2015, www.cnn.com/2015/08/20/politics/jimmy-carter-iran-hostages/.

62. Zegart, *Flawed by Design*, 143, 229–30.

63. FedEx, "In Control, Around the Clock."

64. Ibid.

65. Ibid.; Tronsor, "Business Unusual."

66. Ibid.

CHAPTER 9: ZULU TIME

1. "Profile: Jemaah Islamiah," BBC, February 2, 2012, www.bbc.com/news/world-asia-16850706; Alan Orlob, "Traveler Safety Is Everybody's Business," *Forbes*, January 6, 2015, www.forbes.com/sites/edfuller/2015/01/06/traveler-safety-is-everybodys-business/2/#5e9b3b1b29b1; Tom Wright, "Bombing Suspects Spent Two Days at Hotel," *Wall Street Journal*, July 18, 2009, www.wsj.com/articles/SB124783405799057621.

2. CRS Report, "Terrorism in Southeast Asia," Congressional Research Service 7-5700, October 16, 2009, www.fas.org/sgp/crs/terror/RL34194.pdf, p. 8.

3. Orlob, "Traveler Safety Is Everybody's Business."

4. Ibid.

5. Office of the Coordinator for Counterterrorism, "Country Reports on Terrorism 2009," U.S. Department of State, August 5, 2010, www.state.gov/j/ct/rls/crt/2009/140884.htm.

6. Rich Roberts, "Marriott Tweets to Spread Word During Crisis," *Hotel News Now*, August 3, 2009, www.hotelnewsnow.com/Articles/3279/Marriott-tweets-to-spread-word-during-crisis.

7. Marriott Sustainability Report, 2009, www.marriott.com/Multimedia/PDF/CorporateResponsibility/Marriott_Sustainability_Report_2009.pdf, p. 5.

8. Alan Orlob, "Protecting Soft Targets: How Marriott International Deals with the Threat of Terrorism Overseas," in *The McGraw-Hill Homeland Security Handbook*, ed. David Kamien (New York: McGraw-Hill, 2005), 861–72.

9. Ibid.

10. Their security protections had been ratcheted even higher to incorporate lessons learned from earlier attacks. Keith Bradsher, "Deadly Car Bombing Shakes Marriott Hotel in Jakarta," *New York Times*, August 5, 2003, www.nytimes.com/2003/08/05/international/asia/deadly-car-bombing-shakes-marriott-hotel-in-jakarta.html; "JW Marriott Hotel Bombing," GlobalSecurity.org, www.globalsecurity.org/security/ops/marriot.htm.

11. Orlob, "Protecting Soft Targets."

12. NTDTV, "Security Under Scurtiny for Jakarta Hotels," YouTube, July 25, 2009, www.youtube.com/watch?v=hKakvJcwO2A.

13. APPEL News Staff, "Understanding Near-Misses at NASA," Academy of Program/Project and Engineering Leadership, NASA, February 26, 2010, http://appel.nasa.gov/2010/02/26/ao_1-12_understanding-html/.

14. Indeed, some research finds that people engage in *riskier* behavior after near-miss events. See Robin L. Dillon and Catherine H. Tinsley, "Interpreting Near-Miss Events," *Engineering Management Journal* 17, no. 4 (2005); Dillon and Tinsley, "How Near-Misses Influence Decisions Making Under Risk: A Missed Opportunity for Learning," *Management Science* 54, no. 8 (June 2008): 1425–40; Catherine H. Tinsley, Robin L. Dillon, and Peter M. Madsen, "How to Avoid Catastrophe," *Harvard Business Review*, April 2011, https://hbr.org/2011/04/how-to-avoid-catastrophe.

15. Tinsley, Dillon, and Madsen, "How to Avoid Catastrophe."

16. Apple case from ibid.

17. Ibid.

18. Chapters III and IV of "Report of the Presidential Commission on the Space Shuttle Challenger Accident," Rogers Commission Report (Washington, DC: Government Printing Office, 1986), 157–336, available at https://er.jsc.nasa.gov/seh/explode.html.

19. Rogers Commission Report, 92.

20. AmericaSpace, "Missed Warnings: The Fatal Flaws Which Doomed Challenger," *Space Safety Magazine*, January 28, 2014, www.spacesafetymagazine.com/space-disasters/challenger-disaster/missed-warnings-fatal-flaws-doomed-challenger/.

21. "Engineer Who Opposed Challenger Launch Offers Personal Look at Tragedy," NASA, October 5, 2012, www.nasa.gov/centers/langley/news/researchernews/rn_Colloquium1012.html.

22. "Report to the President by the Presidential Commission on the Space Shuttle Challenger Accident," NASA, June 6, 1986, http://spaceflight.nasa.gov/outreach/SignificantIncidents/assets/rogers_commission_report.pdf, p. 149.

23. Weick and Sutcliffe, *Managing the Unexpected*, 24.

24. "USS Carl Vinson (CVN 70)," Navy Site, http://navysite.de/cvn/cvn70.html; information from USS *Vinson* public affairs office.

25. "Heathrow Airport," Optics and Media Access, http://optimediacc.com/airport-heathrow.php.

26. Kyle Mizokami, "Here Is Every Aircraft Carrier in the World," *Popular Mechanics*, January 25, 2016, www.popularmechanics.com/military/navy-ships/g2412/a-global-roundup-of-aircraft-carriers/.

27. See Weick and Sutcliffe, *Managing the Unexpected*, for more on planning for failure and responding strongly to weak signals.

28. Ibid.

29. Charles Goldsmith, "EU Agrees to Block Merger of Boeing, McDonnell-Douglas," *Wall Street Journal*, July 7, 1997, www.wsj.com/articles/SB868213225416324500; "Brussels v Boeing," *Economist*, July 17, 1997, www.economist.com/node/151796.

30. Goldsmith, "EU Agrees to Block Merger of Boeing, McDonnell-Douglas."

31. BP contracted the *Deepwater Horizon* rig, which was owned and operated by Transocean. A third company, Halliburton, was contracted for cementing and other drilling services.

32. Scientists and analysts are still assessing the long-term environmental impact of the spill. Chelsea Harvey, "The Deepwater Horizon Spill May Have Caused 'Irreversible' Damage to Gulf Coast Marshes," *Washington Post*, September 27, 2016, www.washingtonpost.com/news/energy-environment/wp/2016/09/27/the-deepwater-horizon-oil-spill-may-have-caused-irreversible-damage-to-marshes-along-the-gulf-coast/?utm_term=.3550e883249; Jacqueline Fiore, Craig Bond, and Shanthi Nataraj, *Estimating the Effects of the Deepwater Horizon Oil Spill on Fisheries Landings: A Preliminary Exploration*, RAND Report WR-1173-GMA, December 14, 2016.

33. Devlin Barrett, "U.S., BP Finalize $20.8 Billion Deepwater Oil Spill Settlement," *Wall Street Journal*, www.wsj.com/articles/u-s-says-20-8-billion-bp-spill-settlement-finalized-1444058619.

34. These included violations of existing government regulations; lagging government and industry safety standards and unclear guidelines as offshore drilling grew more technically challenging; unclear management responsibilities between BP (the well owner), Transocean (the rig owner/operator), and Halliburton (the cement and drilling contractor); poor maintenance of electrical equipment that may have ignited the explosion; bypassed gas alarms and automatic shutdown systems; training deficiencies; and a flawed safety management system and culture on board *Deepwater Horizon*.

35. Ian Urbina, "In Gulf, It Was Unclear Who Was in Charge of Rig," *New York Times*, June 5, 2010, www.nytimes.com/2010/06/06/us/06rig.html?scp=1&sq=at%20issue%20in%20gulf&st=cse.

36. James David Dykes, Co-Chair, USCG/BOEMRE Joint Investigation into the Deepwater Horizon/Macondo Well Blowout, testimony before the

United States House of Representatives Committee on Natural Resources, Oversight Hearing on the BOEMRE/U.S. Coast Guard Joint Investigation Team Report, October 13, 2011, p. 9.

37. Urbina, "In Gulf, It Was Unclear Who Was in Charge of Rig."

38. Michael R. Bromwich, Director, Bureau of Safety and Environmental Enforcement, United States Department of the Interior, testimony to the United States House of Representatives Committee on Natural Resources, oversight hearing on BOEMRE/U.S. Coast Guard Joint Investigation Team Report Part I, October 13, 2011.

39. Urbina, "In Gulf, It Was Unclear Who Was in Charge of Rig." See also United States House of Representatives, Committee on Energy and Commerce, Subcommittee on Oversight and Investigations, hearing on the Role of BP in the Deepwater Horizon Explosion and Oil Spill, June 17, 2010, p. 14.

40. SheilaMcNulty,"DocumentsHintatBPPlanningFailures,"*FinancialTimes*, August 26, 2010, www.ft.com/content/752b1c32-b16f-11df-b899-00144feabdc0?mhq5j=e1; United States House of Representatives, Committee on Energy and Commerce, Subcommittee on Oversight and Investigations, hearing on the Role of BP in the Deepwater Horizon Explosion and Oil Spill, June 17, 2010, pp. 99, 109.

41. The results were discussed among members of the crew, and a second test was ordered. This second test was successful, so BP and Transocean officials decided to ignore the first test, explaining the pressure readings as a "bladder effect." According to the Coast Guard Joint Inquiry, the crew continued to overlook "a number of different anomalies" for the next sixty to ninety minutes that should have signaled the influx of leaking hydrocarbons up the wellbore, through the riser, and onto the rig. Michael R. Bromwich, Director, Bureau of Safety and Environmental Enforcement, United States Department of the Interior, testimony to the United States House of Representatives Committee on Natural Resources, oversight hearing on BOEMRE/U.S. Coast Guard Joint Investigation Team Report Part I, October 13, 2011.

42. BP, Deepwater Horizon Accident Investigation Report, September 8, 2010, www.bp.com/content/dam/bp/pdf/sustainability/issue-reports/Deepwater_Horizon_Accident_Investigation_Report.pdf, p. 89.

43. Committee on the Analysis of Causes of the Deepwater Horizon Explosion, Fire, and Oil Spill to Identify Measures to Prevent Similar Accidents in the Future, National Academy of Engineering and National Research Council, *Interim Report on Causes of the* Deepwater Horizon *Oil Rig Blowout and Ways to Prevent Such Events* (Washington, DC: National Academies Press, 2010), 10. In addition, the report, and a second investigation conducted by the U.S. Coast Guard, found that the *Deepwater Horizon* crew disabled or circumvented other systems designed to generate signals of possible disaster. These included bypassing an automatic shutdown system intended to prevent flammable gas from reaching ignition sources. The chief electrician was told by a crew member that it had

"been in bypass for five years" and that "the entire fleet runs them in bypass." Had it been activated, the engine room explosion might have been prevented. See also U.S. Coast Guard, *Report of Investigation into the Circumstances Surrounding the Explosion, Fire, Sinking, and Loss of Eleven Crew Members Aboard the Mobile Offshore Drilling Unit Deepwater Horizon in the Gulf of Mexico April 20-22, 2010*, vol. I, MISLE Activity Number 3721503, pp. 26–27.

44. James David Dykes, Co-Chair, USCG/BOEMRE Joint Investigation into the Deepwater Horizon/Macondo Well Blowout, testimony before the United States House of Representatives Committee on Natural Resources, oversight hearing on the BOEMRE/U.S. Coast Guard Joint Investigation Team Report Part I, October 13, 2011, pp. 7–8.

45. Alan Orlob, "Lessons from the Mumbai Terrorist Attacks," Part II, Testimony to HSGAC, January 28, 2009.

46. Weick and Sutcliffe, *Managing the Unexpected*, 47.

47. Howard Berkes, "30 Years After Explosion, Challenger Engineer Still Blames Himself," NPR, January 28, 2016, www.npr.org/sections/thetwo-way/2016/01/28/464744781/30-years-after-disaster-challenger-engineer-still-blames-himself.

48. Challenger Commission Report, p. 102.

49. Berkes, "30 Years After Explosion."

50. Howard Berkes, "Challenger: Reporting a Disaster's Cold, Hard Facts," NPR, January 28, 2006, www.npr.org/templates/story/story.php?storyId=5175151.

51. Martin Landau and Donald Chisholm, "The Arrogance of Optimism: Notes on Failure-Avoidance Management," *Journal of Contingencies and Crisis Management* 3, no. 2 (June 1995): 67–80, at 77.

52. Darcy Steeg Morris, *Cornell National Social Survey 2009* (Ithaca, NY: Cornell University Survey Research Institute, 2009).

53. One high explosives researcher found that every time an experiment failed, colleagues lined up outside his door offering their assessments about what went wrong. Some of this information could be discovered only in retrospect, but much of it was available beforehand. The researcher began holding "premortem" meetings to surface ideas about potential failures before they occurred. Todd Conklin, *Pre-Accident Investigations: An Introduction to Organizational Safety* (Boca Raton, FL: CRC Press, 2012). Psychologist Gary Klein, who has written extensively about premortems, noted in an interview, "The premortem technique is a sneaky way to get people to do contrarian, devil's advocate thinking without encountering resistance...The logic is that instead of showing people that you are smart because you can come up with a good plan, you show you're smart by thinking of insightful reasons why this project might go south." Interview with Gary Klein and Daniel Kahneman, "Strategic Decisions: When Can You Trust Your Gut?," *McKinsey Quarterly*, March 2010, www.mckinsey.com/business-functions/strategy-and-corporate-finance/our-insights/strategic-decisions-when-can-you-trust-your-gut.

54. Brad Tuttle, "Warren Buffett's Boring, Brilliant Wisdom," *Time*, March 1, 2010.

55. Howard Markel, "How the Tylenol Murders of 1982 Changed How We Consume Medication," *PBS NewsHour*, September 29, 2014, www.pbs.org/news hour/updates/tylenol-murders-1982/; Jerry Knight, "Tylenol's Maker Shows How to Respond to Crisis," *Washington Post*, October 11, 1982, www.washingtonpost .com/archive/business/1982/10/11/tylenols-maker-shows-how-to-respond-to -crisis/bc8df898-3fcf-443f-bc2f-e6fbd639a5a3/.

56. Knight, "Tylenol's Maker Shows How to Respond to Crisis"; Tamar Lewin, "Tylenol Posts an Apparent Recovery," *New York Times*, December 25, 1982, www.nytimes.com/1982/12/25/business/tylenol-posts-an-apparent-recovery.html; Judith Rehak and *International Herald Tribune*, "Tylenol Made a Hero of Johnson & Johnson: The Recall That Started Them All," *New York Times*, March 23, 2002, www.nytimes.com/2002/03/23/your-money/tylenol-made-a-hero-of-johnson -johnson-the-recall-that-started.html.

57. Diermeier, *Reputation Rules*, 11; Lawrence G. Foster, "The Johnson & Johnson Credo and the Tylenol Crisis," *New Jersey Bell Journal* 6, no. 1 (1983); Michael Useem, *The Leadership Moment* (New York: Three Rivers Press, 1998), also calls it the most covered news story since JFK assassination.

58. CEO James E. Burke carried the message personally, appearing on *60 Minutes*.

59. Berge, *The First 24 Hours*; Diermeier, *Reputation Rules*, 11.

60. Diermeier, *Reputation Rules*, 11.

61. Rehak, "Tylenol Made a Hero of Johnson & Johnson."

62. Ibid.

63. See Paresh Dave, "Here's Why Companies Leave You in the Dark About Hacks for Months," *Los Angeles Times*, June 15, 2016, www.latimes.com/business /technology/la-fi-tn-cyberattack-simulation-20160615-snap-story.html.

64. To add insult to injury, Target at the time was an industry leader in cyber security, with state-of-the-art malware detection and a security operations center staffed with more than three hundred analysts.

65. Jim Hammerand, "Target's Redcard Login Website Crashes After Data Breach," *Minneapolis/St. Paul Business Journal*, www.bizjournals.com/twincities/ news/2013/12/19/target-red-card-login-site-crashes.html.

66. Jure Leskovec, Lars Backstrom, and Jon Kleinberg, "Meme-Tracking and the Dynamics of the News Cycle," ACM SIGKDD International Conference on Knowledge Discovery and Data Mining, Paris, June 28–July 1, 2009, cited in Diermeier, *Reputation Rules*, 41, note 60.

67. Diermeier, *Reputation Rules*, 43, citing Philip E. Tetlock, Orie V. Kristel, S. Beth Elson, Melanie C. Green, and Jennifer S. Lerner, "The Psychology of the Unthinkable: Taboo Trade-Offs, Forbidden Base Rates and Heretical Counter-factuals," *Journal of Personality and Social Psychology* 78, no. 5 (2000): 853–70.

68. Thomas Moore, "The Fight to Save Tylenol," *Fortune*, November 29, 1982. See also Glen M. Broom and Bey-Ling Sha, *Cutlip and Center's Effective Public Relations*, 11th ed. (New York: Pearson, 2013), 20.

69. Orlob, "Protecting Soft Targets."

70. Diermeier, *Reputation Rules.*

71. Quoted in "Tylenol and the Legacy of J&J's James Burke," Knowledge@ Wharton, University of Pennsylvania, October 2, 2012, http://knowledge.wharton.upenn.edu/article/tylenol-and-the-legacy-of-jjs-james-burke/.

72. Moore, "The Fight to Save Tylenol."

73. Quoted in Rehak, "Tylenol Made a Hero of Johnson & Johnson."

74. Richard C. Boothman et al., "A Better Approach to Medical Malpractice Claims?," *Journal of Health & Life Sciences Law* 2, no. 2 (January 2009); Kevin Sack, "Doctors Say 'I'm Sorry' Before 'See You in Court,'" *New York Times*, May 18, 2008, www.nytimes.com/2008/05/18/us/18apology.html; Michael S. Wood and Jason Starr, *Healing Words: The Power of Apology in Medicine* (Oak Park, IL: Doctors in Touch, 2007).

75. Munoz is not alone. In the fall of 2016, Wells Fargo CEO John Stumpf appeared before the Senate Banking Committee over a fraud scandal, attracted bipartisan ire for his tone-deaf testimony, and later lost his job. Jeffrey A. Sonnenfield, "How Wells Fargo's CEO Could Have Avoided His Senate Belly Flop," *Yale Insights*, Yale School of Management, September 23, 2016, http://insights.som.yale.edu/insights/how-wells-fargos-ceo-could-have-avoided-his-senate-belly-flop; Matt Egan, Jackie Wattles, and Cristina Alesci, "Wells Fargo CEO John Stumpf Is Out," CNN, October 12, 2016, http://money.cnn.com/2016/10/12/investing/wells-fargo-ceo-john-stumpf-retires/.

76. Matt Rosoff, "United CEO Doubles Down in Email to Employees, Says Passenger Was 'Disruptive and Belligerent,'" CNBC, April 10, 2017, www.cnbc.com/2017/04/10/united-ceo-passenger-disruptive-belligerent.html.

77. Quoted in Julie Creswell and Sapna Maheshwari, "United Grapples with PR Crisis over Videos of Man Being Dragged Off Plane," *New York Times*, April 11, 2017, www.nytimes.com/2017/04/11/business/united-airline-passenger-overbooked-flights.html.

78. Creswell and Maheshwaria, "United Grapples with PR Crisis."

79. "Honesty/Ethics in Professions," Gallup poll, 2015, www.gallup.com/poll/1654/honesty-ethics-professions.aspx.

80. "Tylenol and the Legacy of J&J's James Burke."

81. Alex Kirkpatrick, "A FedEx Driver Will Keep Job After Saving Flag from Burning," KCCI Des Moines, January 28, 2017, www.kcci.com/article/a-fedex-driver-will-keep-job-after-saving-flag-from-burning/8644721.

82. Katie Fratie, "FedEx Releases Statement on Driver Who Saved an American Flag from Being Burned," *Daily Caller*, January 27, 2017, dailycaller.com/2017/01/29/fedex-releases-statement-on-driver-who-saved-an-american-flag-from-being-burned/.

83. "2014 Social CEO Report," CEO.com, www.ceo.com/social-ceo-report-2014/.

84. Rohan Gunaratna, "Marriott in Flames: The Attack on the World's 'Most Protected' Hotel," *Insite Blog on Terrorism and Extremism*, http://news.siteintelgroup.com/blog/index.php/about-us/21-jihad/52-marriott.

85. Diermeier, *Reputation Rules*, 72.

86. Reuters, "BP CEO Apologizes for 'Thoughtless' Oil Spill Comment," June 2, 2010, www.reuters.com/article/us-oil-spill-bp-apology-idUSTRE6515NQ20100602.

87. Elizabeth Shogren, "BP: A Textbook Example of How Not to Handle PR," NPR, April 21, 2011.

88. Lisa Myers, "BP Goes on PR Offensive," *NBC Nightly News*, June 3, 2010, www.nbcnews.com/video/nightly-news/37499024#58503439.

89. Ibid.

90. Elizabeth Shogren, "BP: A Textbook Example of How Not to Handle PR."

91. "Facing Congressional Wrath, BP Chief Apologizes for Oil Disaster," Fox News, June 17, 2010, www.foxnews.com/us/2010/06/17/bp-ceo-tell-congress-hes-devastated-spill.html.

92. Rowena Mason, "BP's Tony Hayward Resigns After Being 'Demonised and Vilified' in the US," *Telegraph*, July 27, 2010, www.telegraph.co.uk/finance/newsbysector/energy/oilandgas/7912338/BPs-Tony-Hayward-resigns-after-being-demonised-and-vilified-in-the-US.html.

93. *Report of Columbia Accident Investigation Board*, Volume 1, August, 26, 2003, http://s3.amazonaws.com/akamai.netstorage/anon.nasa-global/CAIB/CAIB_lowres_chapter6.pdf, chapter 6, p. 122. See also Ben Paynter, "Close Calls Are Near Disasters, Not Lucky Breaks," *Wired*, August 14, 2012.

94. James G. March, "Exploration and Exploitation in Organizational Learning," *Organization Science* 2, no. 1 (February 1991): 71–87.

95. Ibid., 85.

96. Marina Krakovsky, "Charles O'Reilly: Why Some Companies Seem to Last Forever," *Insights by Stanford Business*, Stanford Graduate School of Business, May 31, 2013, www.gsb.stanford.edu/insights/charles-oreilly-why-some-companies-seem-last-forever.

97. "Patients Versus Profits at Johnson & Johnson: Has the Company Lost Its Way?," Knowledge@Wharton, University of Pennsylvania, February 15, 2012, http://knowledge.wharton.upenn.edu/article/patients-versus-profits-at-johnson-johnson-has-the-company-lost-its-way/.

98. Ibid.

99. Erika Fry, "Can Big Still Be Beautiful?," *Fortune*, July 22, 2016, http://fortune.com/johnson-and-johnson-global-500/.

100. David Voreacos, Alex Nussbaum, and Greg Farrel, "Johnson & Johnson Reaches for a Band-Aid," NBC News, April 3, 2011, http://www.nbcnews.com/id/42383262/ns/business-us_business/t/johnson-johnson-reaches-band-aid/.

101. Jonathan D. Rickoff and Joann S. Lublin, "J&J CEO Weldon Is Out," *Wall Street Journal*, February 22, 2012, www.wsj.com/articles/SB10001424052970204909104577237642041667180.

102. Quoted in "Patients Versus Profits at Johnson & Johnson."

103. Fry, "Can Big Still Be Beautiful?"

104. Rockoff and Lublin, "J&J CEO Weldon Is Out."

105. Fry, "Can Big Still Be Beautiful?"

106. Tanya Gazdik, "Johnson & Johnson Struggles with Brand Image," *Marketing Daily*, May 26, 2016, www.mediapost.com/publications/article/276722/johnson-johnson-struggles-with-brand-image.html.

107. Landau and Chisholm, "The Arrogance of Optimism," 75.

108. Ibid., 76.

109. Matt Miller, "Breaking Down the Jim Harbaugh Blueprint for Success," Bleacher Report, September 25, 2012, http://bleacherreport.com/articles/1347305-breaking-down-the-jim-harbaugh-blueprint-for-success.

110. Samuel Chi, "Jim Harbaugh Engineering Another Big Turnaround at Michigan," SFGate, September 27, 2015, www.sfgate.com/collegesports/article/Jim-Harbaugh-engineering-another-big-turnaround-6533638.php.

111. Taylor Price, "You Never Stay the Same," News, San Francisco 49ers, September 14, 2011, www.49ers.com/news/article-2/You-Never-Stay-the-Same/4b2f244d-76be-46dd-8602-f88e7f54a081.

Index

Page numbers of illustrations appear in italics.

About the Authors

Condoleezza Rice is the Denning Professor in Global Business and the Economy at the Stanford Graduate School of Business, the Thomas and Barbara Stephenson Senior Fellow on Public Policy at the Hoover Institution, and a professor of political science at Stanford University. She served as National Security Adviser from 2001 to 2005 and was the sixty-sixth U.S. Secretary of State from 2005 to 2009.

Amy Zegart is codirector of the Center for International Security and Cooperation, the Davies Family Senior Fellow at the Hoover Institution, and a senior fellow at the Freeman Spogli Institute for International Studies at Stanford University. Before her academic career, she was a management consultant at McKinsey & Company.